God's Dust

BY IAN BURUMA

Behind the Mask: *On the Sexual Demons,
Sacred Mothers, Transvestites, Gangsters, Drifters,
and Other Japanese Cultural Heroes*

God's Dust: *A Modern Asian Journey*

God's Dust

A Modern
Asian Journey

IAN BURUMA

FARRAR · STRAUS · GIROUX
NEW YORK

Library of Congress Cataloging-in-Publication Data
Buruma, Ian.
    God's dust : a modern Asian journey / Ian Buruma. — 1st ed.
        p.   cm.
    Bibliography: p.
1. Asia, Southeastern—Description and travel.
2. East Asia—Description and travel.
3. Buruma, Ian—Journeys—Asia, Southeastern.
4. Buruma, Ian—Journeys—East Asia.   I. Title.
DS522.6.B87   1989   89-1548
915.9—dc19

For Richard and Harvey

Contents

Preface

There are many clichés about Asia, as there are about everything. Two in particular have irritated me for years like a persistent itch. One is about so-called Westernization. "Get out of the cities," one is told by Western travelers in search of something they think they lack at home, "they're just like cities everywhere, so Westernized."

The other cliché, linked to the one about Westernized cities, is the sweeping dichotomy of the spiritual East and the materialist West. This idea, often the easiest defense of economically backward countries against more powerful societies, is an old one, held by such different figures as Mahatma Gandhi and Tojo Hideki, the man usually blamed for the Pacific War. The cities of capitalist Asia are materialistic and so, many people presume, they must be "Western."

Naturally, like all clichés, these two contain fragments of truth. Western influence in Asia cannot be denied. And capitalist modernity is to a large extent materialistic. But have rock music, McDonald's hamburgers, and *Dynasty* really made the Thais less Thai, or the Japanese less Japanese? What does it mean, anyway, to be "Thai" or "Japanese" or "Filipino" or "Korean" in the modern world? Does it simply mean clinging to old ceremonies and traditions? Is it a matter of language, or race?

It is the main theme of contemporary Asia—and not just Asia. How to be modern without losing your cultural sense of self. How to adapt your own traditions, ideas, and loyalties to a way of life which came from the West, based on traditions and ideas which might be quite different and are, in any case, often barely understood. Because modernity came from the outside, imposed by or imported from an alien world, Asians often express, in books, films, or political rhetoric, a feeling of discontinuity, of cultural dislocation.

This crisis of identity exists in every Asian country. It plays an important part in almost all social upheavals, rebellions, or conflicts that newspapers reduce to simple political facts. These crises can be destructive. Societies are torn apart when politicians obliterate the past to start again from scratch, or when they seek to remake countries in their own image. The Japanese war in Asia, or at least the propaganda that sought to justify it, was partly a result of Western modernity having been gulped down too fast, causing a kind of cultural indigestion and a consequent return to violent nativism.

But crises can also be creative. The necessity to experiment, to redefine themselves, to find meaning in a world of conflicting values has made the capitalist countries of Southeast and East Asia extraordinarily dynamic. They are alive in a way that old Europe, complacently bearing the burden of its long, miraculously continuous history, is not.

Not that modernity, the brainchild of the West, is without its problems there. The breakdown of organized religion and its resulting spiritual dislocation, the fear that one day the whole world will be an extension of Los Angeles, one huge supermarket filled with Muzak and plagued by anarchic youth gangs, is haunting the West. But it is precisely the contrast between Western ideas and Asian traditions that make the modern condition in Asia so dramatic. It shows, if you like, the modern human predicament in its starkest, rawest form.

My idea for this book was not to add another set of abstractions to the already voluminous academic literature on "modernization," "development theory," and other grand themes. Nor did I have in mind a journalistic wrap-up of a number of Asian countries. The book is not scholarly; nor does it attempt to be exhaustive in its factual coverage. Indeed, by the time you read this, political events will already have made much of what I have described old news. But news is not the point. Political figures come and go; revolts, successful or not, occur. Some of these figures feature prominently in the book, as do events that made headlines at the time, but I am interested mainly in what such people and incidents tell me about the countries whose character they help to define. They are no more than part of the tapestries that make up modern nations.

By spending a year traveling through eight Asian countries, starting in Rangoon and ending in Hiroshima, I have tried to give an account of the dilemmas, the cultural confusion, the endless searching for meaning and national identity that go on there. The trip was not continuous, nor always in the order of the book. Some countries I already knew well, others hardly at all. The Philippine chapter was the result of two visits, one before the February Revolt and one a few months after.

Burma dynamic? you may well ask. Burma rejected the outside world, particularly everything our romantic travelers associate with "Westernization." It has long been the antithesis of the other countries featured in this book, and was therefore the perfect point of departure. I visited Burma in the summer of 1986. It was oppressive and outwardly calm, fatalistic, passive, fetid like a stagnant pool. Two years later the country erupted, finally, in massive demonstrations against the military dictatorship. The uprising, with its demands for elections, freedom of the press, the abolition of one-party rule—in short, democracy—was crushed. Thousands of unarmed demonstrators were shot in the streets. After a summer of violence and euphoria the army took over again, promising elections at some future date. Although things looked worse than they were before, it is hard to imagine Burma ever returning to the same passive state that I found in 1986. Too much has happened; too many lives have been lost. Burma probably will come out of its isolation and eventually join the modern world, but because it is one of the last countries to have to face up to this choice, the stagnant, passive Burma which existed for more than two decades was the ideal place to start reflecting upon the theme that runs through the rest of the book: what happens to people when the loyalties and traditions of the village break down and are replaced by the complexities of the modern world.

Contemplating the condition of modern man sounds like a fine and noble aim. But I also had a less high-minded interest in the subject of national identities, which is autobiographical. My parents were from different countries. I was educated in Holland, but write in my mother's language. And I have lived one-third of my life in Asia. Other people's loyalties, therefore, have always fascinated me. I have always wanted to know what it feels like to be entirely and unselfconsciously at home in one country. The idea fills me with envy, but also with some horror; the feeling of being confined by closed borders strikes me as the ultimate nightmare.

So, like any book based on travel and human encounters, this is a subjective account. If I seem, sometimes, a little harsh in my judgments of other people's illusions, I can only say one thing in my defense: To the extent that I have not found a clear answer to my own loyalties, I shall never condemn others for not finding an answer to theirs. It is those who presume to impose their answers on others who ought to be condemned.

I have encountered so much kindness, hospitality, and help making my way through the various countries that I cannot possibly thank everyone. I would, however, like to single out a few people whose help was indispensable. U Chit Tun, Paisal

Sricharatchanya, Francisco Sionil Jose, Jose Lacaba, Cecil Rajendra, Antonio Chiang, Cha Yun, J. Y. Ra, and Shim Jae Hoon
have been marvelous guides to their respective countries. Carl
Goldstein, Nick Seaward, Richard Nations, K. G. van Wol-
feren, Alan Booth, and Harvey Stockwin have offered me their
encouragement, invaluable expertise, and time to weed out my
more egregious errors. The staff of my former employers, *The
Far Eastern Economic Review*, most especially the bureau secretaries in the various capitals, have been of extraordinary help.
I thank the *Review*'s editor, Derek Davies, for his encouragement and generosity in affording me the time to work on my
own project. I am also much indebted to Robert Silvers of *The
New York Review of Books*, where parts of the book have
appeared in somewhat different form. He must be every writer's
ideal editor; he certainly is mine. Mark Danner of *The New
York Times Magazine*, which published parts of the chapter
on Japan and the chapter on Burma, has also been a delight
to work with. Finally, I would like to offer special thanks to
Margaret Scott, who has had to put up with every neurotic
twist and turn from the first seed of an idea to the final product.

Your idol is shattered in the dust
to prove that God's dust is greater than your idol.

—RABINDRANATH TAGORE

God's Dust

1

The Village and the City

BURMA

The first thing you see as you drive into Rangoon, through the lush green suburbs, past the sturdy old bungalows built for the sahibs and memsahibs of the British Raj, is the Shwe Dagon Pagoda, the most famous building in Burma. And justly so. It is more than six hundred years old, it contains eight hairs of the Lord Buddha, and its graceful stupa, shaped like a reversed ice-cream cone, surrounded by shrines, souvenir shops, gaudy waxworks, and models of legendary Burmese figures that move round and round when fed with coins, is covered with gold and surmounted with priceless gems.

I had visited Rangoon several times since 1978, always, alas, one week at a time, for the government allowed no more.* Rangoon was one city in Asia that hardly seemed to have changed. Here was a place that had succeeded in halting what is commonly known as modern progress, including the progress of isolated communist nations, like North Korea, with their quaintly nineteenth-century devotion to smokestack industries

* During the revolt in the summer of 1988 tourism stopped altogether.

3

and their faceless workers' housing complexes. In Burma time appeared to have stood still. Walking around the Shwe Dagon, I watched the people kneeling in prayer. I saw the gold glitter in the sun and thought of the squalor I had seen in Rangoon. I was filled with a sense of awe, heightened by the fact that, as a secular European, I had no gods to pray to, but also with some doubt. Had these people retained something lost to us, children of modern progress and its concomitant materialism? Or were they, on the contrary, deprived of something we perhaps take too much for granted?

Burma, because of its isolation, its seemingly easy familiarity with the spiritual life, and its traditionalism, is the perfect place to think about the modern world. If our times are marked by the struggle between the temple and the bank, here is a place still ruled by the temple. Here you can leave home without an American Express card; here people don't drink Coca-Cola; here there are no bars with naked go-go girls. But at what price? And is it worth paying?

Every time I visit Rangoon, I am beset by the same, no doubt irrational, fear; the fear of getting stuck behind closed borders. I wake up in a sweat, worrying whether my currency sheet is in order—every purchase in Burma must be accounted for and tally with the amount of foreign currency brought in to the country. I instinctively feel for my passport in fear of losing it and ending up ensnared in the vagaries of Burmese bureaucracy. As I said, these fears are irrational, for I have nothing to fear. But what about the Burmese themselves? What do they have to fear?

Not far from the pagoda there is a more prosaic spot, very much off the tourist track. It is nothing but a field. On this field stood the Student Union Building of the University of Rangoon. It was destroyed by soldiers in 1962, after students protested against the new military government which grabbed power that year. People in Rangoon tell sinister tales of mass graves under the field, containing unknown student demonstrators.

This field has become a symbol. Demonstrations are held there still, as well as around the Shwe Dagon, when students pluck up enough courage to challenge their rulers. They need considerable courage because such demonstrations often result in deaths. It is symbolic because the Student Union stood for something which is being systematically erased in Burma.* I shall call it City, meaning a free exchange of ideas, politics, cosmopolitanism, criticism; everything, in short, which ought to lead to freedom and independence of thought. These are not necessarily incompatible with spiritual life, but they are often crushed in the name of tradition and one holy spirit or another.

The Student Union produced the brilliant men who delivered Burma from British colonial rule in 1948. These men were not lacking in spirituality. Indeed, as far as one can make out, all were devout Buddhists. But having learned about the modern world from the British, they fought, not always successfully, sometimes chaotically, to make Burma a modern nation. This struggle, to the delight of many tourists, at least for seven days at a time, had been lost.

Rangoon is not a modern city. It is in fact an anti-modern city. Unlike Singapore, Jakarta, or Bangkok, where new buildings are obliterating the immediate past, Rangoon has remained much as the British left it in 1948. Old people say that Rangoon was once known as the cleanest and most pleasant city of Southeast Asia. Now the pavements show great cracks filled with refuse. At night the streets are taken over by enormous rats, jostling each other to get at the best bits of garbage floating in the open sewers. The rather pompous 1920s office buildings and trading houses are like tramps in old dinner jackets, several sizes too large. Only the embassies have been spruced up with whitewash. (Burmese love whitewash. Old pagodas are white-

---

* The symbol was revived during the massive demonstrations, resulting in thousands of deaths, in 1988. One of the first demands of the students was the restoration of the Student Union.

washed; Buddhas are whitewashed to make them look new. But apart from the embassies, Rangoon is evidently not deemed worthy of whitewash.) The decaying city center is surrounded by suburbs of brown huts on stilts in slimy water. The once modern capital is being reclaimed by old village Burma.

In some people the dilapidation of Rangoon evokes feelings of nostalgia. They see romantic grandeur in the crumbling porticos and peeling Edwardian façades. Equally gratifying to the romantic visitor is the sight of a whole population in native dress. Men and women wear long skirts called *longyis*, which they constantly wrap and unwrap like birds airing their wings. And, of course, they still smoke the whacking great cheroots celebrated by Kipling in "The Road to Mandalay" (Kipling, incidentally, had never been to Mandalay). Here at last is the "real" Asia, where, to use a dated phrase, people are themselves. It is difficult to feel such good cheer, however, when one is continuously accosted by Burmese who want things bought for them at the foreign currency stores; basic things, like medicine, which can be resold on the black market.

The black market dominates life in Rangoon. It starts in the customs hall of Rangoon Airport. Officers spend endless time checking documents supposed to make sure the visitor spends every cent at the exorbitant official exchange rate. This job done, the officers smile, welcome the visitor to Burma, and ask for "presents": ballpoint pens, key rings; anything that they can sell on the black market. At the same time young men smoking cheroots offer to buy your whiskey, cigarettes, T-shirts, belts, cosmetics. After a day in Rangoon one already feels haunted by the whispered "Want to do business?" This business is not based on greed, but on necessity. Only 8 percent of Burmese imports are consumer goods and most of those, some say, are for the foreign currency stores, where one U.S. dollar is worth seven local kyats. On the street one can get thirty—or at least one could when I was there in 1986. The black market is like a tapeworm eating its way through a bankrupt economy. Everything is sold and resold. Government employees sell their rice rations. Each morning young men rush to the cinemas to buy up all the tickets that they resell later in the day. Many of these young men are university graduates.

The old cars which delighted travel writers in the past are mostly gone; replaced by Japanese pickup trucks. Most cars were privately owned and too many people sold their petrol rations on the black market. In the back streets of Rangoon one sees rotting old Chevrolets and Hillmans, lovingly maintained for decades, now banned from the roads. Pickup trucks are classified as taxis. One gets vague answers as to who owns these taxis. "They are rented by the day," people say. "Yes, but from whom?" "From rich people." Rich people can mean anything from military brass, to Burma Socialist Program Party bosses, to Chinese and Indian traders, to merchant seamen. Most young men want to become seamen. It is a way to get rich, as seamen are allowed to import foreign goods. They work on a ship for three years, save every penny they earn, buy a pickup truck, and live off the profit for years.

Sealing off a culture from the corrupting influences of the outside world has a somewhat similar effect to shutting young girls up in a segregated boarding school—they fall in love with the first bit of corruption that comes their way. Despite the *longyis* and the cheroots, many Burmese make a kind of fetish of modern goods. As one walks barefoot—customary on sacred ground—along the long shop-lined avenues that lead to the Shwe Dagon pagoda, one looks in vain for fine traditional wood carvings or delicate religious objects; instead there are gaudy models of such icons of modernity as TV sets, telephones, or girls in golfing gear. At the black markets teenagers buy T-shirts with Japanese or English words on them—no matter what they mean, as long as they are foreign. The thirst for foreignness stretches to nonmaterial goods too. A Burmese journalist who writes for a foreign magazine often fails to get his copies through the mail; not because of censorship, but because they are stolen at the post office and sold on the black market. I saw bits of an old *Life* magazine sold in the street. It had Lyndon B. Johnson on the cover.

Foreign modernity seeping through the rather porous Burmese wall influences Burmese tradition itself. Wedding receptions are accompanied by loud bands that play sugary pop music. Ancient Buddhist sculptures are "improved" by embossing them with gold-painted concrete or gaudy glass mosaics. Old Buddhas are haloed by colored neon or flashing disco lights. This suggests two things: that Burmese tradition is so alive that Buddhas in neon seem perfectly in order; and that enforced parochialism has done little to protect traditional aesthetics from indiscriminate modern taste. It is hard to say which is worse, the tackiness of Coca-Colonization or the peculiar flowers that grow in a culture artificially but imperfectly isolated from the modern world.

The decay of Rangoon is not simply the result of bad planning. It is part of a deliberate process to strangle the City, to return to pre-colonial village Burma, ruled by a ruler who knows best but is accountable to no one. Rangoon simply does not fit into this vision of Burma. It can only be a source of trouble, as in 1974, when students and monks demonstrated against the government on the site of the Student Union Building and at the Shwe Dagon pagoda, or in 1987 and 1988, when students took to the streets after the government tried to tackle black marketeering by demonetizing the currency. There is another, perhaps more fundamental reason why Rangoon does not fit into the Burmese Way to Socialism: there are still too many foreigners living there.

Modern Rangoon was never really a Burmese city, but, like Calcutta, Singapore, or Hong Kong, a creation of the British. Until 1755, when Rangoon became a commercial port, it was a fishing village named Dagon after the pagoda. Contemporary descriptions of eighteenth-century Rangoon do not sound inviting. B. R. Pearn, in his *History of Rangoon*, quotes one of these descriptions: "The City appeared to me very strange, and such wretched houses I thought I never saw, though they are built with wood. Dogs, rats, hogs, and all manner of vermin, are certainly very numerous, but not more so than they are in a native town in Bengal." Pearn himself remarks that Rangoon "must have been not unlike a modern Burmese village." Only foreigners built houses of brick, as "it was illegal for a Burmese subject to build a brick house, for it was feared that such buildings might become centres of resistance against the authorities . . ."

In 1836, things hardly seemed better. As one C. Bennett reported, "The city is spread upon part of a vast meadow, but little above high tides, and at this season resembling a neglected swamp. The approach from the sea reveals nothing but a few wooden houses between the city and the shore . . . A dozen foreigners, chiefly Moguls, have brick tenements, very shabby. There are also four or five small brick places of worship, for foreigners, and a miserable Custom House. Besides these, it is a city of bamboo huts, comfortable for these people, considering their habits and climate, but in appearance as paltry as possible . . ."

After seizing Lower Burma in a swift, one-sided war in 1852, the British transformed the old port of Rangoon into a modern European-style city, a smaller version of Calcutta, a kind of Palladian fantasy in the tropical swamp. British Rangoon was an urban aberration in a rural society with no tradition to prepare it for the shock of a modern market economy. To the Buddhist Burmans money business was associated with greed and deceitful exploitation. And from their point of view this assessment was essentially correct. The British, the Indian moneylenders, and the Chinese merchants did much better than most Burmans. The Burmans who did well out of the new foreign ways mostly lived in the city. Some peasants began to benefit from British investment and the cash economy, but the Japanese invasion in 1942 stopped rice exports and the peasants, on the brink of becoming farmers, returned to the old life of the self-sufficient village, from which they never emerged again.

The true center of Burma was the royal palace, which stood in the center of the world. It was a movable center, as Burmese kings sometimes started afresh in new capitals, often for astrological reasons. But wherever it was, the palace was thought to be the center of the universe. Burmese kings, as Lords of the universe, ruled in this cosmic center with only the sketchiest awareness of the outside world. All the Burmese knew of international affairs came from bazaar rumors and travelers' tales from Muslim merchants.

Court chronicles hardly mentioned English missions or the causes leading up to the first Anglo-Burmese war of 1824, but they are full of details about a sacred white elephant, who was believed to be the incarnation of Buddha. The holy animal, decked out in the finest silks and covered in gold, rubies, and emeralds, lived in his own palace, where the king would come to worship him. He was bathed in scented water and given human milk to drink. And when the revenue from the elephant's fiefs was reduced by poor crops, the king personally wrote him a letter of apology. This, then, was the world that the British encountered at the Burmese court. No wonder that British envoys were treated with complete disdain. One such emissary, Captain Canning, was actually ordered to be sent to the king in fetters, a fate Canning only managed to escape at the last minute.

The governor of Rangoon, however, knew more about the world than his king in Amarapura, and apologized for this indignity to Canning. "Our king," he said, "is absolute. His commands must be unreservedly obeyed and he disregards the forms and usages of all nations. Indeed, Captain, between ourselves, I sometimes wonder whether His Majesty is quite right in the head, for they say in the Palace he does things which entirely indicate a disorderly mind."

This semi-divine king (at one stage he actually announced that he was Buddha), called Bodawpaya, was described by one

British envoy as "a child in his ideas, a tyrant in his principles, and a madman in his actions." What strikes one about the king, indeed about many Burmese kings, is the pervasive atmosphere of paranoia in their courts. The Hindu-Buddhist god-kings theoretically had absolute power, though they had little control over the outer provinces, which were ruled by autonomous governors, or even over the remoter villages, where the headmen held sway. The king had a council of ministers, the Hluttaw, whose decisions he was supposed to respect, but he picked the ministers himself and could—and some kings often did—throw them in jail without notice. Kings had large harems, but there were no clear rules for succession, so the death of a monarch was usually followed by intrigues and massacres. King Bodawpaya had all possible rivals in the royal family murdered. The last king, Thibaw, killed about eighty of his nearest kin in 1878, allegedly by tying them up in sacks of crimson velvet and having them battered to death. He reported this to the British as "a purging of the realm according to custom." But even the loyalty of one's closest subordinates was often suspect. When Bodawpaya's favorite commander failed to return promptly from a military expedition, as he was held up by physical exhaustion and the rains, the king sent orders "to roast him at a slow fire, taking particular care that none of his bones should be broken or dislocated, which might tend to shorten his sufferings." One understands why Burmese officials are so often described as "trembling with fear." They never knew who was next for the chop.

Nevertheless, when the British abolished the Burmese monarchy in 1886, after King Thibaw refused to let the British dictate his foreign policy, it came as a deep shock to the Burmese psyche. The king was driven past his weeping subjects in an oxcart to the Irrawaddy river, thence to Rangoon, and finally to India. The barbarians had crashed the gates; the sacred Hall of Audience became a British garrison church, the altar placed before the old throne. The king's old summer residence became the Upper Burma Club, where British officers enjoyed their evening drinks. This desecration of the old palace, which later was halted by Lord Curzon, an enlightened Viceroy, spelled the symbolic collapse of a cosmic order.

This is not to say that all Burmese were utterly ignorant of the modern world. King Mindon, Thibaw's predecessor, was a modernizer: he built factories equipped with European machinery, established a telegraph system that transmitted Morse code signals adapted to the Burmese alphabet, and ran a fleet of river steamers on the Irrawaddy. He had a taste for Western novelties such as French mirrors, marmalade jars with royal labels, and clocks. He had a painted Italian room in his beautiful palace, alas bombed during World War II, and the roof was specially made of silver-colored corrugated iron which the king found practical and modern. Mindon's relationship with the British was quite cordial—until relations halted when the British refused to take their shoes off in the palace. His economic ideas, however, based on royal monopolies and Buddhist benevolence, did not fit well with nineteenth-century European capitalism. Mercantile individualism did exist in Burma, but only on the flourishing black markets, clearly a long-standing Burmese institution.

When the British took over the country in 1886 and made Burma part of India, things changed drastically. In the place of cosmic ritual the British imposed secular law, spawning a Burmese elite of Anglicized lawyers and clerks; the lawyers to interpret the new laws to their baffled countrymen and the clerks to help their British mentors implement them. The modern state was there in form, if not always in content. In practice Burmese customs still prevailed. But the wounds inflicted on Burmese civilization were deep and they are far from healed. By removing the king, the Burmese lost the protector of their faith, casting adrift the Buddhist hierarchy. By extending government administration over the non-Burman minorities, who had hitherto only paid tribute to the Burman kings, the basis was laid for future civil wars. Worst of all, by making Burma a province of India and by importing a large number of Indians to man the Burmese bureaucracy, Burmese self-esteem was deeply hurt; especially when Indians proved more adept than they were at modern trade. Consequently the Burmese road to modernity has been marked by a desire to restore the faith, to kick out the foreigners, and to fill the throne with a new protector; an amalgamation of Buddhism, nationalism, and the *Führerprinzip*.

The first Burmese leader after the British were driven out by the Japanese in 1942 was Dr. Ba Maw, a French-trained lawyer. Dr. Ba Maw was a somewhat eccentric figure, so Westernized that he affected a slight foreign accent in his Burmese. He also dressed oddly: baggy trousers and a skullcap he had designed himself. In 1943, when Burma ostensibly became independent but was in effect ruled by the Japanese, Dr. Ba Maw adopted the title of "Adipadi," the Pali equivalent of Führer. He was administered the traditional oath sworn by Burmese kings when ascending the throne. This royal pretension was also couched in terms more in line with the thinking of his Axis friends: "One blood, one voice, one command." National socialism, like most variants of socialism, lent itself well to putting old concepts in modern terms.

The most promising leader of what was to be a truly independent Burma was Aung San, who had learned his politics at the Student Union. He collaborated with the Japanese and served under the "Führer," but then changed sides and helped the Allies beat them. Aung San was associated in the folk mind with Setkya-Min, "the king who will be the future Buddha." Alas, Aung San was assassinated in 1947, the year before independence, at the age of thirty-three. His face still adorns bank notes and his portrait hangs on office walls alongside General Ne Win's.* Aung San's death was perhaps the worst tragedy on Burma's road to modernity, for he was a modernist, a confused one, but a modernist nonetheless.

---

* And his daughter Aung San Sun Kyi came back from England to lead the revolt in 1988.

U Nu, who took over from Aung San, was stuck somewhere between modernism and nativism. Perhaps he never quite knew where he stood himself. He was certainly very adept at articulating traditional ideas in a modern manner. His vision for Burma was that of a Buddhist welfare state. He was opposed to capitalism because it turned people away from religion. U Nu's rule came to an end in 1962, when Ne Win took over by a military coup. After a period of exile, he was allowed to return and he spent his time studying Buddhist scriptures.*

Ne Win in many ways restored the Burmese kingdom. Unlike many post-colonial leaders, he did not have to shape the new society in his own image, for the old blueprint was still there. He is widely believed to be omnipotent.† His alleged irrationality, his extraordinary secrecy, his merciless punishment of the slightest hint of disloyalty, all this reminds people of the royal Burmese style. He even married the granddaughter of King Thibaw. There was the awkward matter of being half Chinese, awkward, that is, for a Burman ruler, so a book was published proving Ne Win's pure Burman stock.

People appeared curiously reluctant to call the ruler by his name. I heard him referred to as the Old Man, Number One, or simply the Top. A Burmese writer called his government "the rule of one man's whims."

In his study of Burma, the American scholar Lucian Pye wrote that "powerful forces for irrationality circulated throughout the traditional Burmese system. Belief in the god-king meant that it was lèse-majesté to suggest or even to imagine any possible limits to his omnipotence . . . since the ultimate proof of high status was the capacity to act beyond the comprehension of mere reason, and the higher the official the less he had to account for his actions, there was a powerful urge at the ruling level to act in unaccountable ways."

---

* He interrupted his studies in 1988 to start his own opposition party.

† He formally stepped down from power in 1988, but still remained in control of the leaders who replaced him.

Courtiers, then as now, have to second-guess their superiors. Getting it right is vitally important. Keeping knowledge from others is an important source of power. A system where people are constantly guessing one another's motives brings on paranoia. Secrecy becomes a way of life. If others know about you, they will dominate you. If those others are foreigners, all the worse.

Since Ne Win came to power, foreign journalists have been banned from entering Burma. Diplomats are discouraged from acquiring, let alone giving out, any information. The more they know, the larger their interest in keeping it to themselves. The Japanese have the biggest foreign stake in Burma and thus the largest embassy. Anything modern in Burma is usually built by the Japanese, from a new hospital to the ubiquitous pickup trucks. There still seems to be a sentimental idea, if only at the Top, that the Japanese are more trustworthy economic allies than the former white imperialists. Ne Win himself was trained by the Japanese army. This is a cause of some ambivalence among the Burmese, who still remember being slapped in the face by arrogant Japanese soldiers.

I was approached in a Rangoon tea shop by a Chinese dentist who seemed genuinely baffled by Japanese success. "Oh, those Japanese, such clever, clever people," he said apropos of the lack of British goods on the black market. He took me to his house, where he worked on his patients with a large hand-driven drill, made in Tokyo in 1942. He showed me a copy of *Newsweek* with a Japanese monster on the cover spewing forth yen notes. He shook his head and jabbed at the picture: "Such clever, clever people." He did not appear entirely happy about this cleverness.

I wanted to see a Japanese diplomat. The phone was out of order, so I went to the embassy to make an appointment with the cultural attaché. I was met at the gate by an anxious Burmese secretary who said the attaché was too busy to see anyone. I said that could not possibly be so. Would he ask again? He returned after five minutes to say that the attaché could not give me the information I wanted. I asked how that could be, if he did not know yet what information I wanted. After another five minutes of consultation with his boss, the agitated secretary informed me the attaché could give me no information at all.

I set off to buy the official pamphlet of the Burmese Way to Socialism. It is entitled *The System of Correlation of Man and His Environment*—written, according to a local newspaperman, by a half-educated progressive journalist and a socialist bohemian who had drifted around Paris. Every state shop will have a copy, I was told. I tried several state shops. None of them had it. In fact, they had hardly any books at all. "Paper shortage," said one of the clerks. He suggested I try the black market. I finally secured a worm-eaten copy from a critic of the government. An old, well-educated Burman, he said he couldn't make head or tale of it. The Burmese I spoke to all dismissed the document. "Socialism," said one, "is just an excuse for the Old Man to nationalize the economy. Not because he is opposed to private enterprise, but because he wants total power." Other old hands say it has little to do with Buddhism either. Dr. Ba Maw probably came closest to the truth when he said: "Because it was socialist it was good, but because it was Burmese it was better."*

He should have said Burman; its peculiar mix of Buddhism, nationalism, and socialism has little to offer the non-Burman minorities, like the Shan, the Karen, or the Kachin, whose insurgent armies control large chunks of the country. Many of them are not even Buddhists. The Burmese Way to Socialism is a nativist Burman response to the modern world. As a blueprint for the perfect Burman society—a society without foreigners, a spiritual welfare state—it is a remarkable document.

The Burmese Way to Socialism became the official ideology in 1962, but its basis was laid long before Ne Win came to

---

* This did not last. By 1988 socialism had become a dirty word—so much so that the ruling party changed its name to the National Unity Party.

power. It is an attempt to reconcile "objective analysis" with a spiritual view of the world. It presents Marxism in Buddhist terms but is opposed to the "vulgar materialism" of "leftists" who are "ensnared by their habitual 'matter matters most' bias and outlook." The Buddhist Law of Constant Change is interpreted in a Marxist way: "The so-called 'immutable' social systems which allow exploitation of man by man (such as the slave system, the feudal system, and the capitalist system) cannot withstand the inexorable laws of change."

The combination of Buddhism and socialism would have surprised and probably outraged Karl Marx, who saw "Asiatic" religions as great barriers to progress. But it is not as absurd as it seems. The new creed is in fact an old attempt to become modern while remaining Burman, which has to involve a merger of science and religion. Awareness of this dilemma, of having to reconcile the otherworldly and the secular, only comes with modern education. It did not bother the taxi driver who took me for a drive through the countryside. He drove like a suicidal maniac, at full speed, never touching his brake, overtaking at blind corners, missing equally insane oncoming traffic by inches. He was quite unruffled. I understood why when he stopped at a roadside shrine to pray to the spirits (Nats) for his safety. It was they—not his own technical skills— who would decide his fate.

It was Burman nationalists, who were both anti-British and modern, who were most exercised by the dilemma. British education had secularized their view of the world, while Protestant missionaries threatened their spiritual life, which was of course Buddhist. The answer was to secularize Buddhism. Anticolonialists like the monk U Ottama, who picked up socialist ideas in India, and the writer Kudow Hmaing came up with something remarkably like Liberation Theology in poor Catholic countries. They argued that Buddhism was really a kind of proto-socialism. Burman modernists aimed at establishing Nirvana on earth. This meant liberation from colonial bondage and capitalist exploitation, which were virtually synonymous;

which meant, in effect, that free enterprise in the hands of
foreign merchants and multinational companies would block
Burmans from reaching spiritual fulfillment; in other words,
from being true Burmans.

At the price of alienating the non-Burmans, and at the price
of keeping a potentially rich country poor, Ne Win has Bur-
manized Burma. The old state monopoly over the economy
has been restored by socialism, or, more accurately perhaps,
by national socialism. The first to go after the military coup
were foreign companies. Then currency and trade restrictions
forced more than 200,000 Indians and Pakistanis to leave the
country without their assets. The ones that stayed still bear the
colonial legacy. Many speak beautiful English, like the emaciated beggar woman from Dhaka who works the tourists in
front of the Strand Hotel in Rangoon: "Spare me just one
minute, would you please," she says, before holding forth on
her misery. Nationalization of land dispossessed foreign landowners, most of whom lived in Rangoon. Apart from providing
peasants with a steady iron rice bowl, these anti-foreign measures had the added benefit of depriving students and other
middle-class urban troublemakers of one of the main causes
for political unrest in Asia: anti-government nationalism.*

Students are deprived in other, more direct ways, too. Their
hopes for social or economic advancement have been effectively
blocked. The military and the ruling party became the conduits
for social mobility. Most university graduates have a hard time
finding jobs, except in the army. You find them reading palms
at temples, or driving tourists around, or dabbling in business
on the black market. Only vocational studies are encouraged,
and students are kept away from the city as much as possible
by setting up provincial schools. According to a student in

---

* It didn't work in the end. Anti-government nationalism is precisely what set
the tone of the 1988 revolt. Students brandished images of Aung San during street
demonstrations. The nationalist rhetoric of the 1930s was now turned against the
government.

Rangoon, "people with the best grades are told to study science, the ones with the worst grades study liberal arts." Politics is banned from the campus.

I asked a teacher of philosophy what his specialty was. "Contemporary philosophy," he said. Eastern or Western? "Eastern." Which Chinese philosophers, for example? "Everything from Confucius to Mao Zedong." You study Maoism? "Oh, no, we cannot study politics."

Some might be inclined to see merit in all this. What use, one can hear them say, are philosophy or politics to an underdeveloped rural country? This, indeed, was the view of some British administrators when Rangoon University expanded its curriculum in the 1920s. One such person, F. S. V. Donnison, has been quoted by the historian D. G. E. Hall as saying that "the courses of study provided were often unrealistic and imperfectly related to the needs of the country." Hall's unusually acerbic riposte is one of the finest arguments for the City that I have read: Donnison's complaint "merely reflects the pathetically wrong-headed attitude of the European community towards university education for Asians. Its real crime to them lay in the fact that it *was* university education and not a superior form of technical education 'related to the needs of the country.' "

Those who seek to destroy the City, seek to destroy books, especially books containing foreign ideas that do not support government orthodoxy. This is the first step in destroying the kind of people who read and write them. Books have not been ritually burned in Burma, nor was the English-educated intelligentsia liquidated as in Pol Pot's Phnom Penh. They were simply made irrelevant, shunted into marginal jobs, and ridiculed in popular entertainment. It is always obvious who the villains are in Burmese plays: they wear glasses and use foreign words. Secondhand bookshops sell off moldy English books to tourists. They belonged to people who died or who are too poor to keep their most treasured possessions. None of these books are newer than the early 1960s. One bookseller said that in another ten years there won't be any more English books left to sell.

Old Burma hands like Tennyson Jesse made much of the fact that under the British system of education the Burmese elite was "left not quite Burmese, not quite English, not quite anything at all." It is the price every colonial elite has to pay. But is nativism the answer? Until the early 1980s, the English language was banned in schools altogether. It is one thing to abolish Dutch in Indonesia, while retaining English. Indonesians were not cut off from the modern world. To abolish English perhaps avoids the cultural confusion of an educated elite, but it also isolates a people from modern knowledge, from the world outside Burma, in short, from the City. English was only allowed back in school curricula, some say, after Ne Win's daughter found she was unable to follow lectures at her English university (the ban on foreign influence does not apply to all). Young Burmese like to practice their English on tourists now. "English is the international language," they say, lest one thinks there is still a linguistic connection with the British Raj.

The old English-language journalists, who once worked for some of the liveliest English papers in Asia, are reduced to writing for the two identical state-run papers. There they pen such front-page leads as "A coordination meeting on cultivating production and purchase of paddy, oil crops, and winter crops for 1986–87 was held in the Mya Eya Hall of Sagaing Division People's Council Office on June 24." Or they survive by filing dispatches to foreign wire services. Complete lack of access to any official information and the sheer danger of accurate reporting stops them from filing much. One journalist I know spends years on one story. He is always waiting for "more detailed information." He clubs together with his colleagues and goes to every embassy function, hoping to pick up the odd crumb of informed gossip. In isolation they have upheld the decency, if not always the standards, of the kind of journalism they were taught long ago. "When we go," said one of them, "journalism will die in this country."

I looked up an old writer whom I shall call U Tin Maung. A highly educated man of the old school with years of experience in Britain, he now lives alone in a cheap hostel. He is certainly not British, however, nor can he be described as "not anything much at all." U Tin Maung, if anything, is an enlightened Burmese nationalist, whose cosmopolitan outlook puts both Burma and the outside world in perspective. His room, filled with books, is opposite the lavatory. Young backpack tourists with mosquito-bitten legs passed his room for their morning wash. "This government has ruined my country," he bellowed to an Irish girl going by. "I need ten different medications for my heart, and I must buy them all on the black market. But I'd still rather be ruled by a Burmese dictatorship than be under the benevolent despotism of the British Raj." The Irish girl laughed. He then wagged his finger at her: "There is one thing we won't forgive you for—your lot killed Mountbatten. We loved Mountbatten in Burma." U Tin Maung smiled at me, grabbed my hand, and said: "As Alice said in Wonderland, things are getting worser and worser."

The overnight train ride from Rangoon to Mandalay can take anything from fourteen to seventeen hours. It was hard to get much sleep. The train stopped frequently and was greeted at every town by swarms of women and children offering to sell water, tea, and snacks wrapped in leaves. The train was old, the tracks were ill maintained, and the chairs were mounted on loose springs, so that one was bounced about as if riding a bucking bull. Someone sitting behind me lightly tapped my shoulder. "Like chicken?" he asked, and held out a shiny piece of brown meat.

My benefactor was a young man dressed in a *longyi* and a cotton Burmese jacket. "I am student," he said, after I asked where he was from. "Go home to Mandalay." His name was

Tin Mya. When he heard I lived in Hong Kong, his eyes shone.
"Hong Kong very good." He fished out an old copy of *Newsweek* and showed me some advertisements for Swiss watches.
"The best?" he asked, as he pointed out a gold Piaget dress
watch. I assured him it was a good watch. His English vocab-
ulary was limited and my Burmese nonexistent, so the conversation soon came to a halt. We both stared out of the
window, into the dark, waiting for the next station and the
next round of drinks and snacks.

Then, another light tap. "You know Browning?" he asked.
I did not know what he meant; another tourist he had met in
Rangoon, perhaps. Could he really assume that all white for-
eigners might know one another?

> *"Had I but plenty of money, money enough and to spare*
> *The house for me, no doubt, were a house in a city*
>   *square;*
> *Ah, such a life, such a life, as one leads at the window*
>   *there!*

"Robert Browning, a fine poet," he said. I asked him where
he had learned to recite the poem. "My uncle in Rangoon teach
me," he said. "Robert Browning, a fine poet," he repeated. I
wondered what the poem meant to Tin Mya. I could only guess
what it meant to his uncle, obviously one of the English-
educated men whose world has been dismantled. I could hear
him instructing his nephew, pronouncing the words with care,
"Robert Browning, a fine poet."

Robert Browning and Swiss watches, what a peculiar view
of the outside world. How inappropriate to Burma. But, and
here an old interior dialogue that had haunted me during my
stays in Burma started up again, who decides what is appropriate? Tin Mya has to make do with what he can get in his
isolated country—isolated, to maintain the political status quo.
At least he has an inquiring mind. Yes, says my devil's advocate,
who is a European liberal, still somewhat haunted by colonial

guilt, but are the Burmese not better off as they are? Does the City really count in a country where 85 percent of the people live in villages, where, it is commonly agreed, they have just enough to eat? Burmese may be ignorant, but ignorant of what? Is the modern world really worth knowing about? Is it worth developing the City if it destabilizes the countryside, resulting in slums and prostitution? Rational answers are countered by fears of Western arrogance. Sympathy for my educated friends in Rangoon is contrasted with the smiling faces of the village children riding water buffaloes. Does the development of the former have to be at the expense of the latter? Images of hideous shopping malls and concrete housing estates go through my mind as I see the picturesque harmony of village Burma pass by.

I turned to the tattered edition of Macaulay's *Essays* which I had bought in an old bookshop in Rangoon. One of the essays, written in 1830, was an attack on a book entitled *Sir Thomas More; or, Colloquies on the Progress and Prospects of Society*, by Robert Southey, Esq. Southey was disturbed by the destruction of rural England by industrial civilization.

" 'How is it,' said I, 'that every thing which is connected with manufactures presents such features of unqualified deformity? From the largest of Mammon's temples down to the poorest hovel in which his helotry are stalled, these edifices have all one character . . .' "

Macaulay's response: "Mr. Southey has found a way, he tells us, in which the effects of manufactures and agriculture may be compared. And what is this way? To stand on a hill, to look at a cottage and a factory, and to see which is the prettier. Does Mr. Southey think that the body of the English peasantry live, or ever lived, in substantial or ornamented cottages . . . If not, what is his parallel worth? We despise those mock philosophers, who think that they serve the cause of science by depreciating literature and the fine arts. But if anything could excuse their narrowness of mind, it would be such a book as this. It is not strange that, when one enthusiast makes the

picturesque the test of political good, another should feel inclined to proscribe altogether the pleasures of taste and
imagination."

Tin Mya had studied engineering. I asked him what he was
going to do. He did not know, but home in Mandalay he could
always guide tourists and practice English. Perhaps I could tell
my friends in Hong Kong about him and he could guide them
around? What about working as an engineer? "Very difficult.
You don't understand our country." He leaned over my shoulder and spoke in my ear, more to overcome the din of the old
train thundering along the tracks than to ensure secrecy: "Our
country, not free."

I find it difficult to respond to such statements. "No, indeed,"
sounds ridiculous, as though the man's views need to be con-
firmed. "Oh, I'm sure it's not as bad as all that," is dishonest
and patronizing. So I said nothing, instinctively felt for my
passport, and felt slightly embarrassed.

Yes, says the devil's advocate, but who are we to impose our
Western ideas of politics and economics on Asian people? They
have their own ways and ideas, which may be just as valid.
Perhaps we can even learn from them.

Again I turned to Macaulay's attack on Southey. Southey
was a believer in paternal government based upon religion.
Macaulay answered: "Now it does not appear to us to be the
first object that people should always believe in the established
religion and to be attached to the established government. A
religion may be false. A government may be oppressive. And
whatever support government gives to false religions, or religion to oppressive governments, we consider a clear evil."

It was the most subversive thing I had read in Burma and it
gave me great pleasure. The problems faced by Europe a
hundred years ago are now exercising much of Asia. The difference is that Europe shaped the modern world; the problems
were of her own making. Modernity was thrust upon Burma
and the rest of the non-Western world. Asians had no choice
in the matter. But is that a reason for rejecting it? Is rejection

of modernity, in the name of kings, secular or divine, not infinitely worse than rational measures to benefit from its fruits? I felt that it was. And it was to test this feeling that I undertook this journey, beginning in Rangoon and ending in Japan.

THAILAND

Cocktails and champagne were served by Thai air hostesses as Burma receded into a distant view of wet paddy fields with the occasional gold or white glint of a pagoda. Purple orchids were presented to the women. The young European travelers in Indian shirts smiled at one another a little guiltily as they tucked into shrimp cocktails and pepper steaks, enjoying their respite from the "real Asia." The cover of the in-flight magazine had a photograph of the king of Thailand, Bhumibol Adulyadej, playing Dixieland jazz on his saxophone.

Arriving in Thailand from more oppressive neighboring countries is always a relief. The taxis smell of flowers. The people are gracious. Hedonism comes without guilt. So what if people want your money. And if the city is a little crass. After the air of slow death of Rangoon, I felt like kissing the ground of the newest Bangkok shopping mall. Here the king plays jazz.

"During this 1987 Year of Tourism, everyone in Thailand's tourist industry is taking special care to make your stay in our country a pleasant and comfortable one, and if possible, improve on our friendliness and hospitality, already well known throughout the world . . ." Thus began the message of the Smile-a-While campaign advertised in the Bangkok papers.

It is charming. But soon, once blind enchantment has worn off, one begins to wonder about modern Thailand, or at least Bangkok. There is something a little over-the-top about the Smile-a-While campaign, the Year of Tourism, the obtrusive desire to please. Delight is replaced with a no doubt puritanical skepticism, which can, it must be said, swing back to delight at great speed. How, one wonders, do Thais preserve their dignity in a world of coarse commercialism? How have decades of tourism, American GIs on Rest and Recreation, and a deluge of dollars and yen affected the urban Thais? Has capitalism indeed corrupted their souls, as some people like to think? Have they lost themselves in greed?

In my hotel room I happened across a column in a weekly entertainment guide for tourists, written by a foreign resident under the name of Nite Owl, and entitled "Out of Respect." "Treated with traditional warm Thai hospitality, the vast majority of residents endeavor to respect the Kingdom's customs and mores . . . Aware that if one breaks the rules, knowingly or unconsciously, it reflects on the others, they keep an eye on one another. I've seen and done this myself." Nite Owl then tells us how he sat on a bus one day with a female acquaintance who was spending some time in Thailand teaching English. "A few little schoolboys (in uniform) got on and I rose to give one my seat. The woman remained sitting. Pointing to the schoolboys still standing, I asked her to give one her seat. 'Why should I?' she asked. 'You haven't learned much during your stay, have you?' I asked rhetorically and walked to another part of the bus." After several more examples of how foreigners in the know keep an eye on visitors as yet ignorant of the finer points of Thai etiquette, Nite Owl, as it were without blinking, goes on to recommend the newest "chicks" in the "founts of Fun City." The chicks are shown in a series of photographs; virtually naked, dancing in high-heeled shoes. One has a chain around her waist, her eyes rolled up in mock ecstasy. Another, in sunglasses, bumps and grinds in see-through panties. Right behind her is a girl sitting on the knee of a foreign customer, mussing his hair.

The two sides of Nite Owl's persona, the self-righteous stickler for social rules and the leering huckster, seem startlingly at odds. Perhaps this is merely the idiosyncrasy of an expatriate hack writer whose cultural confusion has turned into cynicism. On the other hand, perhaps not. Maybe he reflects, in a caricatural form, something of the ethos of modern Bangkok, something Thais like to call pragmatism—a lack of concern for seeming contradictions; a preoccupation with forms which is both conformist and entirely flexible.

The glossy posters, the orchids in the airplane, indeed all the grace of Thailand cannot disguise the basic truth about tourism: More than twice as many foreign men visit Thailand than women. You hardly see any Japanese women, let alone women from the Middle East or Malaysia. Most visitors come from Malaysia, mainly to a city called Hadyai, a kind of Thai Tijuana on the Malaysian border, where the prevalent business is sex. Paid sex is one of the main tourist attractions in Thailand. If isolation has turned Rangoon into a stagnant backwater, Bangkok is beginning to resemble a sexual supermarket, a capital of discos, go-go bars, massage parlors, VD clinics, German beer halls, Japanese nightclubs, and brothels for Arabs. Bangkok is the playground for the world's frustrated men. All this means big business—indeed, at $1.8 billion in 1987, tourism is the largest foreign exchange earner for Thailand. But while the government, businessmen, pimps, girls, and policemen rake in the cash, Thais are deeply concerned about their image, about national Face. In a newspaper article about poor Thais selling the services of their young children to foreign pornographers, a police colonel concluded that the parents "should not be too greedy for money . . . and moreover, the image of the country will be tarnished because of their ignorance."

As an antidote to this bad image, a good image is presented to the world, that of ancient Thai culture. I was given some examples by the editor of a cultural magazine in Bangkok, an intellectual worried about the damage that tourism was doing to his country. Ordinations of monks, an important event in most Thai lives, are sometimes organized around special fairs for tourists, complete with folk performances and parades. When traditions are no longer practiced, they are revived, drained of all the original significance, or invented especially for foreign or even Thai visitors. Ceremonies are designed by the Fine Arts Department in Bangkok and local schoolteachers are put in charge to teach their students how to perform them. The old city walls of Chiengmai appeared to attract tourists. Consequently all towns with walls were encouraged to build tourist facilities. One town even built a fake wall. In the northeastern city of Korath a monument was erected to a heroine of the war against the Lao, 200 years ago. The military were especially keen on it. Nobody appeared to realize that the heroine they worshipped was a fiction of Thai movies. It did not really matter, as long as it attracted visitors. A deep cave, a picturesque waterfall, a ruin, anything would do as an excuse to build a hotel, a disco, a coffee shop, waiting for the tourists. "I think people live in a fake world today. They fool themselves for fun," said the editor's wife. The editor smiled and said Thais think foreigners are gods.

I had heard this said before, in Japan. This does not always mean foreigners are liked. Gods are outsiders with great and unpredictable powers. They are to be appeased, by all means, lest they mean harm and do damage. It is better still if their powers can be exploited. Therein lies the key to your own survival.

The wish to impress visitors with traditional culture and then to exploit it for money seems inconsistent. It smacks of preachers on the take. "No," said a good friend of mine, a prominent Thai journalist, "I don't think so at all. It is pragmatic. The essence of those traditions is still valid. Making money won't affect that."

It is easy for the visitor to Bangkok to feel that he is in a fake world, a world of images, of empty forms, foreign styles divorced from any meaning. It is easy to condemn Thailand, or at least Bangkok, for being so hopelessly corrupted by "Westernization," "cultural imperialism," "Coca-Colonization," or whatever one wants to call it, that it has lost its identity altogether; indeed a place where people fool themselves for fun.

Bangkok, a professor was quoted as saying in the newspaper, "has the Architecture Identity Disaster—AIDS. AIDS is epidemic in Bangkok." Bangkok, like Tokyo, Taipei, or Seoul, is in a constant state of dramatic flux, and thus, like those cities, has something of a film studio atmosphere, a jerry-built look of tinsel and plaster. The effect is heightened by the colorful billboards that show the buildings of the future: condominiums with Doric columns, Bavarian-style cottages, Victorian town houses. There are Japanese department stores, all spic-and-span plastic, and fake-rustic Thai country restaurants decorated with neon and fairy lights. The architect Krisda Arivongse, a man of royal blood, was reminded of Disneyland: "If something like this goes on for a while, we will be the laughingstock of the world capitals." Again this remarkable preoccupation with Face: the laughingstock—as if one builds for foreigners.

Every night in Patpong, two neon-lit streets in the midst of airline offices and international hotels, the pimps wait for the tourists to arrive. "You want fuck? You want live pussy show? Sucky sucky?" Before the 1960s, when Patpong became a major entertainment area for GIs on leave from Vietnam, it was a rather swank district of nightclubs and dance halls frequented by well-to-do Thais. Now it is a cluster of go-go bars, massage parlors, and live sex show joints, with names like Superstar, Limelight, the Lipstick Bar—with an entrance shaped like a huge girl's mouth. Patpong really is a bit like Disneyland, a jumble of displaced images, of erotic kitsch, Oriental decadence for package tours. Dark-skinned girls fresh from the rural northeast dance naked on long bars to deafening rock 'n' roll, while overweight foreigners watch American movies or boxing on video screens. Girls stick cigarettes between their legs and smoke them; or shoot Ping-Pong balls, aiming their crotches at the customers like guns; or soap themselves in transparent bathtubs lit by colored strobe lights; or simply stroll around the bar, stark naked, offering blow jobs to tourists drinking beer. I was taken to such a place, called the Bunny House. Naked girls were carefully drawing the names of customers by swiveling their hips with long ink brushes sticking out of their private parts. Ah, I though, giving in for a moment to the

romantic fantasy of a provincial European, Berlin '29, and in
came a guided tour of white-haired ladies seeing Bangkok by
night. They spoke German.

"You buy me Coke." "You my darling all night." "You want
body massage?" Sexuality in Patpong is so divorced from daily
life, so utterly absurd, that it ceases to be obscene. It is more
like a charade, a show for the benefit of foreigners, a fake
world set up to make money.

There appears to be an almost insulting contradiction between the image of the delicate Land of Smiles, of exquisite
manners and "unique hospitality," and the world of live pussy
shows. Yet, to see these images as contradictory is perhaps to
misunderstand Thailand. Patpong kitsch and Thai traditions
coexist—they are images from different worlds, forms manipulated according to opportunity. The same girl who dances to
rock 'n' roll on a bar top, wearing nothing but cowboy boots,
seemingly a vision of corrupted innocence, will donate part of
her earnings to a Buddhist monk the next morning, to earn
religious merit. The essence of her culture, her moral universe
outside the bar, is symbolized not by the cowboy boots, but
by the amulets she wears around her neck, with images of Thai
kings, of revered monks, or of the Lord Buddha. The apparent
ease with which Thais appear able to adopt different forms, to
swim in and out of seemingly contradictory worlds, is not proof
of a lack of cultural identity, nor is the kitsch of Patpong proof
of Thai corruption—on the contrary, it reflects the corrupted
taste of Westerners, for whom it is specifically designed. Under
the evanescent surface, Thais remain in control of themselves.

Perhaps because of this shimmering, ever-changing, ever-so-
thin surface, Thailand, to me, is one of the most elusive countries in Asia. Thais clearly don't suffer from the colonial hang-
ups of neighboring peoples; they know who they are. And yet
trying to grasp or even touch the essence of Thailand seems
impossible, like pinning down water. But if I did not succeed
in pinning down Thailand I did spend a lot of time talking to
Thais who claimed that they could.

One such person was the architect Sumet Jumsai. "We seem to take over only the veneer of other cultures," he said, "but our essence is still there, like the wooden houses behind the modern department stores." He designed a striking bank building, completed in 1987 in central Bangkok. It is a skyscraper in the shape of a robot—"A Statement in Post-High-Tech," as the brochure describes it. Sumet has a theory about Asians and machines. (Judging by his many newspaper columns, he has theories about most things.) "You see," he said, "machines have no nationality. But Asians humanize them. Computers, they are universal, but also very Asian; a computer exorcises and humanizes the machine. Look at our ten-wheel trucks. They are humanized, decorated like long-tail boats, like boats on wheels, actually—you know, by the way, that our culture is a water culture, Bangkok is a water city—but as I said, they are decorated like boats, with colored cloth, joss sticks, and flowers."

Sumet had just returned from England, where his son attended a public school: "A family tradition, actually. We went to schools in England since 1870. I was at Wellingborough." Sumet's public school accent is impeccable. He smokes a pipe. "Opposites always coexist in Thailand. At one point we were basically Chinese. Then, about seven hundred years ago, our literary culture was Indianized. A basically Sinicized people became Indianized. Quite contradictory, really. Funny thing is that civilizations seem to disappear without a trace here. No continuity, you see. People just start again. Sukhothai, in the thirteenth century, was a great civilization. Nothing much was left. Only two hundred years ago Ayuthaya was destroyed. Hardly had any influence at all on Bangkok. We had to begin all over again. Of course, the unwritten part of our culture, the reflexes, the ceremonies remained. But they may be disappearing now too. Would you care for some more tea?"

Bob Halliday, a genial American who has lived in Thailand for decades, calls it a state of mind. "Everything comes and goes in waves here. High-rise buildings, now there's an example. Suddenly everyone with money wanted one. Tourism is the thing now. But underneath all that, the state of mind does not change at all." Quite what that state of mind, those reflexes are is impossible to define. Halliday, an expatriate who shuns Patpong, speaks fluent Thai, and appears to be content to live the rest of his life in Thailand, describes it as a natural empathy for friends, a certain delicacy of feeling.

Around 1912, King Rama VI devised a slogan to sum up what he saw as the essence of Thailand: Nation, Religion, Monarch. The religion is, of course, Buddhism. "Buddhism," I was told by a Thai writer, "fits Thai ways well. Because we believe that material surroundings are an illusion, and only the internal world is real, to be Thai can be anything we want." It would explain both the lack of resistance against foreign forms, "Westernization" if you like, and the ease with which they are discarded.

The city of Ubon, officially called Ubon Ratchathani, lies in the northeast, not far from the border of Laos. Its people, according to a local tourist folder, "still abide by traditions and culture." And "the Buddhist faith, of which its Dharma Principles are ever abreast of times, has molded the people's psychological makeup." I went there to see Yingsak, a Bangkok writer born in Ubon. He did not meet me at the station because he wanted me "to smell the atmosphere of a typical country town" on my own. Ubon is beautifully located on the Moon River. The shops, like shops in all Thai cities, are mostly owned by Chinese or Sino-Thai families, their Thai names written in Thai, the name of the shops sometimes in Chinese. Yingsak's father, who immigrated from China as a small boy, owns the largest supermarket in town. There he sits, surrounded by the products of modern civilization, still speaking the language of a country he cannot remember. His children only speak Thai. The pace of life is slow, the weather hot. There are some interesting temples, a few hotels with "cocktail lounges," two cinemas, a lively morning market, and a rather gaudy "spirit house," where the town's guardian spirits live.

Ubon is indeed a typical country town with nothing at all to remind the visitor today that less than twenty years ago it housed one of the largest American military bases in Thailand. At its peak, in the late 1960s, there were at least 10,000 Americans in Ubon, flying missions over Laos and Vietnam. Yingsak remembers them sunning themselves in the streets or dancing to hard rock in the bars and discos. Girls appeared in Ubon from all over the north and northeast to work in the bars or live with the Americans as temporary wives. It was a boom time for hotels, restaurants, pimps, and taxi drivers. Young Thais were introduced to rock music, drugs, easy sex, chewing gum, and blue jeans. But in 1973 it all came to an end, the Americans left, almost without trace.

We tried to find at least a few traces. There were some wooden bungalows outside the main gate of the base, where the Americans kept their mistresses. The windows were mostly broken, the girls all gone. A woman who used to live nearby did not know if any of the girls still lived in Ubon. She thought not. One of the old hard-rock bars was now a massage parlor, where young locals drank beer and stared at the girls who watched TV on the other side of a one-way mirror. There were pictures of teenage Japanese singers on the wall. Sentimental Thai pop music came through a scratchy loudspeaker. We asked around if there were still Americans living in the area. Yes, said one shopkeeper, there was one *farang* (white man). She did not know whether he had been in Ubon during the war.

Ed's bungalow was in a dusty row of bungalows on the outskirts of Ubon. The street was littered with garbage—used plastic bags, broken bottles, a dead dog, presumably run over by a car. The bungalow was surrounded by a white wall with bits of glass on top. We could hear the sound of Glenn Miller's "In the Mood" booming from the house. "Come right in, guys," said Ed's wife, a smiling Thai woman in her thirties, chewing gum. She was heavily made-up and must once have been very pretty. It was three in the afternoon and so hot that the slightest physical effort caused one to be drenched in sweat. A tinseled banner saying "Merry Christmas" hung across the front porch. Ed was a heavy man in his sixties, wearing shorts, drinking bourbon on the rocks. His speech was a little slurred, but still coherent. He moved awkwardly, as if every movement was an effort. He had been in the navy in World War II and in the Korean and Vietnam wars. He met and married his present wife in Bangkok about five years ago and decided to retire in Ubon, her hometown. The bungalow had pictures on the wall of battleships, Ronald Reagan, the Thai royal family, and nude Thai girls. There were pink, heart-shaped cushions on the sofa and a kind of altar with Buddhist images and a statue of King Rama V, the great modernizer of Thailand, on top. We could hear Ed singing along with Glenn Miller in the garden. "He often talks to himself," said the wife. Glenn Miller went silent. "Turn the tape over, honey," Ed shouted from the garden.

Ed's conversation revolved around the theme of "whupping ass." "We sure whupped the Japs' ass. They won't start no war again. Now, in Vietnam, we could've whupped their ass too. But the liberals stabbed us in the back." I had seen men like Ed in Bangkok, where they congregate in certain Patpong bars, the sad flotsam of Pax Americana. He seemed to be talking to his wife as much as to us. She looked at Ed indulgently, as a mother to a child about to start a familiar game. "We gotta get those Vietnamese and whup their ass next time, just like we whupped the Japanese. They won't start no war again." Ed poured us another bourbon, slapped my knee, and proposed a toast to General MacArthur: "Now there's a guy I like, an American, number one. Turn the tape over, baby."

I asked Ed how he liked the Thais. "A bunch of lazy free-loaders, that's what they are. They see a *farang* and think he's rich, so they take him for all they can get. Well, not with me they don't. I closed my gates on them. My wife knows, her folks can't come here no more. Fucking freeloaders. I never let them forget I'm an American." Ed poured more drinks and proposed a toast to Jack Dempsey, "an American champion, number one." The talk about Thais resumed. "We don't think the same. They sit on the floor. They eat that shit. Not us, no sir. We eat American food here." The wife smiled and mopped Ed's sweaty brow.

In the bungalow the wife showed us Ed's collection of video tapes—*The Glenn Miller Story*, *Patton*, *The Battle of Midway*. He often cries watching these movies," she said, and giggled. She told my friends in Thai how Ed's talk would drive her crazy, and how bored she often felt. I asked why she put up with it. They said she was simply being realistic. It wasn't a bad life, and she would surely outlive her husband. Despite his crassness, I felt a sneaking sympathy for Ed, who so clearly was the weaker character. His world is based on illusion. Hers seems painfully real.

"Lou Gehrig, Babe Ruth, Joe DiMaggio." Ed banged the garden table. "Those were real ball players." "Show them your baseball, honey," said the wife. Ed stood up, a little wobbly on his feet, and adopted the posture of a catcher in a baseball game, his face creased in intense concentration. He then showed us how to throw a curveball, a fastball. Then he became a batter hitting a home run. He lunged at the imaginary ball, lost his balance, and fell painfully on his bottom. His wife shrieked with pleasure.

"Someday I'd sure like to take my wife to the States," said Ed, "and show her what life is like in a great country. Still, I guess we can't go nowhere. I built this house here. We can't leave it. Sometimes I go to Bangkok with my wife. I buy first-class tickets, so I can close the fuckin' door on everybody. So the Thais can't stare at me 'cause I'm a *farang*. I close the door on all of them. It's worth the money."

The Thais have been both clever and lucky in their relations with foreigners. The Thais were lucky that the British and the

French, the two major colonial powers, neutralized each other, so that Siam became a kind of buffer zone between Burma, Malaya, and Indochina. They were clever in the same way as the Japanese, the only other Asian nation to escape colonialism: they—that is, the elites—"Westernized" themselves to counter the might of the West; they modernized themselves to avoid having modernity imposed on them by others. The phrase used for this by the British pioneer of Japanese studies, Basil Hall Chamberlain, was "protection by mimicry."

The emphasis on monarchy and religion, which seems so atavistic today, was an essential part of this process. The Japanese turned their emperor into what nationalists like to call a "priest-king," a European-style monarch in military uniform, who was at the same time the center of a religious cult. The Thai monarchy turned itself into something similar. King Chulalongkorn (Rama V), whose image adorns Ed's bungalow in Ubon, visited Europe in 1897. He toured the slums of London—quite a remarkable thing to do for a visiting monarch—and saw the problems of European modernity, but was impressed by modern science, by the legal systems and the bureaucratic institutions. Back in Siam, he stated that "there exists no incompatibility between such acquisition [of European science] and the maintenance of our individuality as an independent Asiatic nation." ("We even had trams before the Japs," said Sumet, the architect, sucking his pipe.) This enlightened thought (the king's, not Sumet's), which could not have occurred in a colonized mind, is crucial to the development of modern Thailand. In fact, the king was ahead of the great modernizers of early Meiji Japan, who believed that total Westernization was the only road to modernity.

During his reign, lasting from 1868 to 1910, a collection of regions ruled by aristocratic families was transformed into a state. Buddhism was reformed and institutionalized as a national religion, taught in schools and monasteries all over the country. The supreme patriarch was a Siamese prince. Buddhist monks taught a new standard Thai, as well as science and mathematics, something their counterparts in Burma absolutely refused to do. The chief ingredient in the attitude of the Burmese Buddhist hierarchy was, as the historian D. G. E. Hall put it, "its opposition to what may be termed modernity." Thai monks, in contrast, became the first modern teachers. One thing Burma and Thailand had in common, however, was that a generation later Thai government propagandists and young Burmese anti-colonialists were convinced that true patriotism was inseparable from Buddhism. But Buddhism, unlike the state Shinto of prewar Japan, was always a universalist faith, far removed from the Shinto myths of racial purity. This has contributed greatly to the relative openness of Thai society.

While the Thai elite was educated for government service, Chinese merchants were encouraged to build a modern urban economy, which they still dominate. Chinese businessmen enriched the Thai elite in exchange for status in Thai society, a situation which also still persists. A Sino-Thai journalist in Bangkok told me that "one hundred years ago the Thais knew nothing. The Chinese taught them how to weigh, how to buy, how to sell." To be sure, my friend, who does not speak any Chinese, is a bit of a Chinese chauvinist. But he was not entirely wrong. When I asked him how Thais and Sino-Thais got on today, he smiled as though the answer was self-evident: "No problem. We mix now because of Westernization. TV, discos, Walkmans—we all move to the same point." He was not wrong about this either. But when I asked him whether he would mind if his daughter married an ethnic Thai, he did not hesitate: "That I would not allow."

Chulalongkorn's successor, King Vajiravudh (Rama VI), who ruled from 1910 to 1925, was educated at Sandhurst and Oxford, where he read history and law. There is a picture of him, taken in 1914, on the bridge of the royal yacht, splendidly dressed in white ducks, double-breasted blazer, and cap, holding a brass telescope. It is typical of his chosen image—just as typical as the photograph of the present king playing jazz is of his—the priest-king as a modern naval officer. King Vajiravudh

was fond of the theater and he wrote plays exhorting his subjects to become modern nationalists, more like Europeans. His
hectoring prose could have been written by the moralists of
Meiji Japan:

> *Let us unite our state, unite our hearts, into a great whole.*
> *Thai—do not do harm or destroy Thai,*
> *But combine your spirit and your strength to preserve*
>   *the state*
> *So that all foreign peoples*
> *Will give us increasing respect.*

Respect from foreign people. There it is again. Siam not only
should be modern, but it should look modern, or, rather, if it
looked modern, it *was* modern. Through the king's encouragement, women began to adopt European dress and hairstyles.
He introduced the Gregorian calendar, designed a new national
flag, and encouraged team sports and Boy Scouts. The king
himself was Chief Scout-General and his youngest schoolboy
followers were Tiger's Whelps.

Modernity, however, creates its own monsters. The students
sent abroad by the modern monarch returned and were no
longer satisfied with the rule of the priest-king. In 1932, during
the reign of Vajiravudh's successor, King Prajadhipok, absolute
monarchy came to an end, pushed aside in a coup staged by
forty-nine military and naval officers, and sixty-five civilians,
led by two modern men, both educated in France, one a soldier, the other a civilian: Plaek Khittasangkha and Pridi
Phanomyong.

Pridi and Plaek (better known as Phibunsongkhram or Phibun) represented two faces of modern Thailand, which are still
at odds. Pridi, the son of a Chinese immigrant, was a civilian
intellectual attracted to "progressive" politics. He hoped to
establish a more democratic system in Thailand. Phibun was
a modern military man, inspired by right-wing populist nationalism, like that of King Vajiravudh. The military being a

more powerful and efficient modern institution than anything the budding civilian intelligentsia could muster, Phibun's power grew, while Pridi's declined. In 1938 Phibun became Prime Minister, with Pridi as his Minister of Finance. He belonged to the same school of thinking as Dr. Ba Maw in Burma and the ultranationalists in Japan. He wrote approvingly of Hitler and Mussolini and believed in the *Führerprinzip*. He changed his country's name from Siam to Thailand, as though to emphasize that Thailand belonged to the Thai-speaking peoples and not to outsiders like the Chinese.

This is why many "progressive" nationalists today still insist on using the name Siam. One of the most prominent social critics, Sulak Sivaraksa, believes that the name Thailand "signifies the crisis of traditional Siamese Buddhist values. Removing from the nation the name it had carried all its history is in fact the first step in the psychic dehumanization of its citizens, especially when its original name was replaced by a hybrid, Anglicized word. This new name also implies chauvinism and irredentism." Phibun's most powerful intellectual ally was a writer called Luang Wichit, who liked to compare the Chinese in Thailand to the Jews in Germany; both, in his view, were a noxious and polluting presence.

Like Rama VI, Phibun was eager to impress the world with a progressive, modern Thai image. This meant more Western forms: trousers, gloves, shoes, a national anthem, saluting the flag, and so forth. This was hardly a case of blind adulation for things European. On the contrary, it was a re-creation of Western forms to strengthen Thai nationalism. Western clothes, yes, but made in Thailand.

The full force of modernity, however, only came in the 1950s and 1960s. As usual, it was mixed with tradition, or pseudotradition. In 1958, Field Marshal Sarit Thanarat staged the second coup in two years and formed a "Revolutionary Party." "The fundamental cause of our political instability in the past," wrote Sarit's adviser and later Foreign Minister, Thanat Khoman, "lies in the sudden transplantation of alien institutions onto our soil without proper regard to the circumstances which prevail in our homeland, the nature and characteristics of our own people, in a word the genius of our race, with the result that their functioning has been haphazard and ever chaotic. If we look at our national history, we can see very well that this country works better and prospers under an authority, not a tyrannical authority, but a unifying authority, around which all elements of the nation can rally."* The unifying authority was the priest-king, reinstated as a real force once again. The monarchy lent legitimacy to the new regime, just as the Meiji emperor had done for the Japanese modernizers since 1868.

It is a common theme in Southeast and East Asia, the use of tradition to bolster modern authoritarianism. Ferdinand Marcos saw himself as a tribal chieftain in the Philippines and Park Chung Hee as a Confucian patriarch in South Korea. And as was the case with the other Asian strongmen, Sarit's modern authoritarianism was financed by massive American aid, meant, in the buzzword of the time, to "develop" Thailand. The constitution was abolished, martial law declared, the streets cleaned, crime reduced, and critics arrested. The Vietnam War escalated and U.S. bases grew in size. At the same time there was high economic growth, rapidly spreading education (from five university-level institutions with 1,800 students in 1961 to seventeen with over 100,000 in 1972), the beginning of tourism, and a communist insurgency. Sons and daughters of peasants moved to the cities, the middle class grew, students read Marx and listened to the Rolling Stones—in short, Disneyland came to Bangkok. Intellectuals reacted as they usually do under these circumstances: they wrote about spiritual dislocation and moral drift.

This was the main theme of the novelist Khamsing Srinawk. His best-known stories were written in the late 1950s, when Phibun was in power for the second time, assisted by the Americans to stem the tide of communism, which began to be seen

---

* Quoted by David K. Wyett in his *Thailand: A Short History.*

as the main threat to Thai survival. Communism was associated with foreigners, mainly the Chinese. A British journalist in Bangkok once jokingly called a Thai acquaintance a communist. The Thai failed to see the joke and answered: "No, I am a Thai." Khamsing is not a communist, but very much a modern intellectual concerned about the social costs of development.

In his story "Clash," written in 1969, at the height of the Vietnam War, he describes a provincial town, rather like Ubon. We see all the modern urban ills through the eyes of the main character, a taxi driver. We see cunning insurance salesmen and prostitutes "dressed in red miniskirts with the tops below their navels and the bottom well above their knees." The hero's friend calls them "ambassador's ladies," as they cater to American soldiers: "Who had invented this nickname for camp-following floozies? Had he been more revolted by the rented wives or by the foreign soldiers who, with the immunity of diplomats, swarmed over the brothels and massage parlors?"

Prostitutes, in Khamsing's story, are associated with modern progress: "If it's true that prostitutes bring misfortune to mankind, there would be nothing left in the world. It would be the end of limousines, buses, trains, and planes in the air, not to mention unlicensed taxis. From the smallest roadside stall to the fanciest restaurant with entertainers and singers, from the shops selling diamonds to those selling lavatory brushes, from the pseudo-offices of the country headmen to the great government offices, is there any place that has not known their presence?"

The hero wonders whether to give a monk a lift in his taxi: "I wasn't going to make money off a monk. I thought that if he was going to a place nearby or if he lived along the road to my house, I could do him a good turn and gain a little merit in the process, but when he named a distant town, however, I forgot the merit business."

He finds some rich passengers who wish to go to that distant town and offers the monk a lift after all. Driving along "Progress Road," past the "Progress Villages"—"each displaying a big name-sign in Thai and English"—he swerves to avoid a water buffalo and crashes into a truck. When he regains consciousness he becomes "aware of people running and I could see them shining their flashlights about. Four or five men snatched up the things that lay scattered around the car. On the other side of the wreck, the moans began again. The men moved towards the sounds.

" 'This one's not dead yet,' someone said. Then there was a clunk of something hard, like a lump of earth or rock, striking something." The hero escapes being killed by feigning death as his valuables are removed.

The robbers run away when the police arrive. The rich passengers turn out to have been members of a criminal gang. The police count the bodies and discover that the monk is also part of the gang.

"Dogs barked and bayed. By then all the villagers must have known what had happened. Doors opened and closed as people stopped their cars and got out to look. From the transistor radios carried by the villagers milling around I heard reedy country songs and a sermon on the message of the Lord Buddha."

Khamsing's story is not subtle. His message was clear, and influential among the students and intellectuals who would stage a revolt on October 14, 1973. What was officially understood as progress—capitalism, foreign investment, American aid and culture—was wiping out human values and creating an amoral world. Buddhist sermons on transistor radios sounded hollow: "I forgot the merit business." The correct forms that were left could no longer disguise the leering face of the huckster.

I had met the kind of people Khamsing wrote about in Ubon. I was taken out for dinner by a young Sino-Thai, described to me as "small Mafia." He dressed snappily and drove a gold-painted Mercedes-Benz. After a Chinese meal washed down with French brandy, we repaired to the High-Class Cocktail Lounge, which he partly owned. It was Hawaiian Night, so the pretty hostesses wore paper flowers around their necks and ankles. A portly man in a purple spotlight crooned Tom Jones numbers, some in Thai, some in English. My host had his thighs massaged by two smiling girls. A local politician fondled his girl, gave me the thumbs-up sign, and said, "No bra." The girls giggled. The hostess assigned to me said, "What your name?" When I told her, she answered, "Sorry, English very little." Soon the true generosity of my host was revealed: I was offered one of the girls, any one I liked. They were pure Thai, I was assured, pure Thai country girls, not Chinese from Bangkok. These girls, these pure Thai girls, were not interested in money, only in my well-being.

This turned out to be slightly less than the whole truth. But what interested me was the fact that even Sino-Thais adhered to the cult of the pure, smile-a-while, nonmaterialistic village Thais. Clearly they contrasted these pure Thai girls with their own ethos. But perhaps I should not have been surprised. After all, nobody is as anti-Semitic as an anti-Semitic Jew.

A young human rights lawyer in Bangkok told me that people in rural villages were poor, exploited, and ignorant of the complexities of modern society, but, and this was the important point, they were "spiritually richer than us." The lawyer was educated in Europe, spoke English with a plummy public school accent, and wore beautifully cut suits. He had the long, slender hands of a classical dancer. He spoke a lot of sense. He believed that "democracy, in a metaphysical sense, is universal" and that the universality of this concept is "the right to think critically before accepting things." This, more than anything, is what defines the City. What failed to convince me was the spiritual superiority of peasants. I felt that his admirable desire to educate rural people had as much to do with his own somewhat complex social position as with the lot of the peasants.

A magazine editor called Sujit Wongthes said that "since Rama V started sending Thai students abroad, many Thai intellectuals lost their identities. And so two distinct types emerged, cosmopolitans and those who wish to be very Thai."

Sujit, a chubby man with spectacles, likes to dress in Thai clothes and write articles promoting Thai culture. He obviously belongs to the latter category. But so, in his way, does the young European-educated lawyer. Turning to the Village, as opposed to the confusing, amoral City, is a way of redefining his Thai-ness.

The Village is pure Thai, the City, dominated by Chinese businessmen, is alien. "Traditional ways of life in the village have been attacked and destroyed by the modern culture which occurred during the period of Westernization. In consequence, many social problems came into existence and became more complex in village society," writes Apichart Tongyou in a publication entitled *Back to the Roots*. Apichart was a student leader in the 1970s. Yougyut Trinutchakorn, writing in the same booklet, is a first-generation Sino-Thai who studied political science in the 1970s at a Bangkok university. He was confused about his family life, especially his father, an authoritarian figure. He read books about Buddhism. "I did not know I had deceived myself in pretending to keep strict ethics . . . I never understood why I had to overcome other people and remain with a good heart." After the coup d'état in 1976, which ended the chaotic experiment with democracy since 1973, many of his friends in the student movement took to the hills. Yougyut then "went continuously to the rural areas, which proved helpful to me . . . I felt relieved and happy when I entered the rural area: living with the villagers and doing this and that . . . I cannot describe my feelings of tranquility whilst staying with them . . ."

Wat Wanlyangkun wrote a short story in 1975, entitled "Before Reaching the Stars." The hero leaves his village to study at a university in Bangkok, where his elder brother has already become a successful businessman. The hero is shocked by the poverty of rural people less lucky than himself. He joins a newspaper to fight for justice: "Right now I'm investigating a case of some Thais who are conniving with the Americans to swindle our people out of a huge quantity of the nation's priceless resources, destroying what ought to be for the people's benefit. The accomplices of the *farang* are all big shots with a lot of political and bureaucratic influence . . ."

These sentiments, as well as Marxist books and protest songs from America, supplied the ideas behind the October 14, 1973, revolt that toppled the government of the dictatorial duo Thanom and Praphas. Marxism, a foreign political creed, regarded by the right-wing establishment as anti-Thai, was adopted by many young idealists to protect poor Thais against foreign domination. But the revolt would never have succeeded without the backing of an expanding middle class which, though hardly sympathetic to communism, was tired of being dominated by military strongmen. Even the king supported the students, who often brandished his image in the streets. It was a situation rather like the one in South Korea in 1987, when the prosperous middle class supported nationalist student demonstrations against military rule. The Thai students became more and more radical, however, and revolutionary ideas were met with violent right-wing appeals to "nation, religion, and king." Like their Korean counterparts, Thai professionals and businessmen hate chaos as much as dictatorship and when politics got out of hand they were ready to accept an authoritarian restoration of order in 1976. But unlike in South Korea, one major irritant to nationalist feelings had been removed in the same year, the American military bases.

Today, both Marxism and protest songs seem to have more or less vanished. "We failed. Marxism was not appropriate to Thailand," said the drummer of a rock band called Caravan, the members of which joined the Communist Party of Thailand and took to the hills in 1976. "Young people today know nothing about that period," said Somsak Wongrath, a Sino-Thai writer who was a student in 1973. "They don't understand our generation. They don't even know who Bob Dylan is!"

I met Somsak and the drummer in a lively Bangkok bar called Old West. It is the favorite hangout for young artists, writers, and hangers-on. The pictures on the walls are of cowboys rounding up steers. A Confederate flag hangs over the bar. As we were talking, a drunken sociology professor, also of the October 14 generation, suddenly lurched from his chair and began to rip the pictures off the wall. "Down with American imperialism!" he hollered. My friends looked up as he was taken in hand by the smiling barman. "Ah," said one of my companions, dismissing the professor with a wave of his hand, "he's in the wrong time."

The forms have changed again, but the essence has become more confusing. The perfect symbol of the present period is a rock song by a band called Carabao, which produces some of the most interesting and innovative pop music in Asia. The song is entitled "Made in Thailand." The style is a brilliant mixture of reggae and northeastern Thai folk music. For a while, "Made in Thailand" took over even the foreign bars in Patpong. The girls requested it over and over again, singing along at the top of their voices, as though to challenge, if only for a short time, the white supremacy of Anglo-Saxon rock. The lyrics admonish Thai consumers to buy Thai, to be proud of Thailand and its products, to stop foreigners from flooding the market. The song was taken up by the government to promote Thai industry. The band is sponsored by Coca-Cola. When the musicians were criticized for composing advertising jingles for Coke, they answered that the Coca-Cola was made in Thailand. The leader of the band, called Ad, wears a Khmer Rouge hat and scarf. I asked a Thai friend what this meant, what Ad was trying to show. "Nothing at all. It means nothing. Just fashion."

Meanwhile talk of revolution is still in the air. This time from the army commander-in-chief, General Chavalit Yong-chaiyudh, who wants to revolutionize the countryside and turn Thailand into an "agricultural superpower." He shares with the left-wing radicals a contempt for politicians and business-men, whom he regards as uniformly corrupt. The grand elder statesman of Thailand, Kukrit Pramoj, accused the general of being influenced by communists. Five hundred army officers,

serving under Chavalit, held a noisy protest demonstration at
Kukrit's house. It broke his heart, said Kukrit the next day,
"to see such things happen in this fair country in this tourist
year . . . That is why I was ready to do anything to stop this
sort of thing before the tourists know about it."

"Civilization can kill," said Cherd Songsri, who had just
shown me his latest feature film, entitled *Ploy Talay* (*Gem from
the Deep*), which was, said the *Bangkok Post*, "a perfect advertisement for Visit Thailand Year." Cherd, an independent
filmmaker, is regarded as one of the few directors in Thailand
interested in making serious films instead of standard studio
schlock. *Ploy Talay*, starring Sorapong Chatri, only just past
being a matinee idol, was a commercial success.

The story is about a small fishing community on an island
in southern Thailand. The hero, Rong, when diving for coral,
finds a ruby, which, the synopsis informs us, "spun a web of
greed around itself, and many were trapped." The ruby changes
hands throughout the story. Rong's girlfriend, Kratin, takes it
to the mainland. The first shot of the mainland town, the City
as it were, is of a woman's hand wearing a jade bracelet, lighting
incense in a Chinese shrine—the hand of the daughter of a
Chinese merchant who owns most of the district's fishing fleet.

Kratin marries the Chinese merchant's son and gives him the
ruby. His character is corrupted as "the lust for wealth and
power completely possessed him." When in the end the ruby
is returned to Rong, the hero lectures his former lover: "I
thought it was an evil stone. But now, seeing the way if affects
you, I realize that the stone itself is neither good nor evil. It is
only those who possess it who are good or evil."

The moral of this story is interesting. Fifty-carat rubies are
not normally found in the sea, the synopsis explains. "Our title,
therefore, suggests this displacement and uses it as a key to the
film's underlying meaning." Civilization kills. The Village is
pure, virtuous, and Thai. Cherd pointed out that the story is
like John Steinbeck's "The Pearl," but "in Steinbeck's story the

pearl is thrown away. My message to the Thai people is that
we do not have to throw the ruby away. It does not matter
whether we have it or not. That is our Buddhist belief. The
Lord Buddha said that 'nothing can be truly grasped.' It is all
illusion."

A young girl in Cherd's office, there to interview him for a
newspaper, asked me about my impressions of Thai people.
Did I find them more delicate than Westerners? I asked her
what she meant. She picked up her cup of coffee and put it
down with a noisy clatter. The point of this demonstration was
that "Thai people would try to put it down softly. Westerners
do not care so much." She then asked me about Buddhism,
which, she observed, was "more difficult than all philosophies.
Very few Thai people are real Buddhists." I remembered something that had happened ten years before, a small incident that
stuck in my mind, as small incidents sometimes do. I had gone
down to the Thai-Cambodian border to visit one of the refugee
camps, where people still arrived looking like matchstick men.
A group of foreign journalists asked a Thai colonel whether it
was true that Thai soldiers had shelled refugees to stop them
from entering Thailand. "We are Buddhists," said the colonel,
"how could we possibly do such a thing?"

Thailand is in fact a very violent society, as one can tell from
the lurid crime stories in the Thai newspapers. Packing guns
is a common way of displaying machismo. Hired killers, one
is told, are cheap in Bangkok, and seldom unemployed. Terrible
stories did the rounds: Foreign homosexuals were stabbed to
death in their hotel rooms. Rural policemen were accused of
kicking the victims of a traffic accident to death to get at their
valuables. A man in the Bangkok building where I did some
writing blew his girlfriend up with a hand grenade. Many
crimes appear to involve trickery of one kind or another. During my visit, the police arrested a group of robbers who went
around disguised as monks. Tourists often fall victim to a notorious gang of transvestites.

In a book about Siamese folk tales, written in 1930, Reginald

LeMay commented that "the Siamese are realists. This is a very wicked world, and everyone is trying to get the better of you in some way or other. Your only means of protection is to be cleverer than your neighbor, and if you gain a reputation for being alert and keen in your business dealings, you will be looked up to and admired. There is little sympathy wasted on the dupe . . ."

I asked people about this and got inconclusive answers: modern corruption of morals; morality depends on the nature of your relationship; Buddhist values are humanist, to be sure, but individual behavior depends on time and place, etc. Perhaps statistics, rather than cultural interpretation, would bring light onto the matter. I turned to the Police Research and Planning Division of the Bangkok Police Department. I had made an appointment with the commander, Major General Suwan Suwannavejo. He was a heavy man with long black hair draped around his forehead and a hunted look in his eyes. Our meeting began with smiles and courtesies; name cards were exchanged, one for the general, two for his deputies; iced Cokes were brought in. I asked about the crime rate, the statistics, that is, not the gory details. That is when the conversation took a peculiar turn.

"Are you a friend or an enemy?" asked the general. Well, neither, really, I answered truthfully. "Are you friend or enemy of Thailand? This is Visit Thailand Year." Yes, I was aware of that. "What the general means," said one of the deputies, "is that we cannot say anything. That is our policy and regulations. We have all the data, we do all the research, but we cannot say anything. This is Visit Thailand Year." The problem, the second deputy explained, was that if I wrote something negative it would give the police a bad reputation. All the more reason, I argued, to give me their side of things. No, that was impossible, for I might use it to write something negative. "What the general means," said one of the deputies, "is that you will step on his head."

"You press people all lie," the general said, and asked his

deputy to show me a yellow folder. It contained what seemed to be an innocuous article clipped from *The Observer* of London about the problems of the Tourist Police in Bangkok. It did not mention murder. "All lies," the general said, and whisked the article away, as though it were a secret document. I asked what was wrong with it. "That I am not allowed to tell you," said the general. "What the general means," said the deputy, "is that you must get permission from our superior." This I duly asked for and I was told to write down my hotel and room number.

The next day, the telephone rang in my hotel room. It was a man identifying himself as Major Suphat. He had heard I wanted an interview with the police. He could be of help. Would I meet him the next day for coffee?

We met, exchanged cards, and drank coffee. His card looked well thumbed. He was a young, slightly shifty man. He talked about the cost of hiring a killer and the price of guns. He said General Chavalit was a good man. The government was bad. "All corrupt. Bad for the poor people." He appeared nervous and excused himself for a minute to make a phone call.

I never saw "Major Suphat" again. My wallet had been neatly lifted from my bag. I spent the next days going from police station to police station. I even met the real Major Suphat, whose card I had been given. He told me where to find the crime statistics. In the *Bangkok Post*. And there they were: in 1986, 9,648 serious crimes were committed, and 24,376 petty crimes. Of the serious crimes, 8,726 were murders. And the official source of these figures? The Police Research and Planning Division commander, Major General Suwan Suwannavejo.

Does civilization kill? Has modernity wiped out traditional values to the extent that nothing but empty forms and pragmatism remain? I turned, once again, to cultural interpretation. One of the most interesting theories, by Dutch anthropologist Niels Mulder, is that traditional values, far from being eroded by anonymous modern amorality, have actually been enhanced. Mulder begins by pointing out that Thai Buddhists are still animists at heart. The world is divided into a private sphere of pure moral goodness, exemplified by a mother's love for her children, a teacher's for his pupils, by the Buddha himself, and by the land that provides our food, and a public sphere of amoral powers, called *saksit*. "Basically, *saksit* power is amoral, because it does not ask for intentions and protects the good and the wicked alike. It is unprincipled and reacts to mechanical manipulation and the outward show of respect. It is not concerned with right or wrong, or with the development of moral goodness. Contracts with *saksit* power are guided by their own businesslike logic, and there is no higher moral principle that guides these."

It is good to avoid conflict with outside powers, by polite manners, by hiding one's true feelings, and so forth, and it is also good to manipulate those powers to your own advantage. It is the basic approach to all foreigners. The huckster and the stickler for etiquette are two faces of the same man. But he can also have a third face, that of the devoted friend, an example of the empathy and delicate feelings that Bob Halliday called "the Thai state of mind." In Mulder's words: "The world of modernity is a world of increasingly rapid change filled with self-seeking, impersonal power, and the experience of powerlessness for most. No wonder that the old animist perceptions of power are strongly revitalized, not only in Thailand but worldwide, in the losing battle between the temple and the bank."

He applies the same idea to prostitution: "To sell one's body is an outside phenomenon and so it is to buy—and does not imply any feelings of loyalty or even moral respect for oneself. It is a monetary transaction, and money is widely admired and the preeminent embodiment of power . . . As long as [the prostitute] cares for her relatives and recognizes the *bunkhun* [moral goodness] of her parents in terms of gifts and money, she can still present herself as a good person. When she has accumulated enough, or when her fortunes turn, she may re-settle in her village of origin, marry, and be accepted."

The City is the world of outsiders, the Village the moral home. The trouble is that for more and more people there is no more Village; the City is the only reality they know. Crime and prostitution are but extreme forms of manipulating amoral powers. Impulsive violence is usually a sign of long-suppressed feelings; the behavior of people having to present Face in a pragmatic and increasingly anonymous world. It is often when Face is insulted that sudden violence occurs; a bump of the shoulders in the street, a stranger's glance at the girlfriend in a nightclub.

How to moralize the amoral new world? Boy Scouts, racial pride, and military discipline? Marxist dialectics and learning from the Village? The most common answer in Thailand is none of these; instead people point to the personal example of the king and Buddhism. This is where Thai morality and politics continue to connect.

One of the heroes of the October 14 generation was Sulak Sivaraksa, a genial dandy who goes around in traditional Thai clothes, a cloth bag over his shoulders, and a cane in the hand. His ancestors were Chinese, something he does not hide. He calls himself a Buddhist activist. He is a popular speaker on the international lecture circuit as a leading Southeast Asian intellectual. Sulak was raised as an Anglican and studied clas-sics in Britain.

To Sulak the resurgence of Siam is a moral issue. The modern world is amoral, because it is capitalist, which fills man with greed. What's worse, this greedy new world is foreign. Sulak's very modern response to modernity is profoundly anti-modern. "The present single worst enemy of Buddhism in Siam is of course new technology which comes hand in hand with in-dustrialization and progress . . ."

Society "pollutes," for it makes us crave power and riches.

Western powers "took away a lot from our Buddhist way of life. They provided hospitals for us in the Western way, they provided schools for us in the Western way, they provided everything Western for us, and so the temple lost all its functions." The Buddhist precepts are undermined—for example, the precept that you should not kill. "But now you have all the machinery of killing, you have the multinational corporations dealing with killing, and they are linked to banks, and the first precept on killing relates to the second precept on stealing, and so on."

And then, of course, there is Coca-Cola: "Political awareness and economic awareness are related to our society, and related to our own culture. We must tell our people that to drink Coca-Cola, to drink Pepsi-Cola, is a great sin."

The answer to these modern challenges is to return "to the essence of our Buddhist culture, with its spiritual and moral base, in order to wipe out the danger from modern cultural imperialism." Gandhi's concept of the "Village Republic should be studied more seriously in order to find alternative models to capitalist development ideology . . ." Traditional medicine, administered by monks, should be revived. Bangkok must be developed "Buddhistically—against satanic development models which are now prevailing everywhere, by trying to be big, to be rich and powerful . . ." It is a utopian response resembling Luddite movements in Victorian England. Sulak does not even wish to keep the ruby which "spun a web of greed"; he wants to throw it back into the sea. This seems curiously un-Thai, the response, perhaps, more typical of a lapsed Anglican classics scholar.

I had read about another Buddhist activist, whom the newspapers described as the most famous of Thailand's 338,400 monks: Phra Kittivutho, Abbot of Chitrapawan Buddhist College. "A bad monk," said Sulak, "very egotistical. He's a bad man, so everything he does is bad."

Kittivutho became notorious in the 1970s when he founded a right-wing organization called Nawapol, whose goal was to exterminate the communist threat. "It is no sin to kill a communist," was one of the abbot's more controversial statements. What he really meant to say, he now tells reporters, is that it is no sin to kill communism. Kittivutho was also known to have harbored politically congenial gangsters in his college, as well as using the forty-five-acre spread as a training camp for anti-communist Cambodian guerrillas. A convoy of trucks from Chitrapawan was once intercepted on the way to the Cambodian border. It was found to be full of guns. His latest operation is an ambitious plan to turn some 2,000 Buddhist temples into rural economic nerve centers by manufacturing and operating rice mills. He preaches material as well as spiritual development—the idea being that if people are rich enough they will not be tempted by communism.

The college is a large complex of white buildings just off the main highway from Bangkok to Pattaya, a fishing village turned into a kind of Patpong-on-the-sea. A white Mercedes, belonging to the abbot, was parked in the drive. Part of the college functioned as an industrial park with cars, refrigerators, buses, TV sets, and rice mills scattered around the grounds. Young monks were to be seen, wielding machine tools and blowtorches. Kittivutho sat in a large lacquer chair on the lawn, talking to a well-known Thai TV personality, who knelt at the abbot's feet. His cameramen darted about looking for a good angle. The sound of a Brahms piano concerto wafted from the main office, where bags of freshly milled rice were waiting for buyers. A fussy-looking man in dark granny glasses, who later turned out to be Kittivutho's right-hand man, chief engineer, and social secretary, told us to wait our turn.

Kittivutho is a large man with shrewd eyes and the ready smile of a public figure used to dealing with newsmen. Buddhism, I asked, is known for its tolerance toward other creeds, so how did he explain his active campaign to "kill communism"? "Buddhism is indeed the most tolerant of religions," he answered with a radiant smile, "but the Lord Buddha also said that people should not associate themselves with incorrect thought." Who decided what is correct or not? "The Natural Law of Fact. We can see plainly that communism is wrong. We have seen the suffering in Laos and Cambodia." Kittivutho also made the by now familiar point about people having "desire for power and wealth in their hearts." Christian missionaries, for example. Christianity per se is not bad, but missionaries take advantage of poor countries and are greedy." I asked him about Islam. The Natural Law of Fact appears to show that many people are suffering in Muslim countries. Was Islam, like communism, incorrect? "No, only the people who propagate it. They have greed and power in their hearts." Was it not the same with communism, which, after all, preaches peace and brotherhood? "No, the Natural Law of Fact shows that communism is incorrect."

Commercial greed, says Kittivutho, is the major cause of moral decline. In Western societies and Japan religion was nothing but empty ceremonies. Higher education and science had destroyed faith. "There is no more point in going to church." I asked him whether the same was happening in Thailand. "Certainly not. Technology and science will help Buddhism. The more science, the more faith we will have. Buddhism is rational and scientific. But not in Japan. There it is all empty ceremony." The abbot's Sony tape recorder clicked. The interview had ended. Some Thai journalists from a business publication were waiting their turn. Kittivutho had not been educated abroad. He seemed a great deal more pragmatic and, indeed, Thai than Sulak.

Sulak had mentioned another group of Buddhist fundamentalists, centered in a temple called Dhammakaya. "Very strong," he had told me. "Every university is penetrated. Even the military is afraid of them. You give them money, they tell you, and you will be wealthy in your next life. Appeals to the Chinese, you know."

Wat Dhammakaya is near Dom Muang International Airport, on the outskirts of Bangkok. At more than 1,000 acres, it is the largest temple compound in the country. If Chitrapawan looks like a factory, Dhammakaya is like a sanatorium for very rich patients: lush green lawns, white marble buildings, a large park with lakes and man-made waterfalls. And in a sense it is a sanatorium, for young middle-class people from the city troubled by modern life. It is especially popular among students, which perhaps explains why the place has been accused of being "communist."

In fact, the aggressive promotion of Dhammakaya owes more to the methods employed by American TV evangelists. The visitor, seated on a marble floor, is given a slick slide show, with an American voice explaining that modern education teaches "foreign knowledge and technology, but neglects morality." Individualism, one is told, is bad, for "people no longer trust each other." Thais are alienated from themselves, we hear, as pictures of discos and massage parlors are projected on the screen. This is followed by images of thousands of people, dressed in identical white robes, meditating in odd-looking tents set up in Dhammakaya park. Close-ups of ecstatic young faces are accompanied on the sound track by the theme song from *Chariots of Fire*.

I asked a young woman, dressed in white, smiling at nothing in particular, why this rather extreme promotion was necessary. "To develop people's minds," she said. "Vice is spreading so fast in our society that we must use modern technology to get quick results."

In 1987 Dhammakaya supporters numbered several hundred thousand people. The plan is to open offices in every province of Thailand and mobilize at least one million people to meditate at the temple as part of the king's birthday celebrations. It might have been the sheer scale of this ambition that prompted a middle-aged actor to vow to burn himself to death in protest against Dhammakaya. He claimed the temple was committing lèse-majesté.

It all started modestly in 1970. The founder of Dhammakaya meditation was the late Luang Por Wat Paknam, whose technique incorporated the "Lord Buddha's forty different ways of meditation." The most popular technique at Dhammakaya involves a crystal ball, which, the deputy chief abbot Phra Thattacheevo explained, is "more practical than the old methods. It is nice and smooth and appeals to modern young people." Thattacheevo sat behind a modern desk in his office caressing his crystal ball, juggling it from one hand to the other. "Sometimes," he said, "sexual desires enter the mind when trying to meditate. Then other methods must be found, like opening a coffin in a cemetery." He beamed at me, as though to share a particularly good joke. "But that does not happen often. It's mostly just the crystal ball technique."

Thattacheevo repeated what the young woman had said: The main problem in Thailand today is the deterioration of morals. Why did he think that was so? The monk numbered the reasons: "One, no models of behavior, no aim in life; two, no respect for each other." Yes, but why? "Simple," said the monk, "because of vices." But why had vice increased? The monk stared into his crystal ball for a few seconds and ticked off the reasons again: "One, no models . . ."

The models at Dhammakaya are the monks, who, said Thattacheevo, show the young people that they can be happy without vices. I asked him whether vice might have resulted from the materialist incentives of capitalism (this was, after all, known as a "communist" temple). In other words, were Buddhism and capitalism contradictory? "In the first place," said the monk, "few people understand Buddhism, so no contradiction is felt. Secondly, there is no contradiction between materialism and Buddhism. If you have something, that is fine, as long as you use it constructively." It seemed an honest Thai answer. The solution to modern problems, in short, is not to throw the ruby away, but to have a "good heart," to practice benevolence.

Item in a newspaper: "Thai education authorities are seriously looking toward Buddhism to counter the so-called materialistic approach of modern education . . . When development of the intellect takes place in the forefront, the intuitive or the spiritual aspect of the mind is pushed to the back. This leaves the individual to function with a rigid, narrow, and egocentric outlook on life based on material clinging and false values." Thus the architect Sumet argues in his newspaper column that Thai government should be based on Buddhist benevolence. "The present ill of our nation stems from the fact that the tradition of government by Dhamma has been supplanted by an alien form of government, democracy. With nearly all cultural imports, adaptation has proved awkward and harmful." And thus Sulak writes that law must be based on an "Asian concept of justice," which would stress customs, respect for elders, religious values.

The flaw in these views is that they deal with modern ills in purely personal and moral terms. The attempts to revive or even invent an ideal society, based, it is true, on the traditional forces that helped build a modern Thai nation in the past, now seem inappropriate, reactionary, and at odds with political developments. Thailand is one of the most successful countries in Asia, economically vibrant and politically on the verge of maturity. Military dictatorship and communist insurgency seem to be things of the past. More and more Thais seek to strengthen the legal and political institutions which hold personal excesses—"power and greed in our hearts"—in check. Buddhist fundamentalism, with its distrust of capitalism and secular institutions, would seem to be taking Thailand in the opposite direction. The enormous importance attached to the personal benevolence of the monarch is part of the same worldview. It might work if the monarch is believed to be truly benevolent, as appears to be the case with the present king. There is little reason to believe that the people in cinemas, or other public places, who jump up instantly as the portrait of the king appears, do so reluctantly. But if this were ever to change, the country could become dangerously unstable.

* * *

King Bhumibol spends much of his benevolent energy in rural
areas, bolstering the Village. When communist rebels had in-
stalled themselves in large parts of the northeast, the king encouraged the government to make those areas more prosperous
to undercut the communist cause. Khao Ya, a mountain near
the northeastern town of Petchabun, not far from the Laotian
border, was a communist stronghold until 1982. Now it is the
site of a royal mountain lodge. A visit there seemed a fitting
way to end my trip to Thailand. I had been told it was now a
prosperous place, where farmers lived happily after the guerrillas were defeated by the Thai army in 1982. I also heard it
had become a popular tourist destination.

Khao Ya, and Khao Kor, the former rebel headquarters, must
have been beautiful once. And in a strange way they still are.
What was once a jungle has been transformed into a red desert,
with the occasional tree stump scorched by fire. Great gashes
of erosion, like nasty red flesh wounds, mark the bare mountains. On top of Khao Kor is an army museum and a memorial
to the 1,300 soldiers who died in the battle against the communists. In the museum an officer explained to a group of Thai
tourists how the guerrillas were flushed out of their camps.
There were exhibits of guns, a few rusty AK-47s and M-16s.
There were some tattered red flags, a few Chinese embroidered
portraits of Marx, Lenin, and Stalin, and a book on Kim Il
Sung's thoughts in French.

We drove past the royal mountain lodge, perched in isolation
on the denuded hill. We drove past the newly built villages
along the excellent roads. There were signs in English welcom-
ing tourists in Visit Thailand Year. But there were no people.
The villages seemed completely deserted. In the valley we finally
saw some trees. There were signs warning us not to "make
noise to alarm the animals." We saw no animals. There were
a few souvenir stalls, where Hmong hill tribesmen in their
native dress sold trinkets made by different hill tribes near

Chiengrai, hundreds of miles farther north. The souvenir business was subsidized by the government, they said. But there
were not many tourists around to buy anything.

A group of Hmong men were having soft drinks in a wooden
shack where snacks were served. "There were once ten thousand communists here," said one of the men, before getting up
to leave. "Look at the color of that river," said the woman
who ran the restaurant. She pointed at a river which looked
like fluid caramel. "It was not like that before they came and
chopped the trees down." According to her story, the army
had let loggers in from all over the northeast to take away the
trees. The villagers were paid to grow corn. That way, it was
hoped, guerrillas could no longer hide in the hills. The villages
along the road were deserted because nothing would grow
anymore. The government kept on busing new villagers into
the area, so that tourists could be welcomed. Still, said the
woman, "we feel safe here now that the troops protect us."

She fell silent and I looked at the rather sad-looking souvenir
stalls, the signs about not making noise, the caramel river, the
bald mountains, the empty Pepsi-Cola bottles. "Everything they
try to preserve," the woman said suddenly, "has already gone—
the animals, the trees, everything."

It would be the perfect literary metaphor: the loss of traditional values, the destruction of the Village, the emptiness of
capitalist development, and so on and so forth; Sulak would
have appreciated it. Yet the metaphor would be too easy, too
neat. For every image of loss can be countered with an example
of gain. The mountains of Khao Kor have no trees, but the
political destiny of Thailand is no longer decided by gunfire in
the mountains. More and more, it is decided by debate, choice,
politics. The Hmong drink Pepsi-Cola, as do most Thais, as
do most people. It is sad, perhaps, that popular consumption
is often in bad taste and wasteful, but a poor choice is better
than no choice at all. Modernity in Thailand is sometimes ugly,
and perhaps Thais have lost something in their quest for material well-being. But they have managed to retain the thing

that is most precious to them, their self-respect. This is their most attractive quality and it seems indestructible, in the villages, but also in the cities, among students, merchants, politicians, and peasants, and, yes, even among "the chicks of Fun City," the dancing girls in Patpong.

2

Head of the Chief

THE PHILIPPINES

Olongapo City is a typical Filipino town of about 250,000 people. It has its municipal building, its supermarkets, funeral parlors, hash joints, and roadside jukebox bars, with names like Boy's Place. Jeepneys ride up and down the main street. A jeepney is basically a stretched jeep that can accommodate up to twenty passengers. The first jeepneys were U.S. army surplus. Now they are made in the Philippines, silver-colored vehicles decorated with silver fighting cocks on the hood; aluminum horses prancing on the fenders; decals of Jesus Christ's bleeding heart on the dashboard; sexy slogans and naked women on the windshield; and fantastic Philippine landscapes painted in loud colors on the sides. This wholly Filipino creation is given extra pizzazz by the disco music blaring forth from cassettes, the beat accompanied by flashing disco lights.

On the seafront of Olongapo is Subic Bay, home of the U.S. Seventh Fleet, and the largest American naval base outside mainland U.S.A. The base looks like a neat suburb of San Diego, with cinemas, athletic facilities, churches, minimarts, and social clubs. Well-fed American couples jog up and down the roads in track suits. There are Zen classes, self-improvement groups, and therapy sessions. Outside the base is a large stretch of jungle, well preserved by the ecology-minded Americans, where Filipino tribes, known as Negritos, live more or less in the same way as their great-grandfathers. A number of them train American marines in jungle survival and buried under their land is some of the most lethal weaponry of the U.S. Navy.

Between the center of town and the main gate of the base, or, better put, between "San Diego" and Olongapo City proper, runs a long street called Magsaysay Drive. It is the kind of strip to be found in many base towns, except that it is more garish, noisier, and raunchier than most. On a good day, when the ships are in, about 12,000 prostitutes ply their trade there in bars with names like Hot City, Sergeant Pepper, Rolling Stones, Old West. The main attraction, besides cheap sex, is music. The sex is servile, mostly blow jobs, given under tables, in dingy back rooms, up against walls, anywhere, in fact, where a man can get quick service. The music is loud and in its way perfect. There are Motown bands who perform, note for note, gesture for gesture, exactly like the Supremes or Wilson Pickett or the Pointer Sisters. There are heavy metal rock bands who can do perfect imitations of Deep Purple hits. The members of these groups wear shoulder-length hair, and have that slouching, blurry-eyed, open-mouthed, emaciated look of the habitual dopehead. It is part of the act. Their musical mimicry is so precise, it seems almost too real, like paintings that are supposed to look like photographs. The country and western bands grin like shit-kicking country boys. One "western" bar, very popular with the Americans, has a bull pen with a mechanical bronco. I saw one Filipino with a cowboy hat make numerous attempts to ride the bucking machine, much to the amusement of the Americans, who whooped and hollered every time he was thrown to the ground. The band played bluegrass music and kept on grinning.

I was taken around Magsaysay Drive by a Filipino called Joe. He used to be the chief assistant and PR man and bodyguard of Mayor Richard "Dick" Gordon. Gordon was a Marcos man and consequently lost his job after the February Revolt of 1986. The Gordon family had run Olongapo for two generations. Dick's father was mayor until he was shot dead in 1966. The man who ordered the killing was now a city official, according to the elder Gordon's widow, Amelia, who also had a spell as mayor. Dick Gordon tried to do something about his town's Sin City image. The way he supposedly dealt with criminals who bothered "fleet personnel"—bad for business—was considered to be fairly typical. Criminals were rarely prosecuted, as the victims were usually far away when cases came to court. So the best thing was to get rid of the criminals altogether, by having them shot. The term "salvaging," later associated with military killings of civilians, was said to have originated in Olongapo. Another Gordon idea to boost local morale was to give the workers T-shirts with the slogan "Aim High Olongapo"—a battle cry which also graced the town's jeepneys. "Aim High Olongapo" was replaced after the February Revolt with a new slogan: "Mabuhay ng Kalayaan," literally "Hail to Freedom"—freedom in the sense of deliverance. The fact that Tagalog was used to hail freedom under the new order was part of the drive for "Filipinization."

Joe, the chubby-faced PR man, explained how much better things had been under Mayor Gordon. I asked him about crime: "Very high now. Many get brutally attacked. But under Mayor Gordon . . ." I wanted to know about the number of VD cases. The papers had discussed rather hysterically several cases of AIDs. ("Serves the Yanks right for screwing us," said a woman journalist in Manila.) "It's out of control now," said Joe, "but under Mayor Gordon . . ." I noticed how people would come up to Joe in the streets and ask him for favors. Joe waved them away, telling them to wait for the next election. And we were always treated to free drinks in the bars. I asked the owner of the country and western bar, the one with the bull pen, whether he thought Mayor Gordon would be voted back into office.

"Oh, sure," he said, "Mayor Gordon was good for us. And he is a friend of the Americans."*

One of the more intriguing things about Joe was his membership in the Iglesia ni Christo. I had seen the great Gothic cathedrals of this Filipino church. They have the tasteless and strangely synthetic grandeur that marks buildings of rich new religions in America. The Iglesia was founded in 1914 by "Bishop" Felix Manalo, a confused man who tried most Evangelical sects before starting his own. It was predicted in the Apocalypse that the Angel of the Seventh Seal would rise in the east. Manalo rose in the east and proclaimed himself to be that angel, with the mission to resurrect the Church of Christ. It is customary for Iglesia priests to tell their flock whom to vote for during political elections. For most of his tenure as President, Ferdinand Marcos and thus Mayor Gordon had enjoyed the Iglesia's block vote. The Iglesia commands hefty donations from its members, but acts as a kind of welfare church in return, taking care of the less prosperous believers. Manalo died a very wealthy man and was replaced as bishop by his son Erdy. Erdy, according to a Marcos-era newspaper article, is "an intensely private man" who lives in the enormous palace in Quezon City, with its "lovely Louis XIV-inspired ballroom where he receives his friends, the First Couple, and their children, cabinet ministers, and other government luminaries on his birthday." Joe, however, was not very forthcoming about his religious beliefs. All he would say is that he believed Christ was God and that the apocalypse would surely come. Would anybody be saved? Why, yes, those who believe in Christ as God.

Mayor Gordon was in Manila speaking at a Rotary Club meeting. (There are two Rotary Clubs in Olongapo City; one is run by Dick Gordon and his political followers, and the other by his opponents.) I was able to see Gordon's mother, though,

---

* Mayor Gordon was indeed voted back into office in 1988.

in the family house, which was surrounded by armed guards and furnished with heavy Spanish furniture and an astonishing collection of souvenirs from all over the world. Mrs. Gordon was an elegantly overdressed woman, a bit like an Oriental Pat Nixon, with an elaborate hairdo that looked as if it had been freshly lacquered. Although she had been mayor, she was tired of politics. "I am a Christian and politics is dirty," she said with a sigh. She was disturbed by the many crimes committed after Dick had been relieved of his job. A floating body was found in the Santa Rita River. An American was stabbed. A headless body was discovered in the city center. Who did she think was responsible for all this violence? "The NPAs,* for sure. They're here already. We don't want to be under the communists. Only you Americans can save our country." I asked her how. "Well, during the Japanese times, it was the Americans who saved us . . . But then they helped Japan and left us on our own. Look at Hong Kong and Singapore. They were British colonies. They have improved so much. Why can't the Americans do the same for us." She refused to believe that the prosperity of Hong Kong, Singapore, or Japan had much to do with the people actually born there. No, the Americans had let the Philippines down. What should Filipinos do about it? "Well, we have to be independent, of course. But we must humble ourselves, if it is to help our people."

In the middle of Olongapo, near the beginning of Magsaysay Drive, stands an odd monument: a huge head, with bulging eyes, like a fearsome god on top of a totem pole. Joe explained what it was: "In ancient times, Chief Apo united the tribes of the Philippines. His enemies, the opposition, did not like this and bad guys ambushed the chief and cut off his head. The body was later found but the head was lost. Then, much later, a little boy found it and shouted, "Head of the chief! Head of the chief!"—"*Ulo* [head] *ng Apo! Ulo ng Apo!*"

* * *

* New People's Army, the military arm of the Communist Party.

In November 1985, three months before the revolt against
Ferdinand Marcos, I was taken to a small church in Calamba,
about fifty miles south of Manila. It had a spectacular view:
on one side was a large lake called Laguna de Bay, on the other
was Makiling, a sacred mountain riddled with caves which
peasants believe to be the portals of paradise. They go there
to light candles, often carrying images of the Virgin Mary in
their arms. Between the mountain and the lake lies a relatively
prosperous rice-growing region, traditionally hospitable to rebels and bandits.

The church itself was unremarkable—more like a ramshackle
town hall. The walls inside were covered with murals depicting
scenes from the Passion, the usual thing in Philippine churches.
But there was one peculiar twist: "Christ" was a dapper little
man with a mustache, wearing a nineteenth-century European
suit. Instead of being nailed to the cross on Golgotha, this Christ
was executed by a Spanish firing squad in Manila in 1896. His
name was Dr. Jose Rizal, a medical doctor and nationalist
writer, worshipped by many as a Filipino messiah.

His twelve apostles, all depicted on the church wall, were
fellow nationalists and revolutionaries who fought against
Spanish rule at the end of the nineteenth century. There were
the Fathers Burgos, Gomez, and Zamora, native priests who
challenged the power of the Spanish friars. They were accused
of leading an anti-Spanish mutiny and publicly garroted. There
was Andres Bonifacio, a warehouse clerk from the city of
Tondo (now a slum area of Manila), who founded the Katipunan, a secret society dedicated to violent revolution. (Imelda
Marcos used the society's initials, KKK, to lend an aura to one
of her "people's development" projects.) Then there were Mar-
celo H. Del Pilar, the brilliant propagandist for reforms, and
Apolonario Mabini, the main political thinker behind the Philippine revolution. (Their names now grace the two streets in
Manila collectively known as the "strip," the center of go-go
bars, massage parlors, child prostitution, and VD clinics.) And
there on the wall was also Ferdinand Blumentritt, an obscure

Austrian schoolmaster, who never set foot in the Philippines but who owes his holy eminence to his lifelong position as Dr. Rizal's intellectual pen friend.

This particular church dedicated to the worship of Rizal—there are many others like it—was called the Iglesia Watawat ng Nahi, Inc., or Banner of the Race, Inc. It was founded in 1936, when the American colonial administration required all organizations to be incorporated. The founder, Arsenio de Guzman, claimed to be the new Rizal with the power to lead his followers to the land of promise. Guzman, it is said, could heal the sick, talk to spirits, and fly through the air. A church pamphlet explained that the sect was "purposely organized for the Filipinos to have a Christian religious sect of their own, independent of foreign domination." Rizal, the same pamphlet said, was sent to earth as a "Malayan Avatar who was appointed by Divine Power and ordained to earth in this new cycle to redeem His people from slavery."

In more prosaic versions of history Rizal was the highly educated son of upper-class Filipino parents, who, like all members of the elite, were a racial mixture of Spanish, Indio, Chinese, Malay, even Japanese. He lived much of his life abroad, mostly in Spain, where, like many *ilustrados* (enlightened ones), he picked up modern European ideas, of which nationalism was one. Through his writings, the most famous of which are two novels, *Noli Me Tangere* and *El Filibusterismo*, both compulsory reading at Philippine schools, he propagated these ideas. He was opposed to the power of Spanish friars in the colony, and wanted the Philippines to be represented in the parliament in Madrid, not as a colony but as a province. He was not a revolutionary, but he wanted Filipinos to be treated as equals by the Spanish. This was the message of his Propaganda movement.

Steeped as they were in European culture, Rizal and his fellow *ilustrados* of the Propaganda movement were perhaps not the first modern nationalists in Asia, as many Filipinos like to claim, but they were among the most articulate. Certainly

Rizal was remarkably prophetic. There is a Raskolnikov-like character in *El Filibusterismo* called Simeon, who thinks violent revolution is the only way to liberate the Filipino people from Mother Spain. He poses as a jeweler and encourages greed and corruption in the hope that desperate people will finally realize the need for desperate measures. Then, "when I was about to achieve this spontaneous combustion of all this corruption, this loathsome accumulation of garbage, and when frenzied greed, taken unawares, was rushing about to seize whatever was at hand like an old woman surprised by fire, you showed up with your slogans of pro-Hispanism, with your calls for confidence in the government and faith in what will never come! . . . You ask parity of rights, the Spanish way of life, and you do not realize that what you are asking is death, the destruction of your national identity, the disappearance of your homeland, the ratification of tyranny. What is to become of you? A people without a soul, a nation without freedom: everything in you will be borrowed, even your very defects. You ask for His-panization, and do not blush for shame when it is denied you. And even if it were given to you, what would you do with it? What do you have to gain? At best, to become a country of military revolts, a country racked by civil wars, a republic of the greedy and the needy like some republics of South America."

The irony is that Rizal rejected Simeon's solution, and yet he saw what his own cultural orientation could lead to. (Nat-urally he wrote the novel in Spanish.) The other irony is that this quintessentially upper-class, modernist figure would, like the U.S. army surplus jeep that became the jeepney, be Filipin-ized into a magic totem. The final irony is that despite his European culture, there was probably a Filipino corner in his mind that was perfectly aware that this was likely to happen.

Rizal's holy stature lies in the manner of his death. As the church pamphlet put it (referring to both Christ and Rizal), with slight historical license: "Both their martyrdoms marked the beginning and the end of two once powerful and ruthless empires in the world—the Roman Empire in the case of Christ and the Spanish Empire in the case of Rizal." Or in the words of a more conventional though no less reverent historian, Gregorio Zaide: "Rizal's homecoming in 1869, the last in his life, was his saddest return to his beloved native land . . . Gladly, he desired to meet his enemies and to offer himself as a sacrificial victim to their sadistic lust and unholy designs, for he knew that his blood would water the seeds of Filipino freedom."

There is a pattern in this kind of language which has been little studied. It disturbs middle-class Filipino notions of modernity. But like a primary color which endless paint jobs cannot quite hide, it has a way of shining through even the many layers of American-style education. Catholic imagery of death and redemption, the main legacy of three hundred years of Spanish rule, merged with Malay beliefs in spiritual power, or *anting-anting*. Great leaders have such powers because they are the spiritual incarnations of former leaders. The cult of Rizal is, as it were, a Christian form of ancestor worship. These spiritual links with the dead form of a kind of continuity in a fragmented and mostly unrecorded history.

One of the few historians to have taken these beliefs seriously is Reynaldo Ileto. In his superb book *Pasyon and Revolution*, he traces the forms of peasant rebellion back to folk versions of the Passion, in which the Spanish conquest of the Philippines is likened to the fall from Paradise, and Mother Filipinas must be redeemed by faith and sacrifice, by death and resurrection. Such acts of redemption have been led by a succession of messiahs, not usually from the upper class, as was Rizal, but peasant rebels promising paradise and freedom. The word for this freedom is *kalayaan*, as in the new slogans in Olongapo. New Filipinized Christian faiths have come up, rejecting the false colonial prophets. Rizal himself is said to be waiting in his cave in Mount Makiling for the right moment to emerge and redeem the motherland. In the meantime many messiahs have come and gone.

* * *

General Douglas MacArthur came in October 1944. He was nothing if not a good promoter of himself and he knew more than most Americans about the Philippines. "I shall return," promised matchboxes and leaflets dropped from American planes. After wading through the surf at Leyte, corncob pipe clenched in his determined jaw—a scene made eternal throughout the country by hideous sculptures—he made a remarkable radio speech to the waiting Filipinos: "I have returned. By the grace of Almighty God our forces stand again on Philippine soil—soil consecrated in the blood of our two peoples . . . The hour of your redemption is here." A Filipino newspaper columnist commemorated the event forty years later by stating that the landing "finally brought about a completion of the Fil-American cycle of setback and triumph, of Calvary and Resurrection." There is something extraordinary about a colonized country receiving the general of the colonial power back as a savior. And indeed the spirit of MacArthur hovers around the Philippines as much as Rizal's.

Benigno "Ninoy" Aquino returned to redeem his country from Marcos in 1983. He was perhaps the most Rizalesque of modern messiahs. The *ilustrado* son of a wealthy family of landowners, he was hardly a revolutionary, more a pro-American reformer. At the beginning of his career, he was a typical macho politician, tough enough for Marcos to have respected him more than any other politician, a gun-toting womanizer (so, incidentally, was Rizal; the church pamphlet got around this by stating that women were attracted by "his virtues"). Only during his seven years in jail during the martial law period did Ninoy become more introspective, spending much time reading the Bible and Rizal. In a letter from jail he wrote: "I now realize why Rizal reserved a little book by Thomas a Kempis, 'The Imitation of Christ,' for his beloved Josephine . . . It was from this little book that he drew the strength of his spirituality." He then said that if Rizal had been alive today, he, too, like Aquino, would have been arrested,

and "maybe, reenact his martyrdom . . . If I, however, understand the truth of our tragedy and have been wanting in my
denunciation of the tyrant who dragged back Mother Filipinas
to her dungeon in chains, I hope God will forgive me for failing
to rise up to the occasion."

He did, of course, rise to the occasion. And whoever had
him killed at Manila International Airport on August 21, 1983,
made the same mistake as the Spaniards, who ordered Rizal's
execution. His death released an extraordinary wave of popular
energy. Hundreds of thousands of people demonstrated in the
streets of Manila for months. It was one of the rare times in
Philippine history that the many disparate forces of society
came together in a daily fiesta of tooting horns, stirring songs,
and yellow confetti. "Ninoy you are not alone" was one of the
most popular slogans on T-shirts, key rings, bumper stickers,
and banners. "A Filipino is worth dying for" was another, a
quotation in fact from one of Ninoy's speeches. It was as if
only a martyr's death could unite this fractious society; as if
Ninoy's death proved to Filipinos their worth as a people; as
if this image of suffering briefly gave the nation a sense of
identity.

Opposition papers made much of this image. One of the
more imaginative ones, called Mr. and Ms., had Ninoy's death
mask on the cover. "Gazing at his blood-soaked chest and his
wounded face still bearing its bullet-marks, . . . a grief-stricken
people were actually gazing not only at Ninoy Aquino but
at themselves, bloodied and wounded by a long history of colonial domination, still suffering from foreign and native
suppression."

It is a typically Filipino kind of hyperbole. The empathy with
suffering and death, sometimes bordering on a morbid fasci-
nation, is part of everyday life. The visitor stumbles across it
in the most unexpected places. A bar girl in Manila, after about
ten minutes of desultory conversation, said she wanted to show
me something and proceeded to fish a photograph from her
bag. It showed an open coffin, elaborately decorated with flow-

ers. "My mom," she said matter-of-factly, pointing at the waxen face peeking out of the flowers.

In Escalante, a village on the island of Negros, where, in the autumn of 1985, twenty-seven people were shot dead by paramilitary troops sponsored by a local landlord, a group of nuns passed around a sheaf of color photos of the "martyrs," taken at the local clinic. People casually leafed through the pictures, commenting on the more gory wounds. One person arrived with a little bottle. It contained what looked like a raw meatball: it was the eye of one of the victims.

Suffering and death are a constant theme in Filipino movies. The typical hero is a simple man who gets abused and humiliated, often sexually, all through the film. The audience feels sorry for him, and identifies with him. This is the point of these films. There appears to be little identification with macho killers. The attention is always on the victim. The tension is built up further and further, until the hero cannot stand it any longer and erupts in a climactic scene of extraordinary violence, a kind of frenzy in which brains are blown out, blood splashes over the screen, eyes are gouged. Sometimes, as in a film called *Boatman*, the hero is the victim of this final bloodbath. The boatman is a young provincial who goes to the city to be a film star. He ends up as a live sex show performer, becomes the paid lover of the American mistress of a Filipino gang boss, who, in a jealous rage, has the boy tortured to death. We are shown in great detail how his penis is cut off. Some Filipino critics seriously suggested that the hero be seen as a metaphor for the Philippine people.

In 1985 Filipinos celebrated the two thousandth anniversary of the Virgin Mary's birth. "Happy Birthday, Mama Mary!" it said underneath a huge effigy of the Virgin, richly decorated in jewels, marking the entrance to a section of Metro Manila. The yearly processions of Virgin images are spectacular contests in gaudiness; each one richer, more gorgeous, more glittery than the other. The most lavish procession in Manila was sponsored by a group of wealthy society matrons, who formed a regular entourage of Imelda Marcos, the First Lady. They were collectively known as the "Blue Ladies."

According to the Pastoral Exhortation of the Catholic Bishop's Conference of the Philippines, "our Filipino people have always turned to Our Blessed Mother in times of difficulty, of crisis, even of seeming hopelessness. Always we have asked her, groaning and weeping in this valley of tears, to turn her eyes of mercy upon us." The *Mindanao Daily Mirror*, filled with stories of killings in Davao City by "unidentified armed men," explained to its readers the "right posture in praying."

There is something curious and disturbing about the way Filipinos of all classes turn to cults and fads in times of crisis, looking for otherworldly mercy. Businessmen—not to mention their wives—seek solace in born-again Christianity; students and artists indulge in Zen. One Canadian Zen master set up a successful business in Manila by convincing Filipinos that they, as a people, are especially gifted for spiritual quests. The middle-class fad of 1985 was to share with friends "as a mark of love" a disgusting brew called Kargasok tea. It was brewed from yeast supposed to come from Russia. Among its many benefits are extreme longevity, robust health, weight loss, and sexual vigor. "I hope it works," said a Filipino friend, who also happened to be a Zen meditator and a seeker after that other eternal Filipino panacea, an emigrant visa to the United States.

"What we need in the Philippines is a macho leader," said a government official who had grown disenchanted with Marcos. He spoke in an emotional, exasperated tone, banging on the table. "In the early years of martial law, people were so cooperative. The streets were so clean. No crime."

Marcos was a macho leader, with macho ideas. One of the goals of his New Society was to challenge the power of the "oligarchy"—the old landowning families who had run the country for centuries as power brokers for friends, relatives, and dependents. They managed the country, as dispensers of gifts and privileges, without having the responsibility of actual sovereignty, which lay with the colonial powers, first the Spanish, then the Americans. The old quasi-American system of democracy was not based on democratic principles but on a huge network of patronage, some of which seeped down to the lowliest hacienda worker. The main check on any family's power getting out of control was an election, held every four years, so that different patrons could have their turn at the pork barrel. The Philippines that Marcos took over in 1965 was not so much a nation as a collection of regional, family, and class loyalties. It was a country without a national language, without cultural cohesion. Marcos' long rule proved that national strongmen or communist revolutions can arise not from poverty but from a lack of national union, an absence of common purpose.

Marcos argued that the old democracy, imposed by a Western power on an Asian country, was holding up vital reforms, necessary to make the Philippines a great nation. What was needed was a "revolution from the center." He aimed to break the power of "the few who would promote their selfish interests through the indirect or irresponsible exercise of public and private power." He aimed to wipe out the communist threat, then embodied by about three hundred guerrillas in one area of southern Luzon. He even hoped to diminish the power of the biggest Philippine oligarchy of all: the Catholic Church. But to do all this he needed a new ideology, "a unifying force, an organizing principle for the pursuit of collective ends."

He wrote this in a book entitled *Today's Revolution: Democracy*, an odd work published in 1971, full of learned references to Marcuse, Thucydides, and Edmund Burke. It showed the random reading and Marxist leanings of some of Marcos' intellectual advisers. But there are insights to be culled from the book. About "the knowing tolerance of social corruption and the public show of moral outrage over what it privately indulged in in good conscience," he (or at least his ghostwriter) had this to say: "It is not that we are a corrupt, hypocritical, and unheroic race, nor even such as individuals, but that we become so the moment we 'step into' society. Social mimesis, let us call it: our behavior is an imitation of society—the old, colonial society."

The ideas were not all bad. Land reforms, industrialization, foreign investment incentives, government-guided economic development—all this looked fine on paper. It had worked elsewhere. Other Asian macho rulers, such as South Korea's Park Chung Hee or Singapore's Lee Kuan Yew, though hardly democrats, delivered the goods: strong economies and rising living standards. Ninoy Aquino once made the point that the problem with Marcos was not that he was an authoritarian ruler, but that he was an ineffective authoritarian ruler.

Unfortunately, what Marcos and his First Lady wanted more than anything else was to be king and queen. They wished to shape the kingdom in their own image; like the Sun King, Louis XIV, Marcos wanted to be able to say *"L'état c'est moi."* Marcos was the subject of contradictory forces; on the one hand a nationalist who wanted to modernize his country, on the other an atavistic and divisive figure with monarchical aspirations. Adrian Cristobal, a former left-wing writer who became one of Marcos' chief ideological advisers, said that "Marcos sees the Philippines as a society of tribes." And he saw himself as the great tribal chief, the Datu of pre-Spanish times. He destroyed much of the old network of family and regional loyalties to become the one and only patron, the king of Maharlika.

Maharlika, a pre-Hispanic term meaning "chief" or, literally, "big phallus," was Marcos' nom de guerre as a guerrilla soldier against the Japanese. (Just how much of a resistance fighter he was is open to question; Marcos is said to have made quite a bit of money selling goods to the Japanese.) During Marcos' rule a highway was renamed the Maharlika Highway. There was a Maharlika broadcasting station owned by the government. The main reception room of Malacañang Palace was called Maharlika Hall, where the chief would receive his guests sitting on an elevated golden throne. There was even a plan once to rename the Philippines, Maharlika. "Our people are used to being ruled by royalty," observed the First Lady and former beauty queen. She liked to dress up in the finest, most extravagant clothes "because my little people expect it of me."

The Big Phallus never gave his technocrats much chance. The economy, like the army, became a tool of political patronage to enhance the power of the chief. A new oligarchy of loyal courtiers controlled such vital sectors of the economy as sugar and coconuts. Trusted generals from Ilocos, Marcos' native province, were put in charge of the armed forces. Billions of dollars were secretly invested abroad by Marcos and his friends, more than one-third of the country's foreign debt. The First Lady spent fortunes on projects in Manila: convention centers with murals depicting the glorious achievements of Marcos and Imelda; a University of Life, where students did not learn regular subjects, but "humanist development values" and the "Filipino ideology," as taught by Marcos and Imelda; a Cultural Center and a Film Center, where pornographic films were screened uncensored, to recoup some of the money that had been taken out of the government's coffers. These were monuments to a grotesque sense of inferiority, as if to prove that the Philippines was not just a poor country of "little brown brothers."

A "trainer-facilitator" (teacher) at the University of Life tried to explain the school's aims by drawing diagrams on a blackboard, using terms like "experiential development" and "interactive studies." It was a parody of science. The same trainer-facilitator showed me a book entitled *The New Human Order*, written by Mme. Imelda Marcos. It was an extraordinary work, full of doodles, cartoons, and thoughts like: "The body seeks good, the mind seeks truth, the spirit seeks beauty." There were triangular shapes that showed how the new human order had to be led by one chief. It was a sad parody of philosophy, the deep thoughts of a fiesta queen.

There was something patently false about Maharlika, like

the sign in the lobby of the University of Life which said: "The world is composed of takers and givers. The takers eat better. The givers sleep better." Maharlika was false, because it was based on more than greed. Like many Great Leaders—Sukarno, Kim Il Sung, Mussolini—Marcos was concerned with his place in history. He wrote a multi-volume history, entitled *Destiny*, in which he linked himself spiritually to the great national heroes. Myths were promoted of Marcos having magical powers. "More power to you!" said a newspaper greeting to Marcos on his sixty-eighth birthday from the Le Pena Sawmill Co., Inc. The Philippine Charity Sweepstakers went one step further and had a page-sized picture printed of Marcos as a young war hero. The text ran: "Heroic blood on sacred soil. When Ferdinand E. Marcos' young blood first flowed freely on Bataan's hallowed hills, a deathless covenant of service was forged . . . to all the people—but especially to the most deprived and the underprivileged."

The systematic falseness of Marcos' claims, the way every promise turned into the opposite, is one of Maharlika's worst legacies. Like the Spanish friars or the Japanese conquerors, who promised independence in the Great East Asian Co-Prosperity Sphere, Marcos became a false prophet. He lost his credibility—a much-used word in the Philippines. A Filipino letter writer to *The Far Eastern Economic Review* in Hong Kong put it this way: "In the Philippines today, if President Ferdinand Marcos said that the crow is white, here is what would happen next. Hundreds of people from the provinces will testify that this is so after painting black crows with white paint and then photographing the birds. A court of law will decide on the question with hundreds of witnesses lined up to swear that the crow is white."

The detail about the court of law is telling. Marcos, like many successful Filipino operators, was a lawyer. The rule of law, like so much else, was handed down to the Philippines by a colonial power. Like the English language, like democracy, it did not grow organically out of native soil; it is a system to be manipulated. Those who know the rules best are the best manipulators and consequently come out on top. Marcos was the ultimate shyster lawyer, a man who knew no principles, just forms. The falseness of Maharlika was not only a reflection of Marcos, however. It was indicative of a society adrift, a community of many hand-me-down forms with no real idea of the substance, a country of Rotary Clubs, senators, congressman, and lawyers with no point of reference that can truly be called their own. The confusion of the modern Filipino can be seen right inside the Malacañang Palace, especially in Imelda's old quarters, filled with religious images from China, Spain, and the Middle East, symbols of native superstition mixed with tawdry gimmicks from the world of discotheques and Hollywood stars. Filipinos have no collective memory, no recorded history that precedes the Spanish conquest. This utter rootlessness has led to both a deep cynicism and wild flights of mystical fancy. It has also ensured a pathological dependence on the former colonial master.

"I am getting impatient waiting for the United States to liberate us from two decades of the Marcos regime," wrote a reader to the editor of *Malaya*, one of the many opposition papers that emerged after the killing of Aquino. It was a widely shared sentiment in the dying years of Maharlika. Many blamed America for not stopping Marcos' declaration of martial law in 1972, forgetting how much support it had in the Philippines. Most thought America, the Big White Chief, could get them out of the Marcos mess, just as it had delivered them from the Japanese. A few months before the revolt that toppled Marcos, I asked an old opposition politician, Lorenzo Tanada, what America should do. His hands flew up in a gesture of frustration, and came down again on my knee. Tanada sighed: "It is not right for the United States to intervene, but they can get rid of Marcos. I am not advocating it, but they can. It is their responsibility."

And six months after the revolt, in Honolulu: "It was American support that helped the communists in the Philippines.

And the American media were responsible for bringing Madame Aquino to power." We were sitting in the living room of the Marcos' new home in Makiki Heights. It was luxurious, though not palatial—the kind of place in which a successful building contractor or Mafia boss would live. It was furnished with hideous Chinoiserie and large pictures of the Marcos family. In the dining room was a recent color photograph of Marcos, naked to the waist, flexing his muscles as though in a Charles Atlas ad.

Marcos was dressed in a three-piece suit and a red tie. His manner was affable and had a solemn air of dignity. Imelda ate chocolates and sang American show tunes of the 1940s, an earlier rendering of which, she said, had especially pleased General MacArthur. MacArthur was a looming presence in the Marcos home. Marcos was the general's "favorite student" and later his "favorite guerrilla leader." Imelda, of course, was his favorite entertainer.

Marcos ordered a burly man in a T-shirt to fetch "the article." The man came back with a long essay by Jude Wanniski, a former *Wall Street Journal* writer. The piece was entitled "How the American Media Pushed Marcos Out of the Malacañang Palace." A footnote informed the reader that "Mr. Wanniski is not acquainted with any member of either the Marcos or Aquino governments, nor did he interview any Filipino citizen in preparing this analysis." It was not clear whether this was meant as a sign of added credibility. At any rate, Marcos insisted that we read it. "Very fair," he said.

At lunchtime—pork adobo for us, light vegetables for Marcos—the conversation turned to Ted Koppel, the American TV interviewer, who probably spoke more often to Marcos in his last days in power than anybody else. The Marcoses appeared to like Koppel. "Ted Koppel said that if shoes is all they found in my cupboard, that's pretty good," said Imelda. "I'd rather have shoes in my cupboard than skeletons!" she added, shrieking with laughter.

Rita Gaddi-Balthazar, a former TV personality and friend

of the Marcoses, explained how Imelda had this habit of never throwing anything away. So many admirers gave her shoes, but she never wore them. Imelda then removed her right shoe, stroked it over the table, and said, "Plastic." She added that shoes were not even her weakness. What was her weakness? "Beauty, beautiful people. Beauty is love. That is why I hate the communists. They don't believe in beauty. They are materialists."

Marcos chuckled indulgently at his wife. Only the constant jiggling of his thin legs under the table gave away a hint of impatience. I asked him what his proudest achievement had been. He did not hesitate: "When I became President I found an indolent, passive, unmotivated people resigned to what priests said was their destiny. I turned them into an active, dynamic, vibrant, productive, spiritually rich people. I taught them dignity and the meaning of freedom. That is why the Filipino people rise against a usurping government which violates human rights." For a second I thought I was witnessing an extraordinary confession. Then I realized which government he meant.

What about his biggest mistake? "Negotiating with the communists." Was the snap election itself a mistake? Marcos laughed and said it probably had been. And afterward he should have stood firm and stayed in the palace, instead of being "kidnapped by the Americans—an infringement, by the way, of my human rights." And the assassination of Ninoy Aquino? "Communists did that." Did he respect Ninoy as a politician? "Ninoy," said Imelda, "was all sauce and no substance."

"Sweetheart," said Marcos, "that is the essence of Filipino politics."

It is easy to make fun of Imelda Marcos. She exemplifies the Filipino trait of wishing to be taken seriously, while doing everything in her power to prevent one from doing so. For the same reason it is hard to see the Marcos couple as tragic. Pathetic, yes, but not tragic. They wish to appear tragic, but the tragedy so quickly turns to comedy, to a dream world peopled by Ted Koppel, communists, and General MacArthur.

"It is truly a tragedy," said Imelda as we made ready to leave. Her voiced cracked with emotion. "There goes a great libertarian they call oppressive; a great humanist they call a tyrant; a great democrat they call a dictator." She then appeared to break down and tears streamed from her large, curiously childlike eyes. "Please be kind to us poor, little people. We have nothing left."

Perhaps there is something tragic in this after all. But the tragedy transcends that of the former First Couple. It is the tragedy of a people, of whom the Marcoses are rather symbolic. It is above all the tragedy of a brilliant man who failed, tripped by his own weaknesses. Marcos was the colonial trickster, who learned that the only way to trick the foreign rulers was to bend their own rules. The price of being a trickster is that one loses touch with reality and ends up tricking one's own people and finally oneself.

It might have been better for all concerned if General MacArthur had never returned to the Philippines. To be sure, in that event, many Filipinos would have felt betrayed. Disappointment might have caused bitter anti-American feelings; but at least the Philippines would have been weaned away from that adolescent state of dependence known as the "Fil-American relationship."

By returning as a long-awaited liberator, MacArthur confused an already deeply confused nationalist tradition in the Philippines, which had long been split between reformists who accepted American "protection" and revolutionaries who did not. The great liberator then confused things even more by moving on to Tokyo, where he proceeded to help the old enemy get back on its feet. Worship for his return has alternated ever since with resentment about his abandonment.

Much has been written about the harshness of early American colonial rule; the brutal killing of 15,000 "gooks" (a term

first coined during the Philippine-American war); the racism
of Roosevelt and McKinley. The war was undoubtedly harsh,
the killing was indeed brutal, and Roosevelt was a nineteenth-
century social Darwinist. But to dwell on this is to miss the
point. For the psychological dependency of Filipinos is the
result not of brutal colonization but of a relatively benign one.
Uncle Sam was not an enemy but a "tutor" and a dispenser of
wealth, more a rich uncle than a racist overlord. It is far easier
to attain psychological independence from a hated enemy like
the Japanese than to escape from the clammy embrace of the
benefactor.

The longing for the white messiah and the childish belief in
American omnipotence—communism will never succeed, one
is constantly told, "because the Americans won't allow it"—
show how thoroughly colonial Filipinos still are. It explains
the irresponsiblity of many politicians, both in government and
in opposition, for deep down they do not feel responsible. The
final responsibility lies in Washington. This was true under
Marcos, who would threaten to send his wife to Moscow, or
collect a Soviet war medal, when he wanted to sting the Big
White Chief, while the leaders of his opposition knocked on
Senator Edward Kennedy's door. It remained true under Cory
Aquino, whose ministers blamed American banks for their economic problems and the CIA for every coup attempt, while the
new opposition was in Washington agitating against the
government.

America is both the savior and the enemy, the promised land
and the hated "imperialist." Such influential proponents of
Filipino nationalism as the historian Renato Constantino blame
everything on American imperialism. In Constantino's view,
Washington, through the CIA and multilateral lending agen-
cies, has deliberately kept the Philippines in a state of colonial
dependence, a mere supplier of natural resources. Industrialization did not fail because of incompetence, corruption, and
protectionism, but because Washington prevented it. True nationalism is subverted by Washington by offering bright Fil-

ipinos scholarships to American universities. The International
Monetary Fund and the World Bank wanted to break up Marcos' crony monopolies, not because they were crippling the
economy, but to make way for American corporations. Constantino is a sharp analyst, however, of colonial psychology.
In his book *The Making of a Filipino*, he compares Filipino
resistance to the Japanese during the war with that of the
Vietnamese. The Vietnamese "clearly saw their resistance as a
continuation of the struggle for independence. When the colonizers returned, they were confronted by a people who had
won their independence and refused to give it up again. We
were different. We fought the Japanese not for our liberty but
because we considered ourselves as constituting another front
in America's global battles. And when America returned, we
wanted her to be grateful to us. Mendicancy was further in-
grained in our character when we expected her to rehabilitate
us and to pay us for damages suffered in wartime." In other
words, the Philippines had behaved like a perfect client in a
feudal relationship, but America had not lived up to its duty
as a patron. What distorts the view of Constantino is his attempt to switch the image of the American savior to that of
the American enemy.

This kind of Third World nationalism—not at all unique to
the Philippines—comes uncomfortably close to anti-Semitic
nightmares of an international Jewish conspiracy of bankers
and politicians to dominate the world. It is tinged with the
paranoid envy of the backward provincial for the metropole,
an envy especially acute in the Philippines, where American
products, values, and dreams have been held up as superior for
almost a century. Mainly through the public school system
America succeeded to an extraordinary degree in shaping the
Philippine Islands in its own image.

Nick Joaquin, the most revered contemporary Filipino
writer, sees the 1920s as the watershed years. That was when
overt American imperialism ended and relative Filipino auton-
omy began. "The victory," he wrote in a book about the

Aquino family, "however, was hollow, for, paradoxically, the end of the Empire Days was the start of a truer American dominance in the islands. Through the 1900s the old culture had been sovereign, marking off the American as alien: he was Yanqui or Gringo, the enemy, and his protégés were mocked as 'Sajones' or 'Sajonistas.' But after 1919 the picture changes: it is the people of the old culture who begin to look alien; the Sajones have become the 'real' Filipinos, and America the mother culture."

Joaquin himself was educated in Spanish, but writes only in English. "The Jazz Age," he says, "rather than the Empire Days, was when we lost free will." When Americans ceased being enemies, the Filipino lost his sense of self: "For in discarding the old culture we discarded as well the sense of identity it had achieved during its fight for freedom."

Identification with America, instead of fomenting cosmopolitanism, fostered a new kind of provincialism. "The cultured Filipino of the 1880s was intellectually at home in several worlds: Europe, Spanish America, the Orient (there was a special interest in Japan), not to mention the classic world of the hexameter; and his frame of reference had a latitude unthinkable in the 'educated' Filipino of the '20s and '30s, for whom culture had been reduced to knowing about the world contained between Hollywood and Manhattan."

One could almost say that the legacy of Spanish Catholicism and secondhand Americana are the two things most Filipinos have in common. Even NPA guerrillas wear UCLA T-shirts. America is like a birthmark on the Filipino identity—no matter how hard you rub, it won't come off.

This is why the communist movement is presented as a war of national, as much as economic or political, liberation. The official program of the National Democratic Front of the Philippines (NDF), an illegal front organization virtually indistinguishable from the Communist Party (CPP), begins with a reference to Philippine armed rebellions: "This history," it says, "is not dead and past: our tradition of armed struggle and

resistance in defense of the Motherland and to regain our freedom and independence is still very much alive today. It is alive
for one obvious reason: a foreign master—U.S. imperialism—
still dominates the Philippines."

The program was presented to me a few months before the
February Revolt by an upper-class, American-educated businesswoman in her plush Manila office, "I believe in the NDF
and its programs," she said. "If we look at it from the nationalist point of view and make political programs for the people,
I think there is hope." She thought China might be a good
model to follow, "though we could take some shortcuts." An
equally well-educated lawyer explained to me that "the NPA
and NDF are true nationalists. It's not just lip service. They
have the best interests of the country at heart and they have
always fought U.S. imperialism."

The anti-Western bias ("throw the multinationals out and
start from scratch") of a national front movement directed by
a Maoist party appeals to many in the middle class—teachers,
lawyers, students, in short, readers of Renato Constantino's
history books. It also matches a Filipino brand of Liberation
Theology, harking back perhaps to the old millenarian struggle
against the Spanish church. One priest active in the NDF explained to me how he resolved his problem of reconciling Christianity and Marxism: "As a Filipino and a religious I can only
survive by involvement in the struggle."

"Our history," writes Joaquin, "from the 1790s can be read
as an alternation of Propaganda and Revolution: a period of
peaceful protest exploding into desperate violence to be followed again by an interlude of moderation. But the two traditions, instead of alternating, have been running parallel, for
side by side with the peaceful neo-Propaganda of the middle
class, we have had, since the 1900s, a continuing Revolution,
which forms our underground or outlaw history . . ." Joaquin
is talking about the Great Sellout; or, as Constantino would
have it, the betrayal by the Filipino elite of the popular struggle
against American imperialism at the beginning of the century.

The nationalist revolution against Spain between 1896 and 1899 was one of the few times in Philippine history that the various classes came together in a common cause. The coalition that was formed during those years was made up of *ilustrado* reformers like Rizal, native priests against the Spanish church establishment, and the revolutionary brotherhood—the Katipunan—led by Andres Bonifacio, the clerk from Tondo whose portrait remains an icon throughout the Philippines. The coalition, says Joaquin, showed "a glimpse of nation, as though lightning had revealed another side of the face." It was not to last long. The deep divisions that still plague Philippine society came to the surface even before the first Philippine Republic was inaugurated in 1899. Bonifacio's ideals of armed revolution made him as dangerous to the Philippine elite as to the Spanish, and he was executed for treason by General Aguinaldo, the man who was to become the first President of the new republic.

Aguinaldo, whose house in Cavite with its collection of Filipino and American national icons—American eagles mixed with Filipino flags—can still be visited, had little choice but to surrender to superior American force. In 1901, after he was captured, he issued his last wartime proclamation, recognizing American sovereignty over the Philippines and recommending that the Filipinos make the best of American rule. Perhaps because of this, perhaps because he lived to a contented old age, Aguinaldo never became a national hero of the same rank as Bonifacio or Rizal. His portrait is not on the wall of the Rizalist church in Calamba. It has often been said that Rizal became a greater hero than Bonifacio because of American propaganda aimed at fostering peaceful reforms instead of violent revolution. Rizal's legacy is certainly safer to deal with for a colonial power than Bonifacio's, but the truth is more complicated. Rizal's image was more congenial to the Philippine elite, which benefited most from American rule. This is where the Great Sellout comes in.

By sailing into Manila Bay in 1898, ostensibly to help the

Filipino struggle against Spain, America effectively aborted the revolution, turning the first steps toward nationhood into a false start. Although Aguinaldo fought on for a few years, much of the Philippine elite did what they had done for centuries to survive, and as they have done ever since, even, until the last few years, under Marcos: they made deals with the new power, acting as power brokers for their dependents. And by and large they have prospered by doing so. It is they who became the best disciples of American ways, from party politics to Lions clubs.

And it is they, the Aquinos, the Laurels, the promoters of traditional, moderate politics, who took power in February 1986. But rural groups, from the Sakdalistas in the 1930s to the Huks in the 1940s, kept on erupting in revolts, often inspired by nationalist visions of martyrdom and redemption. The communist movement is still trying to convince people that they are the true heirs to the first revolution, taking up the thread of history where it was so rudely cut off by the Americans.

Jose Maria Sison, founder of the CPP, made a speech in 1964, on the 101st anniversary of Bonifacio's birth. He stated that "after the death of Bonifacio, the revolutionary initiative of the peasants and workers of the Katipunan and the anti-colonialist struggle in general was undermined and debilitated by the liberal compromises made by the *ilustrado* leadership . . . U.S. imperialism was not only superior in industrial might but also well versed in a liberal jargon which could easily deceive the newly emerged Filipino bourgeoisie."

Deception through the sweet talk of foreigners—that is precisely what the earlier revolutionaries said about the Spanish friars: Mother Filipinas must be delivered from alien lies. Marcos himself used a similar argument when he declared martial law. Struggle against the false foreign prophets is what lends legitimacy to every Filipino nationalist movement. It is a potent message at a time when "credibility" becomes a precious commodity. Having said that, in 1985 there was a backlog of more than 450,000 Filipino applicants for emigration to the United States. In 1987, a year after the fall of Marcos, the number had grown to 483,000.

The most remarkable thing about Lorenzo Tanada's eighty-eighth birthday party was the cake. Tanada has had a long and consistent career as a "nationalist." One of his proudest possessions, prominently displayed in his Manila law firm, is a large painting of "Tani," as his friends call him, being shoved into a police wagon by Marcos' riot troops. On first sight it is hard to see Tani, leaning on his cane, more like an old Spanish landowner than a rebellious Indio, as an activist. He is sympathetic to the left, though Filipino wits like to say that Tani hardly knows the difference between Groucho and Karl Marx. His brand of nationalism is a struggle for liberation from, among other egregious enemies, the CIA, the IMF, multinationals, the U.S. military bases, in short, American imperialism. As Renato Constantino pointed out in a speech during Tani's birthday party, the senator was born in the same year that Commodore Dewey sank the Spanish fleet in Manila Bay. He is still battling what Constantino calls "the forces responsible for our lack of independence . . ."

The birthday party in August 1986 was organized by a group called Bayan, a nationwide organization of so-called cause-oriented groups with strong links with the Communist Party. The wild cheers that greeted the representatives from the Cuban and Vietnamese embassies were thus to be expected. Even the almost hysterical joy with which a whole row of nuns acclaimed a birthday message from the NDF did not seem out of place. Nor, this being the Philippines, did the entire congregation singing "Happy Birthday to You" in English seem especially incongruous.

It was, as I said, the cake that was most curious. It was a huge slab of confectionery upon which artful chefs had re-created the February Revolt. There were sugar barricades in front of Camps Crame and Aguinaldo; there were little toy nuns defying little toy tanks; there were chocolate signposts pointing to the U.S. embassy and the Subic Bay naval base; there were minature helicopters hovering overhead. This splendid cake was further embellished with marzipan hand grenades. What was peculiar, however, was the depiction of People Power itself: there were no yellow banners signifying the spirit of the Aquinos—the late husband and his widow—just red ones representing militant trade unions and leftist groups. This was strange because it was false. People Power was overwhelmingly yellow, moderate, and religious. The left had missed the bus in February. History was rewritten in the icing of Tani's cake.

It was the traditional leftist version of history, in which the communists are the only true nationalists; the only legitimate heirs to the 1896 revolution against Spain. The February Revolt was only the beginning. It was now up to the left to finish the job. As a writer in a left-wing magazine put it, "People Power must be transformed into People's Power"—as in People's Republic.

The birthday cake was also an example of the extraordinary confusion, sometimes deliberate, sometimes not, of symbols in the Philippines. This is partly a question of language. An editorial writer for a Sunday newspaper pointed out that "the top leaders and private educators speak English while the masses speak the vernacular. Because of 'the lack of a common language from which flows the soul and aspirations of Filipinos,' we remain today still a divided and weak nation." One only speaks Tagalog to the servants, I was told by the son of a landowner. But the language problem goes deeper than class; it is regional too. At a mass rally in Manila that same summer, the Minister of Education, a lady from Cebu, addressed the crowd in English. She had misjudged her audience, which was nationalist and left-wing. They booed and jeered and shouted, "Speak your language! Speak Tagalog!" She answered that Cebuano, not Tagalog, was her own language, so English was more appropriate. The crowd kept on jeering, and she finished her speech in her native language of Cebu, which hardly anybody understood. Perhaps because no language can properly articulate the national experience, past or present, Filipinos tend to express the common cause in symbols—hand gestures, religious objects, jokes, T-shirt slogans, colors, pictures. This is why it is always dangerous to take words at face value in the Philippines; language itself is so often symbolic, based on borrowed rhetoric, expressing a vision of reality instead of what merely exists. After February there were more than twenty daily newspapers in Manila, mostly in English. From one sensational headline to another, they offered widely different interpretations of the same events. This points to a problem that goes beyond language. A problem hinted at in this poem by Alfredo Navarro Salanga, entitled "A Philippine History Lesson."

It's a history that
moves us away
from what we are.

We call it names,
assign it origins,
and blame the might
that made Spain right
and America—bite.

This is what it amounts to:
we've been bitten off, excised
from the rind of things.

What once gave us pulp
has been chewed off
and pitted—dry.

The Rashomon-like quality of almost any event, beginning with the February Revolt itself, was striking. To some it was a revolt, to others a revolution, to others yet a religious miracle. Jaime Cardinal Sin reminded his flock in a pastoral letter in August that Divine intervention brought about the success of the February events. He called it a modern-day Exodus that was the gift of Mary to the Filipino nation after the one-year celebration of her two thousandth birthday. This is not merely overblown rhetoric; these are the terms in which many, if not most Filipinos think.

There was an exhibition in Manila of paintings and sculptures depicting the revolt, revolution, or miracle. Most of the works were symbolic: M-16 guns with yellow ribbons tied to them; nuns praying for liberation from the "Marcos-U.S. dictatorship"; ghastly skulls draped in a bloody American flag; nice middle-class people dressed in yellow holding back tanks; rosary beads held up to a vision of Benigno "Ninoy" Aquino smiling from heaven; barbed wire from the barricades in the shape of the sacred crown of thorns; NPA guerrillas marching to a glorious future, arm in arm with workers and priests waving red banners; a wounded Mother Filipinas, raped by American Imperialism; and so on and so forth. The only image lacking in this exhibition was the poster I saw elsewhere of then Defense Minister Juan Ponce Enrile looking like a bespectacled Rambo, bravely leading his armed troops to victory in Manila. After the exhibition I attended a PEN club meeting. Members discussed the topic for a forthcoming lecture. National Renewal and the Filipino Writer, suggested one person. No, National Revival, said another. No, Restoration. No, Reconstruction.

An item in a Sunday newspaper social column, called "People Incorporated": "My nominee for the most colorful attempt to turn back the hands of time is Ado Escudero's reunion of friends at his villa. Most of them came in turn-of-the-century costumes. So their recent cook-out at Bobby Borja's fantastic villa could be another chance to plan for the Casa Manila patroness to project once again one more aspect of Philippine culture. Bobby insisted it was simply a potluck despedida for dinner members Patis & Tito Tesoro, Ramon Zaragoza, Cathy Veloso, Ado, Dr. and Mrs. Kevin Wong. Patis is going to Washington, no,

not to join the President's entourage but to enroll her son;
Ramon is going to Spain . . ."

The feverish search for symbolic significance, for common
cause, for anything to keep the February spirit alive, lent a
mythical quality to the most banal, even sordid events. In July
a worker named Stephen Salcedo got caught up in a demonstration by Marcos supporters. Because he wore the wrong-
colored shirt, or made a provocative gesture, or perhaps both,
he got beaten to death by a group of "loyalist" thugs. It caused
a huge rumpus in the local press. One letter writer to a national
magazine stated: "The innocent and hapless Stephen Salcedo
died a martyr. Together with others like him, he is one of the
YELLOW MARTYRS of our exodus to the promised land. May
the blood of Stephen and his companions hasten our people's
passage to reconciliation." The same magazine came out several
weeks later with a serious article entitled "What Two Martyrs
Had in Common," comparing Salcedo with Ninoy Aquino.
Among other things: "Both their surnames have three syllables
and end with an o." Perhaps, as an old Philippine hand pointed
out, it is their misfortune that Filipinos have to express Malay
mysticism in English. A month later a provincial prosecutor
and prominent Marcos loyalist, named Felizardo Lota, was
shot dead in front of the Manila Hilton. Several unsavory fellow
loyalist types, including two former movie actors, were said to
be involved. A sympathetic radio announcer said that "loyalists
are proud to produce a real martyr" and that "Fiscal Lota
sacrificed his life for the restoration of peace against violence,
love against hatred, and democracy against slavery."

I met Adrian Cristobal, the former official spokesman for
Marcos, at a radical-chic party where society ladies looked on
adoringly as Jose Maria Sison, the communist leader just released from jail, sang "Dreaming the Impossible Dream" at the
piano. "Much though I hate to say this about my fellow countrymen," said Cristobal, "Filipinos are not a serious people."
The wild flights of rhetoric, the instant mythology, the constant

jokes, the substitution of analysis with sensational rumor, all these do indeed suggest an extraordinary degree of frivolity.

The Filipino word for it is *palabas*, meaning ostentatious show, combining the flamboyance of a fiesta with the solemnity of Hollywood melodrama. Marcos' habit of cloaking his deceit in earnest legalisms was *palabas*. Imelda's monarchical pretensions, her diamond tiaras, her parties for Hollywood stars and minor royalty, her "beautification" projects were all *palabas*. Even the opposition during the Marcos years was full of *palabas*. In 1985 I was on the same plane to Manila as Senator Jovito Salonga, an opposition politician returning after years of exile in the United States. He was accompanied by a crowd of fellow oppositionists, including Tanada, grinning from ear to ear; Ninoy's brother "Butz" Aquino, flirting with the air hostesses; Jose Diokno, just out of a hospital in the United States. "I shall return! I shall return!" shouted several members of the entourage, echoing MacArthur's words, as the plane banked toward Manila. "I am prepared to share the brutal fate of Ninoy," said another man, his face flushed with emotion. Salonga, a quiet-spoken Protestant, looked a little embarrassed by it all as he was escorted off the plane by his friends, who, as one put it, were "protecting him from the dictator's bullets." The group was greeted in the arrival hall by a hysterical mob of press people and more oppositionists, one of whom told the television cameras that "neither wind nor rain can wipe out the blood of the martyr." It was clearly *palabas*. Yet at the same time these men were deadly serious. But their seriousness could only find an expression in comic melodrama.

With nothing but borrowed language, borrowed ideas, borrowed points of view, theater becomes a way of life. Fantasy is the last recourse of the dispossessed. And to quote that old but still delightful cliché, three hundred years in a Spanish convent and forty years in Hollywood have left Filipinos culturally dispossessed. One is rather lost for words when a Filipino businessman tells one that "at this point in time we are not yet fully Filipino." The quest for meaning and national pride may be pathetic but it is certainly serious.

It was to a large extent what the February Revolt was all about. Marcos and his discredited government were the enemy, or, in the parlance of the Church, "the forces of Evil"; Cory Aquino and her yellow crusaders were the forces of Good. But the ultimate aim of this moral revolt went further than ousting Marcos; it was the assertion of national pride, the celebration of a common cause, an occasion for feeling truly Filipino.

James Fenton, in "The Snap Revolution," described the chaotic scenes in the Malacañang Palace after Marcos fled in a helicopter. Fenton went out into the street with a happy Filipino. "All was quiet again. He had a glass of whiskey in his hand. He had been celebrating. 'You don't realize,' he said, 'how deep this goes. Nobody will call us cowards again. We've done it. We've had a peaceful revolution. We've beaten Poland.' " This may sound like *palabas*, but it expresses a serious emotion.

Courage is what Ninoy Aquino's martyrdom signified to most Filipinos. The manner of his death gave courage to a people anxiously aware of their reputation for spinelessness. It was, as editorials liked to point out over and over again, a national awakening. Cory Aquino's government did everything to keep the symbols of February alive. Videotapes of the Revolt were replayed endlessly on TV and sold at department stores and domestic airports. Philippine Airlines pilots announced the arrival in the New Philippines. The Filipina beauty at the Miss Universe contest proudly said she was from "People Power Philippines." A three-hour TV movie was planned. It was to be a depiction of, and here I quote from a newspaper, "the history of the Filipino people from 1986 to the present and projecting into the future up to 1996." The death of Ninoy was commemorated on August 21 with a morbid passion. The assassination itself was shown over and over again in photographs, TV documentaries, special exhibitions, and in the theater. Ninoy's bloody clothes were exhibited in an art gallery, as was the Aviation Security Command van that took his corpse away from the airport. The martyr's death was reenacted in a musical entertainment with the entire Aquino family in attendance—Ninoy's brother Butz was said to have been asked to play the part of the martyr. But the glamorous figure tumbling down the silver steps amidst dry ice and disco music was an actor. There were songs celebrating the February events, and a large number of coffee-table books.

"The Filipino is worth dying for," announced the Government Service Insurance System in a newspaper advertisement. "We Carry a Truly Filipino Identity," said an ad for the Chico Computer Research Corporation. The Philippine Transport Company commemorated Ninoy as "the great Filipino martyr of our time . . . who, with his death, gave life and a new beginning to the Filipino people." Now the company has opened a new route, linking the main islands, so "that Filipinos may work closely together . . . sharing their hopes and aspirations with one another, as they commune in the spirit of unity, freedom, and national progress."

It remained a fragile spirit and no amount of coffee-table books and TV spots could hide the deep anxieties expressed in such letters to newspapers as the one that asked: "Is the Filipino worth dying for? Certainly not now . . . The Filipino flesh is one of the weakest in mankind." Or the one after the murder of Stephen Salcedo which lamented: "We cannot wash ourselves of Stephen's death . . . Has the country of heroes once again become a country of cowards?" Or in Cardinal Sin's statement that the gains of the February Revolt are "little by little being lost . . . Faces have indeed changed, but the ugly head of the evil one still shows itself in many ways." Or in the fact that Filipino businessmen still refused to invest in their own economy.

Just as Cory Aquino stood up at the Manila Hotel to make a speech about Ninoy on the anniversary of his death, and just as the TV documentary about Ninoy was reaching its fatal climax, the blackout hit. The whole island of Luzon was in the dark, causing pandemonium. A local radio station called on People Power to protect the New Philippines against a coup. Laoag International Airport in Ilocos Norte, where Marcos grew up, was closed, lest he might use the opportunity to fly home. The papers the next day speculated about sabotage. Ominous conclusions were drawn from the fact that the last blackout of similar magnitude—it lasted for eight hours—had been in 1983, on the day after Ninoy died. As the President rather hurriedly left the Manila Hotel ceremonies without delivering her speech, a member of her entourage said: "They cannot even let us enjoy our anniversary dinner."

Who did she mean by "they"? The military? Defense Minister Enrile, who was otherwise engaged that night? The NPA? The loyalists? A simple branch of a tree? All these possibilities were feverishly discussed in the press. No culprit was found. But, said one editorial, "the nation must maintain its vigilance . . . for the forces of evil are abroad in times of darkness."

Some would call the rather pathetic group of people who gathered every morning for breakfast at the 365 Club evil. The club was a coffee shop in one of the large hotels. The members were mostly overweight men, wearing expensive but tasteless jewelry. Almost all lost their jobs after the February Revolt. Most hoped, rather against their better judgment, that Marcos would come back. But until that day they jumped up to shake hands with Enrile when he came in on Saturday mornings with his bodyguards, and laughed uproariously at the Defense Minister's jokes. The 365 is where Enrile relaxed with friends and talked about the Red menace in the government and other such popular topics. One of these friends, a fat man in a silk T-shirt, held forth about how the failed coup at the Manila hotel had been set up by the Americans to discredit the loyalists. Heads nodded all around. This was the way it was.

The doyen of the 365 was not Enrile, however, but the newspaper columnist Teodoro Valencia. "Doroy," as he was nicknamed, died a year after the Revolt. He was a tall, thin man with a rasping voice and a cackling laugh. He spoke in the manner of his daily column, in wisecracks, observing his audience with the shrewd eyes of an old comedian, always watching the effect of his words. Doroy, through many years of service to the Marcos regime, became a symbol of sycophancy. He did well out of the last twenty years and under his own motto that "if you don't brag in the Philippines, people will step on your head," he liked to tell people that he was the best-paid journalist in the country.

There is no reason to believe that Doroy especially liked the Marcos couple; rather, as do so many, he liked power. He never rallied around Cory Aquino's flag. It was too late for that. But he gave Mrs. Aquino his favorite Jaguar, as a token of his esteem. He claimed to be happy remaining a Marcos loyalist. "If you support Cory, her people won't like you, because they think you want a slice of the cake. If you are a loyalist, people like you, as there is no cake to share. And never forget that this is a cake-sharing country." His point was well taken. Tired of the rhetoric of unity, February Miracles, and Yellow Revolution, I decided to leave the capital, to see how things had changed in the provinces. If Manila was given to wild flights of fancy, cynicism and raw power were more in evidence out in the country.

Since the turn of the century two families have shared most of the cake in Tarlac, a flat, rice- and sugar-rich province in central Luzon: the Aquinos and the Cojuancos. Cory Aquino was born a Cojuanco. The Cojuancos, as the name suggests, are of Chinese stock. Her cousin Eduardo "Danding" Cojuanco was Marcos' most powerful "crony." During the *ancien régime* he virtually owned the coconut industry and he also ran Tarlac. He fled with Marcos and moved to Los Angeles. "He had a soft heart," said his supporters, who, according to one of them, felt "like lost sheep without a shepherd." The towns in northern Tarlac, where the softhearted Godfather lived, all have good roads, neat plazas, and were ruled by Danding's "boys." These boys lived in large houses, surrounded by armed men. The former provincial governor, Federico Peralta, was such a boy, as was his son, the former mayor of San Manuel. The son was last seen staggering around town shooting his revolver off into the air. The Officer in Charge who had taken over his job was the son of Peralta's predecessor, one of Ninoy Aquino's boys.

Governor Peralta is said to have made some of his fortune from American aid, which Danding procured for his boys' towns. He is also said to have demanded a standard 10 percent of every contract for building roads, supermarkets, drainage systems, or anything else that brought in cash. He lived in a lavish mansion, built in the middle of a rice field behind Vic's Minimart and Snackhouse. There, in the courtyard, next to the swimming pool, his body is now enshrined in a marble tomb bearing the somewhat ambiguous words: "Here lies a great and lowly man." For Peralta was stabbed in his bed one night shortly after the February Revolt. A large black-and-white photograph of Peralta, looking like a burly mafioso, a vicious good ole boy, adorns his shrine. The new OIC thinks it was a simple case of robbery.

According to another one of Danding's boys, Rolando Sembrano, former mayor of Gerona, "what happened to Peralta was political." Why? "Why? Well, we are all politicians, in or out of the government. We all have our interests to protect." Sembrano was known by his opponents as the terror of the town. He took care that people voted Danding's way during elections. He handled, as they say in the Philippines, the guns, the goons, and the gold. He was most indignant that he had been replaced after February by an OIC appointed by the revolutionary government. "I was ousted from my position mandated by the people. We are no longer governed by the rule of law." When people talked about the rule of law, you knew you were dealing with a loyalist. They had a point, of course, but one of the unfortunate ironies of the Philippines was that the wrong people were saying the right things for the wrong reasons. The rule of law was invoked, once again, as part of *palabas*.

The man whom people like Sembrano suspected of protecting

his interests by having Peralta killed was Jose "Peping" Cojuanco, brother and former campaign manager of Cory Aquino.
He ran the family hacienda, Luisita, at six thousand acres the
biggest sugar-growing hacienda in the province. It was once
managed by Ninoy Aquino, who had a huge golf course built
there to attract rich industrialists who might invest in the family
enterprise. Peping used to be on excellent terms with his cousin
Danding. They shared a passion for fighting cocks. "An expensive hobby," explained the hacienda manager, as he pointed
to the long rows of cages surrounding the family compound.
It was an impressive sight, those thousand or so cocks crowing
at the Voice of America radio masts in the distance. The split
between the cousins began in 1963, when they backed different
mayors in their hometown. In 1965 they ran for election as
congressmen. Danding was a Marcos man and lost; Peping
backed Aquino and won. But when Marcos came to power,
bank loans to Hacienda Luisita dried up. The towns to the
south of the hacienda were Aquino's territory. Most of them,
including Concepcion, where Ninoy was born, did not get good
roads and neat plazas.

Liborio de Jesus campaigned hard for Cory Aquino. He had
been a lawyer in the town of Tarlac, a dusty, charmless place
with little more to offer than some Chinese shops, jukebox
joints, and a few shady motels. After February he became director of the Philippine Charity Sweepstakes, a highly profitable
government enterprise. "Bor" also owned a restaurant in Tarlac
called Los Angeles Freeway 101. I asked him about Peping.
"He has a soft heart," he said. "He takes good care of his
people." Bor cited the example of a retired colonel in Peping's
private security force who was kept on the payroll as a con-
sultant on the golf course. "With Peping's blessing anyone can
win an election in Tarlac. His mere presence as brother of the
President is enough." Bor hoped to run for congressman himself
in the coming elections.

I asked him about the Peralta case. He did not believe in the
political angle. He then went through the other possibilities:

Peralta had some outstanding deals with building contractors, which he could no longer pay off after February; there might have been gambling debts; then again, he might have been involved in dispensing money that Danding left behind; and besides, he was seen entering motels with married women. One of them was the wife of the prime suspect, a local police officer.

I said goodbye to Bor. In parting he said: "Our main problem is the economy. It all depends on you Americans. If our Big Brother can't help and things don't get better, we have to go back to the guns."

It you take a bus from Tarlac, straight up the MacArthur Highway, you hit the Solid North, Marcos country. There, at the northern tip of Ilocos Norte, is a grand hotel in the colonial Spanish style called Fort Ilocandia. It was built in 1983, the year Ninoy died and Marcos' daughter Irene got married in Sarrat, where Marcos was born, about five miles from the hotel. Fort Ilocandia was meant to accommodate the wedding guests who wished to stay on for a few days. It had about three hundred rooms, a nice pool, an excellent restaurant, and a discotheque. Things were not what they used to be before February; I was just about the only guest. I saw one other solitary figure, quietly drinking wine in the bar. A constant din of disco music kept all outside sounds from penetrating this palace in the dunes. But the discotheque was empty, the air conditioning was turned off, and long-distance phone calls were impossible. The hotel, I was later informed, had difficulties paying its utility bills.

In the dunes, not far from the hotel, is another palace, the Malacañang of the north, where Marcos used to spend a few days a year playing golf. I asked the people who were sticking tags on the furniture—the place was being "inventorized"—why there were so many rusty golf carts in the garage. I was told they had been used once to transport the funeral procession for one of Marcos' stillborn granddaughters, who was buried in the nearby lake. This, the people said, was an old Ilocano custom to ward off bad luck.

Ilocanos are a clannish people with a history of emigration, a bit like the Scots; industrious, dour, and loyal. Most Filipinos in Hawaii are Ilocanos. Almost the entire upper echelon of Marcos' armed forces was Ilocano, including General Fabian Ver, who was born in the same town as the former President. I once asked a girl in Manila what she thought of Marcos. "I loved my President," she said. Why so? "Because I am an Ilocana. And the President, he gave us all the American things." She mentioned the nice roads, the overhead city railway in Manila, and some of Imelda's white elephants, like the Cultural Center of the Philippines.

"Welcome to Laoag, Town of Discipline and Order," said a sign as we drove into the main town of Ilocos Norte. There were quite a few "American things" to be seen. The main roads were excellent—though not the back streets. There were a conspicuous number of banks offering special U.S. dollar accounts—to handle remittances from abroad, I was told. And there was a recruitment office for the U.S. Navy, which handled hundreds of applicants a month. Two family names dominated the place: Marcos and Ablan. Among other family monuments, there was a Marcos Hall of Justice and a Marcos Museum of Costumes, "Given to President Ferdinand E. Marcos as a birthday present by Madam Imelda Romualdez Marcos." There was an Ablan Hall of Heroes, a Roque Ablan shrine. And "Ablan Day" is celebrated every year on the anniversary of Governor Roque Ablan, Sr.'s birthday.

I wanted to meet Ablan, Jr., or Roquito, who had been acting governor for Marcos' son, "Bongbong," but he was not home. Instead I saw his mother, who was receiving a large number of people. She was a friendly woman, with a surplus of nervous energy, the political wife par excellence. "You see how people still come to us," she said, pointing at a group of sad-looking people waiting in the hall who beamed pathetically every time Mrs. Ablan looked their way. "No matter what they say about him, Marcos did a lot of good for us. Look around you, all those roads and new bridges, the Cultural Center." Why had things gone wrong? "All because of that woman," she said. "It's those Romualdezes. They were too greedy." What about Marcos himself? "In any country, if a high official does something for you, you show him gratitude with gifts. It is only natural, no?"*

I managed to catch Roquito a week later in Manila, where he managed the affairs for Aeroflot. He was one of those fat men with jewelry one met at the 365 Club. He smelled strongly of after-shave lotion. There were a lot of muscle-bound men around the office, to whom he would distribute hundred-peso bills. "Thanks, boss," they grunted in unison. Our conversation was interrupted several times by messages which the boss would read and then burn with his lighter. My eyes wandered to the pictures on the wall of Roquito with Marcos, Roquito with General Ver, Roquito in a paratrooper's uniform—he was a volunteer in Vietnam, "helping brothers fight the communists." I asked Roquito about his reputation as a gunslinger: "They accuse me of having a private army. It's not an army. They're just friends." Roquito would run for governor again, he said. He was not worried about the OIC, a lawyer in his seventies called Castor Raval. Raval, an amiable old lawyer, whose wife was Mrs. Ablan's cousin, had been tolerated for many years as a harmless opposition figure, "because," as he himself said with a melancholy smile, "it gave the Marcos rule a semblance of democracy."

"Hey," said Roquito, leaning back in his leather swivel chair like a redneck sheriff, "most of his mayors are my boys. I told them which opposition parties to join before the elections. I also told Raval that he may be the OIC, but I'm still the governor."

The Solid North, hitherto relatively immune to the communist insurgency, had been the scene of an increasing number of killings. The only local factory, a tomato paste plant, was

* In 1988, Mrs. Ablan switched her allegiance to Cory Aquino and ran for governor.

raided and a guard was killed. Several people were murdered in a village called Ferdinand, part of a township called Marcos. A number of soldiers and constabulary officers, including a relative of Marcos, were ambushed and killed. "The NPA is emboldened by the new democratic space," explained a lawyer. "They are not NPAs, but loyalists in disguise," said a local newspaper editor. "The loyalists have joined the NPA," said the priest in Sarrat.

Picture this situation, five years on from the February Revolt: Cory Aquino is still President; Bongbong Marcos is a loyalist guerrilla in the hills of northern Luzon; Kris Aquino, Cory's daughter, is a movie star. Bongbong kidnaps Kris to force Cory to allow his father to come back, so he can die in his own country. Kris falls in love with Bongbong and is sympathetic to his cause. They stage People Power II and declare their love in front of shrieking fans and TV cameras at Camp Crame. Marcos returns in his wheelchair, makes his famous V sign, pisses in his trousers, and keels over to die. He is buried next to Ninoy Aquino. Imelda, who has become a nun in Mindanao, joins Cory at the graves. The president places a yellow flower on Marcos' grave; Imelda puts a red rose on Ninoy's. The women embrace. Reconciliation, that elusive Philippine dream, has come true.

It is an odd notion, impossible even, but it has the ring of Filipino truth. It is the plot of a successful play, called *Bongbong and Kris*. The play is witty, in a way that Asian plays rarely are. Filipinos laugh at anything, including themselves. Humor, as well as fantasy, is a refuge of the dispossessed. But the play is also sentimental, the product of an extraordinary capacity for wishful thinking. The last scene at the graves is not at all meant to be funny; it is supposed to be moving.

The play, or at least the emotions it engendered, was typical of the new Cory era. Cory Aquino, the hitherto withdrawn housewife, became a religious figure, a kind of patron saint of a country yet to find its form. She belongs to the landowning Filipino aristocracy, studied in America, speaks fluent French and Spanish. In short, she represents Nick Joaquin's ideal cosmopolitan Filipino. With her plans to restore Democracy and all its institutions, she struck the pose of a truly modern leader. But at the same time she stuck to the Filipino folk tradition, presenting herself as a medium of her assassinated husband, whose spirit was evoked in almost all her speeches. Cory Aquino was the long-awaited folk Messiah. Can a Filipino leader really be both: a modern democrat, sharing power, making compromises, strengthening institutions, as well as being the voice of God? Can the City be built on pure charisma?

In one of the post-Revolt coffee-table books, called *People Power*, there is a fascinating account by Cardinal Sin of the way in which Mrs. Aquino decided to run for President: "Cory said to me: 'Cardinal, Ninoy is inspiring me. It seems that he is talking to me, telling me that I should run.' " The cardinal asked her to kneel down: " 'I will bless you. You are going to be President. You are the Joan of Arc.' At that moment I thought God answered the prayers of our people."

The press added to her iconography:

We voted in the past for Presidents for all sorts of reasons, but those who voted for you in the last elections did so because they also *loved* you.
—Luis D. Beltran in the *Philippine Daily Enquirer*, August 1986

When our leader-by-example exhausts all options given a democratic process, she is labeled weak and indecisive. Let us remember that it was never Cory's own Will to become President, but rather God's and the Filipino people's.
—Letter to the *Philippine Daily Enquirer*, August 1986

During the campaign, Cory would sense Ninoy's presence helping her, pushing her on during the difficult moments in the campaign . . . "It's what we Catholics call the communion of saints," Cory said. "I pray for him, as I believe he prays for me."
—*Weekend*, magazine of the *Sunday Express*, March 1986

This is not the language of politics, but of miracles, of faith. Bishop Francisco F. Claver, one of the most impressive Jesuits in Manila, caught the Cory spirit perfectly: "The revolutionary class was not just the proletariat, the mass of people at the lowest socioeconomic levels of society, but people from all ranks of society sparked by a common purpose—and a common faith ... If action for justice cannot be a merely political act, but must at all times be led and guided by faith, so must a people's 'analysis of the situation' not be a purely rational exercise, but one that must, from start to finish, be infused and illuminated by a truly discerning faith." It was as if the Marxist faith could only be countered by the *anting-anting*, the spiritual power of Cory and her Catholic Church. This is the thinking of a pre-modern world, confusing to the Western observer, especially if that observer makes the mistake of taking Filipino rhetoric about democracy, rule of law, etc., at face value. In a perverse way the language of the Church has more in common with that of the Marxist revolutionaries than either have with democracy.

As always, the modern gloss of the Philippines was endorsed by the Big White Chief. Cory Aquino became *Time* magazine's Woman of the Year. She spoke to Congress in her yellow dress; the praying Mother Filipinas transformed into a female Mr. Smith going to Washington. It was a moving experience watching her on television, moving in the way good Hollywood melodramas are moving. One wished her well, one hoped for a happy ending. But, however much one tried to resist it, one was left with a feeling of unreality, of make-believe.

Friends in Manila received a Christmas card from a very wealthy Filipino family. "Dear Friends," began the printed text:

From the turn of the year came the revolution. Then the long hot summer and soon the thunderous rains, and before we knew it, the solemnity and serenity of Xmas is here again. Motions are so swift that oftentimes we do not realize movements in our own lives. Then we say: It seemed like only yesterday!!! 1986 . . . Never before have we seen so many changes. Never before have we been so proud of our country, our people, and our leaders. We, the Cagayanos, stood up to be counted. We, Filipinos, were proud and united in the kindred spirit we shared. The chain reaction of love and rebellion shook this young vibrant nation of ours and made it known throughout the world that we were a peace-loving people who wished to enjoy our freedom in our way.

Cory's speech at the U.S. Congress was exceptional—one of the best I've ever heard. Kudos!!

To you—our love, a memory, and a wish for all the best—MERRY CHRISTMAS AND HAPPY NEW YEAR!!!

I thought of Franky Jose, the novelist, who told me more than once that "as long as the American bases are here, we cannot become a modern country." I thought of a conversation I had had in the back of a taxi with Father Edicio "Ed" de la Torre, who spent many years in jail as an alleged communist rebel. He was released at the orders of Cory Aquino. In the taxi, we discussed the bases. Infringement of national sovereignty, said Father Ed, exploitation of Filipinas, cynical use of the Philippines in a global imperialist game. I dropped him at his office. The taxi driver turned around and said: "Sir, you know where I'm from?" I did not. "From Olongapo, yes, sir." He told me how he had tried to stow away on an American ship when he was a boy; how he later tried to join the U.S. navy; and how he wanted his two daughters to marry Americans and live in San Diego. Finally he said: "If any politician in our city talked like your companion just did, he'd be a goner for sure."

And I thought of another driver I had spoken to in the summer. He had supported Cory. He had been there in February. But now he was disgusted, with the politicians' quarreling, the crime, the murder rate, the coup attempts, the communists, the lack of any change in the country. He still loved Cory, he hastened to say. She is sincere. "But if our country doesn't change, something is going to happen. Or maybe . . ." Maybe what? "Or maybe nothing."

3

Sensitive Issues

MALAYSIA

Malaysia begins in Singapore. More precisely, it begins at the railway station, a shabby old building with a dusty main hall and a well-known bar frequented by Indians who look conspiratorial and whisper about Special Branch agents always assumed to be in their midst. It seems out of place in spotless new Singapore, like a relic of a more raffish past, the kind of landmark that Singapore's rulers tend to tear down to make way for something more in keeping with the modern republic. Another shopping complex, for instance. The station, in fact, belongs to Malaysia, as does the land on one side of the railway line. Near the border, where the line stretches across the causeway to the Malaysian city of Johore Bahru, there is a Malay village, or kampong; on the other side of the tracks, barely visible through the coconut trees surrounding the kampong, are the last buildings of Singapore: a shopping complex, a cinema, a video center.

The kampong is little more than a few ramshackle houses on stilts in black, stagnant water. Compared with the rather forbidding government housing estates that fill much of the land in Singapore, the kampong looks human, even idyllic, in the way airport paintings of tropical villages are supposed to look idyllic. Three elderly women sat on the porch of one of the houses, two of them dressed in colorful sarongs. The third wore a flowered dress and a jade bracelet. Her house, next door, looked neater than the rest in the row, with a well-tended garden in front, showing a pride in ownership. She was Chinese, married to a Malay, a man with a mustache busy tending the flowers. The two Malays appeared to be teasing their Chinese friend. My companion, a young Indian-Singaporean woman called Ghita, translated part of the conversation. The Malays were praising the Chinese woman's sons, who were at university. They will go very far, they said. They are very clever. They work very hard. You must be very proud. The Chinese woman smiled. The Malays screeched with mirth. "They are a bit envious," said Ghita.

Up the road was a small café, which looked to be on the verge of collapsing into the black lagoon. To get there you had to pick your way through a pile of refuse, rotting in the balmy afternoon sun—the tropical idyll gone to seed. A group of young Malay men sat around a table laughing and preening in their neatly pressed jeans and flashy Japanese T-shirts. They were slender, almost pretty, yet powerfully built, more like dancers than the dock workers they turned out to be. They asked me whether I would like to pay for their tea and showed their teeth in merry smiles. Ghita explained that they were Malaysians working in Singapore. Why? "They say the money is better here. They can wear nice clothes and have more fun." The boys giggled. Did they prefer to live in Singapore? "Oh no. They say Malaysia is much better. It is their country. They say there are too many rules in Singapore." When they got up to leave for the docks, Ghita said: "They are quite content. Malays don't care about material things. They are happy to relax."

Happy to relax. It was the usual image of Malays in Malaysia, as common as the other image, of the corrupt Malay politician, living in his grotesquely palatial home, driving expensive European cars, keeping Chinese mistresses, and taking in kickbacks from every big deal in town.

I was driven around a rich suburb of Kuala Lumpur by Mr. and Mrs. Lim, who wished to show me some of the larger houses in the neighborood, so I could see "what is wrong with our country." Various grand mansions were pointed out, owned by friends of Prime Minister Mahathir, or the minister of this or that. "The *bumis*," said Mr. Lim, "they get rich here from government loans. Then they build big houses. That's the first thing they do, la. Build big houses. They live in them and then they go bankrupt in them." Then I was shown what the Malays aspire to. There was a Disneyland castle, complete with turrets and watchtowers and what looked like dungeons on the basement floor, called "Camelot." Across the road was an even larger mansion, known to the locals as "Costalot." It had cast-iron gates decorated with gold; it had a long drive, like an English country house. The effect was that of many Hollywood homes, expensive yet somehow a little flimsy, as if not built to last very long. Camelot belonged to a Chinese general, and Costalot to a Chinese tycoon, jailed in Singapore for involvement in a business scandal.

Mr. Lim, a dapper Chinese entrepreneur in his early forties, was a kindly man who spoke about the state of his country with a kind of gallows humor. He chuckled as he explained that "this is a make-believe economy. The corruption is too bad. It will all collapse soon." He would come home in the evening and, asked by his wife how his day had been, he would answer in terms of the stock market. "Stock market down ten points today, la." After dinner he spent hours on the phone talking deals: "You play ball with me and we both make a killing, la." Mrs. Lim, a beautiful woman who liked to dress in shorts and high heels, explained what a shock it had been coming from Penang, an almost entirely Chinese town, to K.L.: "I never had to deal with *bumis* before." She did not express horror at the thought, but simply surprise at this new experience.

Bumis are the *bumiputras*, literally the sons of the soil, the Malays and the tribes of Sarawak and Sabah, who altogether make up a little over half the population of Malaysia. As sons of the soil, they regard the Chinese and Indians as immigrants. Since independence from the British in 1957, they have tried to shape the country in their own image: Islam is the official religion, Malay the official language. It is government policy to favor Malays, in education, in business, in the arts, indeed in every sphere of public life. It is the Malays who receive the government grants, scholarships, special loans, and plum government jobs. Malays run the country. Yet it is the Malays who look dispossessed in Kuala Lumpur, many of them huddled together in shabby estates on the city's outskirts, their children skulking in shopping arcades with nothing to do, taking to drugs or religion, dressed like punks or in the pseudo-Arab gear of Muslim fundamentalists. Mrs. Lim indeed deals with *bumis*, a few shopkeepers here and there, the odd business contact of her husband's, a taxi driver on occasion; otherwise they might as well not exist. Not a word of Malay is spoken in her house. The maid is Chinese. Her friends are Chinese. She speaks English to her husband. She watches American sitcoms on TV and Cantonese soap operas from Hong Kong on her video machine. It all points to the basic fact of Malaysia: the Village is Malay, but the City still belongs to the immigrants.

"Essentially because of environmental and hereditary factors, the Malays have become a rural race with only a minute portion of them in the towns. Rural people everywhere are less sophisticated and progressive than urban people. Our solution to this problem must be to attempt a reversal of this state of affairs. In other words, we must seek to urbanize the Malays." Dr. Mahathir bin Mohamed, the present Prime Minister of Malaysia, wrote this in 1970, in his book *The Malay Dilemma*.

It is an astonishing book, which was banned for years before
he became Prime Minister. Dr. Mahathir, a former medical
doctor, believes in social Darwinism. "The history of China is
littered with disasters, both natural and man-made. Four thousand years ago a great flood was recorded, and subsequently
floods alternated with famine, while waves of invaders, pred-
atory emperors and warlords ravaged the country. For the
Chinese people life was one continuous struggle for survival.
In the process the weak of mind and body lost out to the strong
and the resourceful." The Malays, on the other hand, always
had it easy. "There was plenty for everyone throughout the
year . . . Under these conditions everyone survived. Even the
weakest and the least diligent were able to live in comparative
comfort, to marry and to procreate. The observation that only
the fittest would survive did not apply, for the abundance of
food supported the existence of even the weakest."

It is interesting how the racial theories that justified Western
colonialism—the white man's burden—survived in the East,
from Malaysia to Singapore to Japan, while being discredited
in the West. Both Dr. Mahathir and his counterpart in Singapore, Lee Kuan Yew (whose English name is Harry), profess
to despise the decadent West of our times, but admire the spirit
of their erstwhile colonial masters.

In Singapore I was told a story by the former President,
Devan Nair. I later heard several versions of the same story
from others. Here is Nair's: When George Brown visited Singapore in the 1960s as British Foreign Secretary, Lee hosted a
garden party for him and launched into a long diatribe about
the loss of Western will, the rotten state of England, the lack
of discipline, the overall decline. When he had finished, Brown
reportedly replied: "Harry, you're the finest Englishman east
of Suez." Harry for once was at a loss for words.

Dr. Mahathir shares Lee's views on the decline of the West:
"The fall of the West means victory for the East which the
West once colonized. If the Western nations bemoan the loss
of their colonies, the Eastern peoples should rejoice over their

independence. If the Western nations react to their loss by rejecting old values and creating new ones, the Eastern peoples should hold fast to the values which brought them success . . . There is no reason why the Eastern peoples should reject the values and norms developed during their colonization by the West, unlike the Western nations who have cause to be disillusioned in their old values and norms." Much is made by the Prime Minister of "propriety in attire." He speaks approvingly of the Englishmen who used to swelter in tropical heat dressed in suits and ties. This showed discipline and seriousness of purpose. He decries modern Western habits of dress: "Just as copying proper attire once led to the East adopting Western values regarding discipline, copying improper attire has infected the East with the values behind the Western change in attire." Behind this obsession with appearance one senses a cultural anxiety, the unease of a people who have lost their inner direction. Modern influence is seen as a threat, because there is nothing indigenous strong enough to absorb it. "Whereas the non-Malays have easily adjusted to Western civilization," writes Dr. Mahathir, "the Malays seem to be more attracted by the forms than the substance of that civilization." One suspects this also applies to the doctor himself.

As a postwar European, one is inclined to reject Dr. Mahathir's Darwinism out of hand. The associations are too painful. Fortunately one can find other reasons for the failure of Malays to cope with the City. The British were happy to let the Chinese, rural folk themselves, run the plantations and build the cities. After all, the Malays were quite content to stay in the kampongs, ruled by their sultans. The division of labor worked well, so why change it? The Chinese, not being allowed to acquire land, had little choice in the matter. And so the City was built before the Malays had a chance to participate. As a former British colonial civil servant still living in K.L. said: "They had their charming customs in the kampongs. All is lost when they move to the cities, I'm afraid." This was a common attitude among the British in Malaya. The underdogs are more

loyal, more pliable, indeed more charming. I called the former
civil servant, now a man in his eighties, for an appointment:
"Make sure you get a Malay taxi driver, old chap, the Chinese
are an unreliable lot."

One does not have to be a Darwinist to explain why the
Chinese immigrants built cities. They were forced to live off
trade and made their own communities to survive. To stop the
village Malays from being swamped by the immigrants, the
British protected the Malays' way of life, their religion, their
native rulers, their charming customs. Just as these were protected in the constitution of independent Malaya in 1957. But
at the same time, the British nurtured a Malay elite along
Western lines, installing a Western legal system and Western
political institutions. "Proof of our goodwill, you know," said
the civil servant.

This Westernized elite, exemplified by the father of Malaysia,
the first Prime Minister and son of a sultan, Tunku Abdul
Rahman, took over after independence, as the administrators
of modern institutions and defenders of Islam, the Malay language, the charming customs—in short, all that is implied by
so-called Malay rights. The two tasks began to clash when the
patrician elite was gradually replaced in power by new men,
less sure of themselves, their place in the world, their religious
values—in short, by men like Dr. Mahathir. They have lost
touch with the traditional Malay way of life, but lack a strong
commitment to democratic institutions. They are confused
modernists who rely upon the kampongs for their votes. The
Malay rights they are beholden to protect are a source of power,
but also an increasing menace. They divide the races, for one
thing. And then there is the problem of definition. The power
of the sultans was more or less limited to religious affairs.
Everything else, the British took care of. Ever so politely the
Malay elite was shorn of real power; face was saved by offering
pomp, titles, and money. The result was something unlike Thailand or Indonesia: the Malay identity came to be defined almost
entirely by religion; to be a Muslim was to be a Malay, and

vice versa. Because the cities were Chinese and the villages Malay, Islam never urbanized; it became part of a nostalgic cult of the kampong.

Dr. Mahathir hopes to Malayanize the City, by dragging the sons of the soil from their kampongs through what Americans call affirmative action, institutionalized in Malaysia as the New Economic Policy. The aim is to make sure Malays own at least 30 percent of the nation's wealth by 1990. He argues that Islam, far from being an obstacle to modernization, is in fact a modernizing force. Muslims, he says, falling back on an old face-saving canard, invented modern science, medicine, law, mathematics: "The education and knowledge that the West has and that the Western people have spread throughout the world are in reality Islamic." The Malay dilemma in Dr. Mahathir's view has nothing to do with religion, but with the contradiction between being protected and learning to be competitive. With too much political protection, "they will become softer and less able to overcome difficulties on their own. Because of this, political power might ultimately prove their complete downfall. But the alternative is equally without promise. Removal of all protection would subject the Malays to the primitive laws that enable only the fittest to survive." The fittest, of course, are the Chinese. Pride is of the essence here, and for that Dr. Mahathir returns to the world of forms. It is essential that Malays are seen to rule the City. Malays must become company directors, and "by virtue of their status . . . acquire riches. At first sight this might seem grossly unfair. These few Malays, for they are only a few, have waxed rich not because of themselves but because of the policy of a government supported by a huge majority of poor Malays . . . But if these few Malays are not enriched the poor Malays will not gain either. It is the Chinese who will continue to live in huge houses and regard the Malays as only fit to drive their cars . . . From the point of view of racial ego, and this ego is still strong, the unseemly existence of Malay tycoons is essential." Dr. Mahathir's Malay City is openly built on the "make-believe economy." Urban

Malays have been given a make-believe identity, by Dr. Mahathir, but also by his enemies, the religious fundamentalists. Drugs and religion, corruption, the baroque mansions, all have the same source: racial ego, the desire to match the Camelots and Costalots.

The skyline of Kuala Lumpur tells its own story. In few cities of the world has so much deliberate effort gone into expressing national identity—that is to say, Malay identity—in architecture. Some of the older landmarks are attractive and indeed impressive. The most famous is the railway station, the third one built since the Chinese tin-mining town turned into a regional capital. (Malay schoolteachers now claim that the city was not really founded by Chinese at all, but by a Malay prince.) It was designed in what was known as the Moorish style: mosquelike pinnacles and Buddhist domes, loggias, columns, and archways. The effect is, well, Oriental. Then there is the Sultan Abdul Samad building, housing the federal and high courts, along the Padang across from the Selangor Club (where women are still barred from the Long Bar, one of the finest colonial saloons in Asia, filled with silver trophies and pictures of cricket teams). As was the case with the railway station, an effort was made to make it look Oriental, to incorporate Islamic details, delicate pinnacles, arches and domes, a mixture of Arabian Nights and Victorian Gothic. Both buildings, the former completed in 1910, the latter in 1897, are full of character, but it is a character utterly remote from the Malay past. They were designed by British architects. The style is that of the British Raj attempting to incorporate Mogul India. "Like mules," wrote Robert Byron about the town hall in Bombay, "these crosses are infertile." They are the expressions, not of Malay rights, but of British Empire.

The modern buildings, symbols of Dr. Mahathir's Malay City, so to speak, are almost as impressive. The huge Dayabumi complex, financed and built by the Japanese; the brand-new Islamic Center; the imposing government buildings. Unlike the

older landmarks, these additions to the K.L. skyline were designed by Malays, but they are as alien to the Malay tradition
as the railway station. In this case the forms were borrowed
from the Middle East.

The Islamic Center, for example, is supposed to express "Islamic values." It has an Islamic library, Islamic exhibitions, and
a large courtyard where annual National Koran Reading Com-
petitions are held. According to a brochure of the Center, it
"was designed with the aim of reviving the traditional Islamic
architecture, like those found in Baghdad and Jidda. Before
coming up with the design, Datuk Nik Mohamed made a survey
and study abroad, especially in the Middle East countries, to
obtain a glimpse of Islamic architecture there."

The Islamic Center is not unattractive, but in the midst of
Chinatowns and kampongs it looks out of place. It belongs to
the world of Expos, the world of make-believe.

Perhaps closer to Dr. Mahathir's modernist heart are the
new shopping complexes, such as the towering Mall. This time
the model is a shopping center in Toronto. Hundreds of fashion
boutiques, video shops, restaurants, and record stores fill an
enormous glass dome. There is a constant din of rock music
and clattering fountains. On the top floor is a kind of film set
replica of an old street in Malacca, with Chinese shophouses
and noodle stands. Somewhere between this fake street and a
computerized cosmetic center, frequented by young Chinese
ladies dressed like Mrs. Lim in miniskirts or shorts and high
heels, is a rather sad-looking stall selling Islamic literature,
Koranic quotations, and Muslim veils. The female attendant,
looking forlorn, like an extra who wandered onto the wrong
set, was covered from head to toe with a pseudo-Arab robe.

Shades of Jidda are much in evidence in the government
building that contains the television station and the Information
Ministry. I had made an appointment to see a parliamentary
secretary by the name of Datuk Haji Dusuki Ahmad. He had
caused a controversy by blaming the remarkable number of
rape cases in Malaysia on women dressing immodestly. The

fact that some of the more egregious recent cases concerned children made his statement especially unfortunate. Like many Malay civil servants, he had tried to impress on me how busy he was, as if constantly aware of the Malay reputation for idleness: "I am very busy, very busy indeed. Call me tomorrow. Perhaps you can come now. I am very busy. Welcome to Malaysia, you can come now."

There were few non-Malays to be seen in the building. Koranic quotations decorated the walls. Women wore long dresses. "Welcome to Malaysia," said Datuk Dusuki, slouched on a leather sofa. He called for an interpreter, a young man in a business suit, who seemed painfully nervous, tapping his feet and polishing his glasses. The young man explained what he did at the various ministries. "We are interchangeable," he said.

I asked Datuk Dusuki about Western influence on Malaysia. The problem, he said, was that Western influence brought useful knowledge but had a bad effect on morals. There were taboos in Oriental culture which did not exist in the West, exposing the body, for instance, and social relations between men and women which were, well, not good. "What we want," he said, "is a united perception of a modern Malaysia. We must take the good things from all cultures." What about cultures in the Middle East? "We take only the good aspects which conform to our culture." Which aspects of Middle Eastern culture would not conform? "That is very sensitive. Many people cannot distinguish between Islam and the Middle East. But we must unite as one modern Malaysia." How do the Chinese fit in? What are the good things in their culture? "We are all part of one united Malaysia. The Chinese are good at business. That we can't deny." What else, apart from business? At this point the interpreter, furiously polishing his glasses, engaged in a discussion with Datuk Dusuki. Then he repeated that "Chinese business is good." And Indian culture? "We cannot separate Indians and Chinese and Malays. We must learn from all the races and build a truly Malaysian heritage."

I asked him about a suggestion made by Tunku Abdul Rah-

man that all converts to Islam should be given the same status
as Malay sons of the soil. "That would not do," said Datuk
Dusuki, "for we don't mix race with religion. We Malays are
protected by the constitution because we are weak." Did this
include Christian Malays? "Not protected by the constitution."
What about Chinese Muslims? "How can they be protected?
They are not Malay."

How to define the elusive "true Malaysian heritage" has been
debated for almost twenty years. Which elements should be
included in the "national culture"? The Chinese lion dance?
No, said the Acting Culture, Youth, and Sports Minister (this
was before culture was transferred to the Ministry of Culture
and Tourism) in 1982, for the lion dance could not be accepted
by all the people in the country. National culture, he said, had
to be based on the culture indigenous to the region, on features
of other cultures suited to the national culture, and on Islam.
"Based on these three principles, the national culture will elim-
inate racial cultures." The Foreign Minister joined the debate
and declared that "only characteristics of art which are based
on the Malay identity should be accepted as elements of the
national culture." The Chinese did not like this idea of national
culture and protested. Lion dances became a political issue.
"The national culture policy should not be used as an issue to
arouse racial sentiments," declared the Culture, Youth, and
Sports Minister, Anwar Ibrahim, the following year. The status
of national culture, he said, was the same as that of Islam:
"This means that the issue of national culture cannot be
raised."

A basic flaw in the concept of a national culture based on
indigenous tradition is that Malays, unlike the Chinese or the
Indians, lack an urban tradition. There is no urban Malay
culture to speak of. To base a new urban culture on kampong
life won't work. The forms can be borrowed to some extent,
as in the Penang airport, and a few other public buildings,
shaped like giant Malay huts, but otherwise urban life is too
different and, literally, too alien to incorporate much from the

kampong. There is, however, a kind of official Malay or Malaysian culture promoted by the government: food festivals in international hotels, enlivened by traditional song and dance. (Food, in fact, is one of the few instances of integrated culture: the delicious Nonya cuisine mixes Chinese and Malay dishes in ways that add an extra dash to both.)

The Malaysia Fest in 1987 was such a manifestation. It was considered a great success by the Ministry of Culture and Tourism and 1990 has already been designated Visit Malaysia Year. *The New Sunday Times* called the festival a celebration of the spirit. "For what was on show were the many cultures that Malaysian life is made up of. And the spirit that moves these cultures to keep them alive. Without culture, we won't have people visiting us." The Malaysia Fest, said *The Star*, a newspaper close to the Chinese community and less controlled by the government, was about image. "Thailand sells itself as the Land of Smiles, while our southern approach is bound by instant Asia / Garden City Singapore. But say Malaysia and it draws a blank for most tourists."

Looking for an image. An image which avoids racial conflict, but is nevertheless based on Malay culture. Perhaps the closest thing to such an image was provided by a singer and movie star named P. Ramlee. He was discovered singing at an agricultural fair in 1948, a thin youth with curly hair and a thin mustache. He captured the Malay imagination, made a large number of successful records and films, and died in 1973, aged forty-five, bitter and overweight. He lives on, though, as an officially supported icon of identity: a street in K.L. is named after him, his house is a museum, and his films are often shown on Malaysian TV. I watched a tape of one of his movies—a melodrama about a kampong boy, played by Ramlee, who becomes a rich and successful entertainer in Singapore, only to see his pampered son, also played by Ramlee, turn into an evil gangster—at the house of Chinese friends. They were astonished by my interest. "How can you torture yourself watching that Malay stuff?" they asked. "The *bumis* needed a hero, that's why they built him up," said one who had actually seen his films. "But he is no good, isn't it?"

Ramlee clearly had talent. And his morality plays about the urban Malay, both as a success and as a failure, genuinely struck a chord. But his films, mostly directed by Indians and following the pattern of Hindi musicals, seem as confused, culturally, as the buildings of K.L. In one film, the hero ends in heaven, a bizarre place with angels playing harps behind Greek columns. "That," said Malay playwright Syed Alwi, "is the Malay idea of heaven."

Syed Alwi is a man of liberal ideas, a cosmopolitan. There are, of course, more Malays like him. I met a Malay woman reporter who found the New Economic Policy humiliating; she constantly felt the need to prove to her colleagues that she was worthy of her job. I met another Malay woman who lived with an Indian, a rare case indeed. But I was asked not to write about them, for it would surely get them into trouble. That is the problem: such liberals are a small and increasingly threatened minority. "What can an artist do in this country?" asked Syed Alwi. "People just laugh at us, or, worse, ignore us."

A Chinese journalist named Thor Kah Hoong wrote a series of skits for the stage entitled *Caught in the Middle*. This satire of life in the Malaysian city included a scene about a young middle-class Malay couple, whose behavior is modeled entirely after TV commercials and American soap operas. (In an earlier version of the play, a scene showing Malays sitting in a bar was banned by the censors, who declared this was "not Malay behavior.") They talk like people in commercials, walk like them, dress like them, and, if such a thing could be imagined, think like them. The point of the scene is that for new middle-class Malays there is no other model to turn to. All commercials are placed in a make-believe world, but Malaysian commercials especially so. To fudge the racial differences, the models look vaguely Eurasian, neither obviously Malay nor Chinese, and almost always fair-skinned. Their behavior, when they are confronted with dazzling detergents, chocolate products, or automobiles, is marked by the barely contained hysteria of TV commercials everywhere. The interiors of their homes look American. They are modern, modern, modern! I was told that an American Express commercial, showing a Malay-looking man coming ashore in a rescue dinghy, tired and in tatters, but in the sure knowledge that Amex would take care of things, was taken off the air by the Information Minister. The reason? To show the man in tattered clothing was thought to be denigrating to Malays.

Only occasionally does the deep Malay sense of insecurity slip through the sterilizing filter of international advertising. "Is your BMW performing as it should? Meet Mr. H. Führer, our BMW service engineer on a short visit from Germany. He understands BMW with the cold logic of science and the intuition of a man who loves the machine." As Dr. Mahathir wrote in his analysis of "racial character": "The Malays are spiritually inclined, tolerant and easygoing." The cold logic of science and love of the machine are evidently alien to the modern Malay. The model has to be a German, Mr. Führer.

It is, then, as if there is not much to choose for the new urban, middle-class Malay between Costalot and the spiritual inclination, which leads to the religious veil. Although it would seem that most Malays still support the former, offered as an incentive to success by Dr. Mahathir and his ruling UMNO Party, more and more are turning to the latter, to the religious state, promised by the Parti Islam Se Tanah Melayu, or PAS. The big house and the BMW, let alone Mr. Führer's cold logic, are out of reach for most migrants to the city. And the hypocrisy of Dr. Mahathir's "unseemly tycoons" who profess to be good Muslims is too blatant, the contradiction too harsh.

"You see," said Subky Latiff, a PAS politician described to me as a relatively liberal man, "it is quite simple. There is conflict between Westernization and Islam." I asked him to give him an example. "Everything. Political, social, economic, everything. Islam is not just a religion, it is a way of life. Western culture is also a way of life." Yes, but what was the area of greatest conflict? "Simple. It is religion. Westerners are not religious. For us everything is religious: politics, social life, economics."

Subky is a thin, scholarly-looking man with old-fashioned glasses and a wispy black beard. He seemed as preoccupied with appropriate forms as Dr. Mahathir. The idea was not to imitate Arabs, he said, but to emulate the prophet Mohammed. He demonstrated this by tying a scarf around his head in the way the Prophet himself would have done. I expressed interest, as his two unruly sons, dressed in jumpsuits, bounced up and down on the sofa and tried to shove sticky cakes into my face. His daughter, in an Arab robe, scowled from the kitchen. Subky wished to illustrate his point about proper forms further. "Look," he said, jumping up from the sofa in the small living room of his concrete bungalow, "there is only one proper Muslim way to pass water." Subky hunkered down, as if perched over a toilet. "You see, if I would pass water like this in Western trousers, they would get wet. That is bad because a good Muslim must be clean when praying in the mosque. So we wear Muslim robes. It is good."

Subky Latiff is in favor of an Islamic state, ruled by good Muslims, who enforce Islamic laws. The other races would have to abide by such laws. I thought of Mrs. Lim, shopping for pork at the market, wearing her shorts and high heels. The Chinese could be persuaded over time, thought Subky, and then he offered two examples I was to hear from many PAS members, obviously part of a well-rehearsed argument: "When our Prophet Mohammed ruled in Medina, the majority of the people were non-Muslims, but they obeyed our Prophet because they saw he was good, his life was good, his religion also good." The other example was more surprising: "When the communists first went to Russia and China, the people disagreed with them. Communism was foreign. But later they accepted. People thought it was good."

I asked whether Dr. Mahathir was a good Muslim. Subky's face creased in an indignant frown. "No, no, no," he said. "He was born a Muslim, but he does not understand Islam. His experience is too narrow. He does not live like a Muslim."

To carry this idea to its extreme, to live as much as possible like the Prophet, one has to leave the City entirely and start from scratch. That is what Yussuf, a handsome man in his thirties, dressed in a long green robe and a turban, decided to do. He was working for a British company sponsoring musical entertainment when he dropped everything to live in a Muslim commune outside K.L. We were sitting on the floor, drinking tea. Young men, dressed in the same green robes, some with kohl painted around their eyes like Arabs, recorded our conversation on tape recorders, video, and film. "Just for the record," said one of the men, his face hidden behind a video camera. Only his white turban, tied in the fashion of the Prophet, was visible.

Yussuf's parents were well-off and they sent their son to an English-language school. "I was trapped in the rat race by the colonial influence," said Yussuf. "We were Muslims, but my religious background was not stressed, only my academic record. I got married, had children, and got involved in the music industry, you know, the high life, women, wine, and temptations. I never thought of my spiritual life. Then one day I was watching TV when prayers were announced. My brother went off to pray. But not me. Then my daughter asked me whether I prayed. It was like ten thousand tons of rocks hitting my head. Should I lie to my daughter? I felt that if I failed to teach my daughter how to be a true Muslim, I would have ruined my life. So I looked around for a religious movement and I found Al Arqam. It was great. I left my job and everything."

Could he not have lived as a true Muslim and continued his job? "Impossible. That life, freely associating with women, drinking, it was too different from Muslim laws. Too many temptations. I had to choose. I chose to have a life of the spirit."

"Yes, yes, the spirit," whispered the other men in the room, while maneuvering their cameras and tape recorders, red lights blinking, flashbulbs popping, as though at a press conference.

Three visitors from Sweden entered the room, beaming good-will, bubbling with pleasure at all they had been shown. They soon left, bubbling something about traditional Muslim hospitality. A man with kohl around his eyes turned to me and said: "See, we have connections all over the world." Would I like to see a videotape they had made of a very famous French journalist who had liked Al Arqam very much? I declined the offer, and asked what all this filming and recording was for. It began to make me nervous. "For us technology is a tool for the worship of Allah. Cameras, tapes, all that is to worship God." I jotted this down. "Now repeat what I said," ordered a burly man called Abdul Halim.

Mr. Lim had warned me about these men in their green robes. "They will kill you!" he said. In fact, they were friendly in the slightly obtrusive way of all religious groups. I asked Abdul Halim about his encounter with V. S. Naipaul, who had visited the commune for his book *Among the Believers*. "Naipaul," said Abdul Halim, with a look of great disapproval, "is a freethinker." "A freethinker, a freethinker," repeated the cameraman.

The women of the kampong, who lived in strict seclusion behind a wall, occasionally appeared, looking like giant ravens in their black robes that concealed all but the eyes that peered through tiny slits. I was allowed one peek through the wall. Two young women—at least I assumed they were young—were working on electric typewriters. They quickly looked away, as if I could see anything immodest. Even children were covered from head to toe. Some women wore glasses wrapped around their hoods, creating a ghostly effect. There were about one hundred families in the village, all trying to live like Arabs at the time of the Prophet. They made their own food—"clean food," said Abdul Halim, "in line with Muslim law. Before, all the food was made by Chinese, who are only interested in money. We can provide good, clean food." They also had their own entertainment, which was part of Yussuf's job. "We offer good entertainment," he said, "minus the music and other things not in line with Muslim laws. Islamic songs, poetry. People will accept it as beautiful. No vice."

To say that Yussuf and his fellow believers are anti-modern is not entirely accurate. They seem obsessed with modern technology. But it is all put to a single-minded use: their religion. Technology is regarded as neutral, as Abdul Halim had said, a tool. By using the tool to propagate their religious way of life, they can be modern, without being tainted by Westernization. It is a very limited concept of modernity, to be sure, but there is a certain extreme logic to the idea. Unlike the politicians of UMNO, the Malay mainstream, as it were, members of Al Arqam do not pretend to uphold Malay culture at all. According to Abdul Halim, only about 5 percent of traditional Malay life conformed to Muslim law. "This new Islamic consciousness has only been understood for the last twenty years." Abdul and his fellow believers, almost all young people, are a bit like American hippies seeking salvation in communes in New Mexico, reading Carlos Castaneda. But with one basic difference: The hippies escaped the complexity of modern life by turning to a form of anarchy, a world without rules, where people did their own thing. Al Arqam is the exact opposite: A world of uncertain values, borrowed laws, confused goals, and no clear principles is replaced by a community based on nothing but rules and principles of the most extreme kind.

I was reminded of something Subky Latiff said: "Only ideological people can rule an ideological country." Dr. Mahathir, despite all his books, has no ideology. The political supremacy of UMNO, the New Economic Policy, the protection of Malay rights, these are all political aims. Power and economic development do not offer a moral universe, which is precisely what PAS and the Islamic communards do promise. At a time when an increasing number of Malay graduates, having been promised power and riches, find themselves without jobs, confused and lonely in the City they cannot handle, at such a time the religious veil becomes an attractive option. It does not simply promise a return to the kampong. Much better than that: Modern gadgets in the service of Islamic orthodoxy promise domination of the future City. As Abdul Halim put it, when I asked him why he chose to live in a village: "One day this village will be a town."

The Muslim fundamentalists reject nationalism as being against the tenets of Islamic brotherhood. That is the reason they give. A more plausible motive might be that they find it hard to identify with a country in which they feel defensive, as though they were a threatened minority, despite the political supremacy of Malays. Malaysia is too vague a concept. It is defined politically and geographically, but, apart from tourist festivals, not culturally. As the Malay playwright Syed Alwi once said in his pained voice: "Malaysian culture does not exist." A very talented artist, he has more or less given up writing plays, because his audience is too small. Indians and Chinese have no interest in Malay plays, and the urban middle-class Malays prefer American pop culture. The problem for Malaysian artists, one feels, is the lack of a civilization, a Great Tradition to draw upon, to challenge, to be inspired by. The yearning to be part of something larger, something beyond the confines of racial culture, is pervasive in Malaysia. The Chinese have their Hong Kong soap operas on video, many educated Indians send their children to Indian universities, and Malays seek Muslim brotherhood. But it is not entirely satisfactory. As the memories of shared history fade, the element of make-believe grows. China and India become more and more abstract, while identification with the Middle East, let alone the ancient world of the Prophet, remains artificial at best.

There is another way out of racial culture. Cecil Rajendra is a poet and a lawyer. His parents were Indian, his wife is Chinese, and he writes his poems in English. His son is called Yasunari, after the Japanese novelist Kawabata. His art cannot really be placed in any tradition, unlike the writing of, say, V. S. Naipaul (one thinks of him often in Malaysia) or Salman

Rushdie, both of whom are self-consciously aware, and derive their creative spark from the confrontation of the cultures of their childhood and the Great Tradition of English literature. And so Rajendra turns to an abstraction, to a make-believe civilization he likes to call the Third World.

> *Do not ask*
> *who am I?*
> *i am what i am*
> *child of the sun*
> *ashes & quinine*
> *jade and jasmine*
> *i am lamentation*
> *i am celebration*
>
> *i am Pocahontas*
> *Tutankhamen*
> *Buddha, Shaka*
> *Bolivar, Zapata*
> *Hannibal and Ho*
> *Chi Minh, Toussaint*
> *Gandhi & Guevara*
> *i am Lumumba.*
>
> *i am a city of shanty*
> *towns, blood & chancre:*
> *i am Kingston & Brasilia*
> *Bangkok, Montevideo*
> *Manila, Dhaka, Rio*
> *Calcutta & Jakarta*
> *Hanoi & Addis Ababa*
> *i am Santiago . . .*

And so on he goes. He is Hiroshima, Sharpeville, Shatila; he is sitar, tabla, reggae, calypso. He is "a symphony for the tongue primeval: watermelon & pineapple, saltfish & mango curry . . ." He is the Rubaiyat of Omar Khayyam, Basho, Neruda,

Tu Fu, and Tagore. "My name is Jose Rizal." He is who he is, "child of the almighty sun."

Rajendra has found something larger, but it is too large, too indiscriminate, and too diffuse to have much meaning. Syed Alwi, who is anything but a deracinated man of all cultures and none, said that Malaysians still tended to adopt the racial caricatures bequeathed by the British colonialists, the lazy Malay, the money-grabbing Chinese, and so on. This may be so. But the Third World persona, also, is an image borrowed from the West, from social activists in Berkeley and concerned poetry magazines in London. The Third World concept is a product of post-colonial guilt. In the work of a Southeast Asian poet it looks as out of place as the green Arab robes in Al Arqam.

Rajendra wants to be an engaged artist, speaking out on progressive causes. He has written poems about nuclear war, about ecology, about rivers being poisoned "by progress's vomit." He hates that "mammon DEVELOPMENT," and what it is doing to "our customs, our culture, our traditions." Foreign brand names, Benson & Hedges, Marlboro, appear in his poems as icons of everything that is loathsome. He hates airport art, he despises America. Yet his voice is not that of a son of the soil, or even of a kampong intellectual. Rajendra is a city boy educated in England. His poetry is published in London and heard at Third World poetry readings in Islington.

He lives in Penang, an island off the west coast of the peninsula, not far from the Thai border. It is a congenial place for a radical poet. A bit like Kyoto, San Francisco, or Amsterdam, it has beauty, gentility, and history, and unburdened by the responsibilities of government, it can afford to be comfortably anti-establishment. Compared to the confusion of K.L., Penang also has a pleasing sense of cultural cohesion. George Town, the main city of Penang, is a Chinese town. Its shophouses were built by craftsmen imported from China; its wedding rituals, burial customs, its clan associations, its restaurants, and its temples make up a small, self-contained world where the way of life of southern China is still more or less preserved. George

Town is in many ways more traditionally Chinese than the old towns in Canton and Fujian, whence most of the immigrants to Malaya came. The culture of George Town is an expatriate culture, which often tends to be anachronistic and exaggerated. The expatriate mentality is still there even among generations born in Malaysia, among people who have only the haziest notion of contemporary China. People like the Chinese taxi driver who slammed on his brakes to avoid another taxi that suddenly swerved in front of us. "Malay driver, terrible, la! They do anything they like; it's their country." Wasn't this his country too? "No, la. We are Chinese. We just rent the land. This country no use."

Tunku Abdul Rahman blames it on the British, who allowed Chinese schools in Malaya. I saw the Tunku in his large bungalow in Penang, decorated with tiger-skin rugs, sporting trophies and an enormous number of photographs and paintings of the Tunku: the Tunku and his favorite racehorse, the Tunku in front of a mosque, the Tunku with a football team, the Tunku with the British royal family. He is an amiable man in his eighties, given to telling jokes and presenting reporters with outrageous quotes in the offhand manner of the born aristrocrat. Pictures of the young Tunku make him appear as a noble good-time Charlie, which, to all accounts, he was. "In my day," he said, "we had none of this Islamic bigotry. When I gave a party, champagne flowed, oh yes, champagne flowed." I could well imagine it. But he also seems a decent man, whose jovial manners are a useful adjunct to his political shrewdness. His prestige is still such that he gets away with criticism of the government which would be intolerable coming from anybody else. For years he has been writing a provocative column in *The Star*. He is the traditional and now fading voice of reason and tolerance.

It was the Tunku who presided over the deal made at independence whereby the Chinese and other minorities accepted the special status of Malays, the position of Malay rulers, Malay as the national language, and Islam as the official religion.

In exchange they were given citizenship and granted rights in language and education. I asked the Tunku about this. "Well, they wanted to be Chinese. We couldn't really stop them. So why not?"

They were allowed to remain Chinese, but were barred from visiting China. They adopted the identity of expatriates without a motherland. To be Chinese in Malaysia is to have a culture cut off from its source. The political part of the Malaysian deal was to form a coalition of racially based parties, dominated by UMNO. It was a practical compromise in the best British colonial tradition, but it effectively politicized culture, language, and religion, which, in Malaysia, means racial identity.

The racial divisions were not a problem as long as the British acted as umpires and the minorities had countries to return to. But now the umpire is also the dominant race—the Malays. Any encroachment on minority cultures is seen by the Chinese as a political threat to their rights. Any attempt by the Chinese to assert their language and culture is regarded by Malay politicians as an attack on racial harmony and unity, code words for the state as defined by the ruling Malays. These are what are known as "sensitive issues." Which is why criticizing the official view of national culture is a sensitive issue; or challenging the preferential treatment of Malays under the New Economic Policy.

The Tunku seemed exasperated by these sensitive issues and slapped his thighs in a gesture of frustration: "What have the Malays got now? All the wealth is still in the hands of the immigrants. If we don't protect the sons of the soil, they are finished, totally finished." When will the Chinese stop being regarded as immigrants? The Tunku sighed. He explained the tolerant nature of Malays. He tapped my knee and said with a friendly smile: "Look, what do you do if half the population is loyal to this country and the other half is not."

In that same week the sensitive issue came to the boil. It started as a bureaucratic problem. More than one hundred ethnic Chinese teachers, who had not been trained in Mandarin

Chinese, had been promoted to be deputy heads of Chinese primary schools, where the language of instruction is Mandarin. This was done after searching for qualified Mandarin speakers and failing to find enough of them, as most Malaysian Chinese speak the dialects of their ancestors in Fujian and Canton, where Mandarin is not much used even today. Still, the appointments sent the Chinese community into a frenzy. Boycotts were announced. A common Chinese front was formed. The Malaysian Chinese Association, or MCA, which is part of the National Front coalition with UMNO, agreed with the mainly Chinese opposition party DAP and various Chinese associations that they would not "sell off Chinese rights." An UMNO youth rally was held in K.L., denouncing the MCA, calling for the resignation of a Chinese cabinet minister, who was later stripped of his honorary title by the sultan of his state. "Long Live Malays," said the banners at the youth rally. "Malay dignity must be preserved!" shouted the speakers. "Don't test the patience of the Malays!" said the Chief Minister of Malacca. Warnings about a repeat of the racial riots in 1969, when several hundred people died, were issued. Dr. Mahathir accused opposition groups of purposely blowing up racially related issues. "Zionist writers of the foreign press" were denounced for fanning the flames of racial conflict. A Malay gunman ran amok with an M-16 in K.L. The Deputy Home Minister had to reassure people that the killings "were not racial in nature." Terrified of riots, many people stayed home from work. "Racial polarization has got out of control," said a normally placid Indian friend in Penang. "This place is going to blow," said a British journalist in K.L. "The stock market is crashing," said Mr. Lim.

It all ended in the arrest of more than a hundred people—some prominent, some not, but most of them Chinese—under the Internal Security Act. Three newspapers, including *The Star*, were banned. The Tunku lost his column and protested against dictatorial tendencies. Being the Tunku, he escaped arrest.

George Town was the center of Chinese agitation. I met Mr.

Khoo in a noodle restaurant called the Sun, in a dreary back street called Drury Lane. Not a word of Malay was spoken in the Sun, and there was little evidence of Mandarin either. Most people, a motley group of elderly, heavily made-up Chinese ladies, politicians, and journalists from the local Chinese press, spoke Hokkienese. I asked Mr. Khoo, a politician of one of the opposition parties, why Mandarin was so important to Malaysian Chinese. "Otherwise we cannot communicate." What about Malay? "No, la. Very unnatural. We learn Malay. We accept it as the national language. But we are Chinese. Mandarin is our mother tongue." When I expressed some skepticism, noting the prevalence of other dialects, he got excited: "Mandarin is the language of the Chinese people, of China. We love our mother tongue." But surely adopting the official language of China instead of sticking to local dialects or Malay is a political decision? "Ah, very sensitive, la."

I heard the same argument from another Chinese politician, Mr. Tan, sitting in his office, which he had turned into a kind of shrine to the Lions Club, covered with Lions flags, pendants, pictures, and stickers. "Mr. Tan agreed that Chinese had to accept Malay as the national language. But having one language was not necessarily the recipe for peaceful integration. He gave the examples of Switzerland, a peaceful country despite several languages, and Northern Ireland, where people speaking the same language were at war. He did not want his children to identify with China, but with Malaysia. Why, then, the insistence on Mandarin? Ah, well, the mother tongue.

The confusion between China as a civilization and China as a nation has always been a problem for overseas Chinese. Mr. Tan was probably quite sincere in his desire to identify with the state of Malaysia and the civilization of China. But somehow the two don't quite jell. There are too many sensitive issues. The frustration goes too deep. His normally calm voice and placid manner became agitated when he spoke about his son, who had the highest marks at school but was denied a place at university because of racial quotas. "This is very disheartening," he said, turning red, his voice quivering. "Ah, ya! We cannot stand!" It is people like Mr. Tan, and if not Mr. Tan himself, then his son, who will answer the numerous newspaper advertisements that say: "If you are interested in the business migration to Canada, an immigration officer from the province of Quebec will be here soon to brief interested and qualified persons on the business and investment opportunities and prospects available." Fifty thousand Malaysian immigrants, mostly Chinese, already live in Australia; many more have applied. But the problem goes deeper than sensitive political issues and job prospects. A Thai Chinese can easily speak Thai, worship the king, and live as a Buddhist. Even in Indonesia, a Chinese can be absorbed in the national culture without having to become a Muslim. And this is not just a matter of numbers. It is a matter of having a national culture in the first place. The problem, then, for Mr. Tan, or Mr. Khoo, or Mrs. Lim, is that, as a culture, Malaysia does not yet exist.

The east coast, many people had told me, was where you could see the real Malay culture. "It is like another country," said an Indian lawyer in George Town. I took the bus to Kota Bahru, along the East-West Highway, which cuts through the jungle that still harbors the remnants of what only a few decades ago had been a serious communist insurgency. Traffic is still allowed to pass only in daylight.

This sounds more dramatic than it was. The jungle on both sides of the road has been cut back for miles. All one saw was eroded soil and tree stumps, a landscape too bare to give shelter to even one communist guerrilla. Our driver, a friendly Malay with rotten teeth who smoked incessantly and had frightful hacking fits, was reckless in the extreme. It did not seem to bother any of the other passengers, whose eyes were all fixed on the tiny video screen above the driver's seat. First we saw an Italian film about European mercenaries slaughtering Filipino extras by the thousands to capture a golden cobra. Then we saw clips of American professional wrestlers jumping up and down on one another's throats. Meanwhile the driver carried on his suicide mission, hacking green gobs onto his steering wheel. The kampongs along the way looked Malay all right: women in sarongs worked along with the men. I saw very few men in long robes or women in veils.

Kota Bahru is not an attractive town. It has the dusty, somewhat menacing sluggishness of Mexican towns in old Westerns. The shops were mostly owned by Chinese. But there were some rather grandiose government buildings in the familiar Jidda style. And there was one luxury hotel, the Perdana, where lavish parties were held every night for Malay notables, who arrived in fleets of white Mercedes-Benzes. The men were mostly overweight and wore white caps as badges of their pilgrimage to Mecca. The women were elegantly dressed in silk robes. Both men and women left a trail of expensive perfumes.

I went to see the local PAS politicians—PAS won 46 percent of the vote in Kota Bahru—who repeated what I had heard before, that Medina at the time of the Prophet had a majority of non-Muslims, who nevertheless were happy to accept Islamic rule, and that Russians embraced communism despite the fact that Marxists began as a minority. They spoke bitterly about the corrupt UMNO politicians, "the most anti-Islamic group in the country," whose double standards were scandalous; they sent their children abroad, where they "take on the feelings of foreign societies." They pointed out how men and women should never be alone together, unless they were married, because—and here one of the politicians clucked his tongue suggestively—human nature would not tolerate it; and how most gangsters were Chinese, because Malays, being good Muslims, were not inclined to commit crimes. When I countered that most drug addicts were young Malays, they agreed, and said that was because their parents did not teach them Islam. "Our only barrier against foreign influence," said the man who clucked his tongue, "against pessimistic society, is religion. Without Islam we will lose against pessimistic Western society."

"Brother Anwar does not mean pessimistic, he means per-missive," said a young man in granny glasses.

It had all become depressingly familiar. The struggle (a word Muslims use a lot) for meaning, for an identity which could hold its own, seemed so hopeless. And meeting a truly excep-tional person, the first person, in a way, who could be called a true Malaysian, brought relief, but, being so exceptional, not much hope. His name was Anwar Tan, a Chinese Muslim. Sipping coconut juice, we watched the sun come up over the "beach of passionate love," as the tourist brochures call a beautiful stretch of sand just outside the town. He was born a Muslim. His grandfather came from China to seek a better life and ended up living in an entirely Malay kampong. "He had no choice but to convert," said Anwar. Anwar went to a Chinese school—"I kept my Chinese identity"—but took re-ligious instruction from the village teacher. I asked whether there were many Chinese like him in Kota Bahru. "No, very few. See, Chinese have the wrong assumption that to convert to Islam is to become a Malay. In our country Islam is Malay." We gazed at the sea, the empty beach of passionate love, the few Australian backpackers sipping from their coconuts. An-war, a young and successful businessman, who had the same kind of BMW as Mr. Lim, complete with a car telephone, seemed sure of himself; not the cocky swagger of Mr. Lim or the defensive arrogance of some Malay politicians. He seemed at peace with his world. He talked about PAS and UMNO, how both wanted to be more Islamic than the other. Who were the better Muslims? "That is very sensitive," he said. He gazed at the sea a bit longer, as if deep in thought. "Only God can judge that."

A tropical cloudburst did not improve my mood, as I stood in the pouring rain, waiting for a taxi that never came. Instead there was an endless procession of white Mercedes-Benzes, whose occupants, the fat men in white caps, grinned at me, pointing at the funny-looking stranger getting wet. I decided to escape across the border for the afternoon. Thailand was

only half an hour away from Kota Behru. The Golok bridge
between Malaysia and Thailand is one of the strangest, and
because of politics and geography, one of the few open border
crossings in East Asia. In Malaysia there are lugubrious billboards showing a hangman's noose, warning about the fate of
drug smugglers. There are a few Chinese shops, waiting taxis,
a sleepy kampong, and a distant mosque. Streams of Malaysians, Muslim fundamentalists in robes as well as Chinese, cross
the bridge from the Thai side loaded down with goods: TV
sets, cassette recorders, fake Italian leatherwear, designer
watches, and silk shirts. Some of the men smiled like happy
children after a satisfying school excursion. When one mentions
the name Golok to Malaysians, they usually smile like that,
roguishly. They know what Golok is all about.

For Golok, the small Thai border town, is the great outlet
for Malaysian frustration. The town is little more than a market, a few shopping streets, several large tourist hotels with
discos, massage parlors, and louche barbershops. The town
thrives on sex. That and counterfeit luxury goods. One would
imagine a place like Golok to be unbelievably sordid, one large
brothel promising, with the sickliest of smiles, temporary relief
from repression. In fact, Golok is not depressing at all. Its
complete lack of hypocrisy, the self-assured, even graceful manners of the people, the enormous vitality, even those Thai
smiles, offer an extraordinary and welcome contrast to the not
unfriendly, but oppressive sluggishness (I can think of no other
word for it) of Kota Bahru. The people of Golok, one feels,
have taken to this world, however sordid, however much ruled
by naked greed, with gusto. They are at home in it. Kota
Bahru—unlike the kampongs around it—does not look like a
place where anyone feels at home.

The border crossing closes at six o'clock sharp. I asked a
young Malay who had kindly lent me his pen whether he had
had a good time in Golok. Oh, yes, a nice place, Golok. He
looked like a student—a wisp of a beard, a woolen hat over
longish hair, jeans, a flak jacket. His name was Ahmed, and

he was a student, in Pakistan. He spoke unusually good English and evidently had been around. Bangkok, oh, yes, he had friends there, and in Singapore, Hong Kong, India. "Traveling is good for my mind," he said, munching an endless supply of sunflower seeds. He seemed rather like students in Europe and America, casual, open to adventure, broad-minded, a rock-and-roll fan. Perhaps I could have known by the permanently pained look on his face, or his whiny voice: when it came to his own country, Ahmed the traveler was a zealot. Almost as soon as we met, he began to whine: "Look around you, we are second-class citizens in our own country. The immigrants, yes, the immigrants get so many privileges here. Anything they want, they get. Can a Chinese be a cabinet minister in your country?" I was about to answer, but he carried on: "Of course he can't. Here they have everything, own everything, all the business, Chinese."

What was he planning to do? "Maybe business." Was he studying business or economics in Pakistan? No, he was studying Islam, learning the Koran by heart. "Material success in this world is not our priority. What we do in our lives is just a stepping-stone for success in the hereafter. Anyway, it is not necessary to study business to have success. If we truly understand our religion, everything will be easy." His intelligent face looked even more pained than before, as if he was suffering from indigestion. He showed me a photograph of himself and his Malaysian friends in Karachi. They looked a melancholy group, frowning at the camera, dressed in long Pakistani shirts, standing in front of the memorial to Mohammed Ali Jinnah, the secularist Anglophile who founded a country constantly threatened by religious and ethnic strife.

SINGAPORE

"Chop," said the Chinese businessman sitting next to me in the train to Singapore, "chop, chop, chop!" His short right arm, fingers stretched, crashed down on his armrest. "When the Japanese were here, there was discipline. We were afraid. If you were bad, they cut your head off." He illustrated his point with another crashing chop. "Now, no more discipline. Many bad people in Singapore."

I judged the man to be in his late fifties. He was neatly dressed in a suit. His hair was dyed black. He explained what he did for a living, something to do with medical equipment. He referred to his fellow Chinese as "Chinamen," not a term one often uses in the post-colonial West, but still commonly heard in former British colonies. I was a little surprised, though, to hear a Chinese speak with a certain nostalgia about the war. After all, the Chinese had suffered terribly under the Japanese, while the Malays were often favored. But after spending some time in Singapore, the novelty of hearing such opinions wore off; expressions of awe for the Japanese are common in the Garden City.

Surely, I said, Singaporeans are still very disciplined. No, said the man, it might appear that way, but it isn't true. Singaporeans are selfish, stubborn, and greedy. They only think of money. That is all Chinamen care about. They lack spirit. The Japanese, now they have spirit. They are strong, they work hard, they sacrifice, they are number one in the world. Their cars, their machines, their technology, all number one.

Such undisguised respect for the Japanese—unusual among Asians, who more frequently regard Japan with a defensive hostility—is, as I said, common among Singaporeans. It is an indication of their obsession with success, with being number one. It has something to do with being a prosperous little island, a minute modern enclave of industrious Chinese (well, mostly Chinese) surrounded by millions of Malays, whose relative backwardness could so easily—so the Chinese fear—turn to hostility. It points to a deep, Conradian fear of being swallowed up by the jungle, a fate that can only be avoided by being ever more perfect, ever more disciplined, always the best.

The creation of Singapore—the republic, that is, not the city—was an accident. When Singaporean nationhood actually began is still a matter of some dispute. Singapore ceased being a British colony in 1963, but it then became part of Malaysia. Singapore as a mere island state would be a political joke, said Lee Kuan Yew, who still retained his title as Prime Minister, or as Singaporeans say, PM of Singapore. Two years later, Singapore split with Malaysia and became an independent republic. The PM announced the split on television with tears in his eyes. In 1984, the Singapore government decided to celebrate its national history in a grand jubilee. Radio jingles proclaimed it, schoolchildren sang about it, TV spot commercials featured it; billboards, double-decker buses, and soft-drink cans announced it: "25 Years of Nation Building—Stand Up for Singapore." Why twenty-five years, and not twenty-one years, or nineteen years? Typically, this latest count of Singapore history was entirely political: Twenty-five years before, in 1959, Singaporeans voted in their first wholly elected legislative assembly. And that election began the ascendancy of Lee Kuan Yew and his People's Action Party, the PAP; both have held power without interruption ever since.

Singapore island—there are fifty-seven smaller islands, little more than rocks in the sea—is only 27 miles long by 14 miles wide. The city itself is about the size of the Bronx, with a population of about two and a half million people, of whom 77 percent are of Chinese descent, 15 percent Malay, and 6 percent Indian. It is a neat, clean, prosperous place. A city of joggers, of suburban condominiums with swimming pools and squash courts; of shopping complexes; of recreation centers, cricket clubs, green lawns, and $250 fines for spitting in the streets. A city of first-class hotels, of news broadcasts read in perfect Oxford English voices; a city without slums, where women can safely walk the streets at night. It is a city where food stalls, offering noodles and other Sino-Malay snacks are rounded up, cleaned up, and concentrated in hygienic "hawker stall centers."

Singapore is a city of homeowners—around 80 percent of the people. It is in many ways an ideal society, promising prosperity for all, a perfect suburban paradise, whose imperfections and blemishes are quickly swept out of sight, like shameful spots of dust in a fussy housewife's parlor. It is also a city of fear.

To prepare an article on the twenty-five years of nation building in 1984, I visited a wealthy Chinese lady named Mrs. Ho. She lived in a comfortably sumptuous house, filled with rather good Chinese antiques. Mrs. Ho was an influential lady, well connected, as they say, in government circles, and she had served as an adviser to the producers of a popular television soap opera called *The Awakening*. It was a rather anodyne and wholly celebratory series about the long-suffering rubber tappers, noble society girls, and dutiful Chinese sons, who, through hard work, perseverance, and discipline, created Singapore. The drama was very much part of the national jubilee, hence my interest. Seeing the videotapes of the show neatly numbered and stacked on Mrs. Ho's bookcase, I asked whether it would be possible to watch an episode or two. Oh, no, that was quite impossible, quite out of the question. I asked her why. "Classified material." A TV drama, classified? How could that be possible? Well, maybe not quite classified, but still very sensitive. Showing these things to a foreign journalist. It was bad enough even talking. Internal Security Act, you know. Could she then kindly help to draft a request to the TV station for a viewing? This suggestion made Mrs. Ho so nervous that I stopped pressing the point. We switched to another subject. But I am reminded of Mrs. Ho every time a Singapore secretary tells me her boss doesn't have the information I want before I have explained what I'm looking for. It is the sort of thing one expects in Peking or Hanoi, but hardly in modern, suburban Garden City.

In fact, Singapore can be more frustrating than Peking, where people, high and low, still have the easy manners of citizens of a great empire. The anxious suspicion of outsiders in Singapore is not merely a matter of political oppression, which is clearly worse in Peking. In Singapore it is social as much as political: it is the fear one finds in a very small town, where everybody knows everybody, where all walls have ears, where careers are destroyed by neighbors who tell tales, where those that stick out, behave oddly, speak out of turn, are seen as threats to the perfect order and must be dealt with, as the fussy housewife deals with those shameful specks of dust.

Big Brother in Singapore is less a tyrant than an authoritarian father worried that his family will one day disappear. Singapore was an accident of history, like a bunny that popped out of the magician's hat by mistake. One sleight of hand and the bunny could vanish as swiftly as it appeared. Political rhetoric in Singapore is obsessed with this fear. "My deepest concern," said Lee Kuan Yew in his Eve of National Day address in 1982, "is how to make the young more conscious of security. By security I mean defense against threats to our survival, whether the threats are external or internal . . . Civilization is fragile. It is especially so for an island city-state." The word "civilization" is telling—the civilized oasis, so vulnerable in the steaming Malay jungle. Lee, a Chinese educated in Cambridge, "the finest Englishman east of Suez," fathered Singapore and now holds it in his jealous, stifling grip. Any form of dissent, of nonconformism, of restlessness with the status quo, could lead to catastrophe. As he put it on another occasion: "In the case of Singapore, the disaster, if it comes, must be total, irreparable, and final. There is no second chance for us." The PM's son and possible successor, Brigadier General Lee Hsien Loong, also known as BG, warned about the loss of faith in Singapore (meaning the PM and his PAP government): "Far from cheerfully muddling through, we would vanish without trace, submerged into the mud of history." *Après nous le déluge*; the jungle will close in.

This anxiety about impending doom seemed at odds with the solid British colonial government building where I met S. Rajaratnam, founding member of Singapore, Foreign Minister for many years, and the republic's chief ideologue. If there is such a thing as a Singapore identity, "Raja" is its author.

He is a man of grand words, learned quotations, great theories, and threatening speeches. He is like one of those clever dwarfs at medieval European courts, a jester with poison in his words. None of this was apparent from his toothy smiles and jovial manners in the massive reception room, clearly built to last for eternity. He was casually dressed in a shirt and blue suede shoes, like a natty professor. "Identity is like a photograph," he said, "you need shades between black and white. When a Chinese Singaporean goes to China, he will feel Singaporean. That is the negative part. The positive part is, well, some might call it jingoism, but I define it as a sense of feeling at home here. Singapore is our home." He beamed down at me, baring his teeth, pleased with his words, no longer a professor but a clever student who had found the right answer. But then fear struck, as it invariably does: "But all this can break up"—his hands fluttered in the air, like particles of dust floating away after an explosion—"and disappear totally. All might be totally lost." Again he beamed, wide nostrils flaring, white teeth dazzling.

He continued speaking eloquently, dropping bon mots and quotations from the likes of Herman Kahn and Alvin Toffler. He spoke about politics and the necessity to control the press. He likened society to a brain: conflicting information would "make it go bonkers." He banged his balding pate as if in a state of madness. "How many Singaporeans really want free speech anyway? They want orderliness, a decent living." He was concerned about the revival of sensitive issues, race, religion, and language, which he compared to TB germs. "We must keep them under control. If your constitution is weak, TB will take over and kill you." His choice of words did not seem entirely in character. They appeared to echo the concerns of the PM, a man obsessed to the point of paranoia about germs, cigarette smoke, any kind of dirt or dust, a man who demanded that the former President, Devan Nair, undergo a medical inspection for skin diseases before allowing him to use the presidential swimming pool. This in turn is reflected in the sterility of Singapore itself. Few countries have so clearly taken on the characteristics of their leaders as Singapore, again a function not so much of political coercion as of the smallness of the place, just as an isolated boarding school becomes like its headmaster.

Singapore used to be famous for what the PM called "yellow culture": sailors' bars, Chinese brothels, and the transvestites in Bugis Street, who drove the sailors wild with fashion parades, held late at night, vying with the girl prostitutes for the sexiest, most outrageous looks. The johns would climb on the roof of the century-old pissoir and holler their approval as the boys and girls simpered in their slit silk dresses. Bugis Street was torn down. The drag queens dispersed. But in 1987, stung by a report in *The Economist* which judged Singapore to be one of the most boring countries in the world, the Singapore Tourism Board announced that Bugis Street would be re-created, stone by stone, including the old toilet. This time, however, it would be clean, "for family entertainment," as a spokesman for the Board put it. "Give Bugis Street a chance," said the *Sunday Times* of Singapore. "The place was popular with the tourists because it offered the queer and the quaint, fulfilling the kind of Far East fantasy image on which the common imagination had long been nurtured."

We were in a large Western-style restaurant, which served hamburgers, chips, and beer. The chairs were done up in red plastic, the tables were of fake wood. We had just been to see a British film at the Goethe Institute. I was sitting next to a young Chinese woman, dressed in the latest London fashion, who worked for an American advertising agency. Opposite me was a local Chinese culture vulture in glasses who chatted about Bertolucci, Wim Wenders, Robert De Niro. To make his rather commonplace points, he quoted Western film critics, and used grand words like Rajaratnam. On the stage was a stout middle-aged woman in an ill-fitting brunette wig, playing an electronic organ and singing Taiwanese pop songs rather badly. A sign on the wall said: "Patrons are expressly forbidden to sing songs on stage." I asked the chic lady next to me why this should be forbidden. "Ah, well," she said, in almost flawless British English, "we Singaporeans don't go in for that sort of thing." I was about to say something scathing. It must have shown on my face. For the culture vulture quickly explained: "You see, patrons are not professionals. They lack the proper skill to sing."

The proper skill. Number one. " 'Excellence' encapsules in one word how Singapore can survive in a very competitive world" (Lee Kuan Yew, National Day Dinner, 1987). The negative side of the photograph, as Rajaratnam might have said, is a crippling fear of failure.

"The Japanese worker can be a model," said the PM. "A Japanese waiter is proud to be an excellent waiter and goes about his work efficiently, with grace and style. A Japanese cook is proud of his excellent training." I watched the Japanese sushi chef at work in my hotel, skillfully cutting the slabs of raw fish into neat slices. Not one superfluous gesture, his entire body a finely tuned machine, an instrument of the highest precision. While his delicate fish knife went chop, chop, he spoke in the clipped, theatrically macho Japanese that is the mark of members of his trade. "Yes, I had trouble adjusting to life here," he said. "You see, we just don't think in the same way." He then launched into the chauvinistic tirade about "the natives" that one comes to expect from Japanese abroad. They are selfish, materialistic, undisciplined, rude, lacking in respect for their elders, and so forth. I had heard it before and took it with a pinch of salt. I felt inclined to defend the natives or at least to shut the man up by pointing out some deficiencies in the Japanese. But then he said something which rang true. "They never apologize. They never admit a mistake."

Are there absolute standards to measure excellence? It is a pertinent question in Singapore. For if excellence is a matter of taste, of fulfilling the expectations of a given place and time, of measuring up to the rules of a style, shaped by many years of experiment and change, then excellence cannot have absolute standards; there must be a culture as a basis for achievement.

In the case of Singapore, which culture? The ethos of Cambridge of the 1940s or the colonial culture of Malaya? Or should one look at the hybrid, immigrant culture of the Straits Chinese, who spoke Malay and spiced their southern Chinese cuisine with chili? What, indeed, about Malay culture itself? Malay, after all, is the national language, even though few Chinese speak it well. Then there are the cultures of Indian and Sri Lankan Tamils, of Kerala, Bengal, and Punjab. There are Chinese whose first language is English, as in the case of the PM; Chinese who speak Mandarin, or Hokkienese, or Cantonese.

The answer is that none of these cultures will really do, for to stress one over another raises those sensitive issues, those germs that attack the constitution. Earlier in Singapore history, after independence, but before the republic was born, the founding fathers thought of creating a new culture from scratch. Rajaratnam, naturally, was the most eloquent advocate. In an anthology of Rajaratnamiana, entitled *The Prophetic and the Political*, we find the following statement, made in 1960: "It is as essential for us to lay the foundations for a Malayan culture as it is for us to build hospitals, schools, and factories and provide jobs for our rapidly expanding population. Malayan culture is, for us, an essential part of nation building. It is not something to be worshipped from afar but an instrument for reshaping society along lines we think desirable." Already in those days there was the familiar menacing tone of the aspirant social engineers: along lines we think desirable. Quite what Malayan culture was or should be remained vague, as vague as the Singaporean culture which soon took its place.

"You cannot assume that once you are born a Singaporean, you will always remain a Singaporean," said the PM. "Singapore has no history to speak of," said Rajaratnam. "We can show the Raffles statue. I can tell people what we have achieved. Tomorrow? The Mass Rapid Transit system. Yesterday? Maybe, Lee Kuan Yew, that's all."

* * *

"Evening brought the breeze, channelled by the concrete blocks, blowing across Singapore . . . Evening brought light, flooding the corridors of the concrete blocks and lining the roads. The daytime of tinted windows and air-conditioning was giving way to the night-time of fluorescent tubes and halogen headlights. White then red flashed the cars speeding past on the road outside Ah Leong's window. Across the country televisions were coming on and video cassette recorders plugged in. Husbands greeted wives and changed channels . . ."

It is a familiar scene of modern anomie, described many times in American and Japanese novels. It is the first paragraph of a Singaporean best-seller, a novel by Philip Jeyaratnam, entitled *First Loves*. The fact that the author is the son of the only opposition leader in Singapore might have added some glamour to the book and helped sales, but the main reason for the novel's success must be its theme: the Singapore identity, who and what are Singaporeans? This is also the chief weakness of the novel. The individuality of the characters is undermined by their duty to play roles, to wear the badges of racial identity. Their personalities serve as comments on the Singaporean quest for a culture, for something to identify with. The story is structured around love affairs between members of different races. An Indian boy falls in love with a Chinese girl: "How do I explain this to my parents? It is easy for Chinese people to make concessions on private personal matters when they control public life. After some hesitation her parents welcomed me into their home. But my parents see integration as endangering their identity. How many of us are there after all who speak Malayalam? How many my age? I speak English, I struggle when my mother lapses into her own tongue. And the English I speak, my mother says, English with a Chinese accent. I say Singaporean, but now draining my glass of beer I have to admit that she is probably right."

The third of the three main founding fathers of Singapore—the other two being Rajaratnam and the PM—is Devan Nair, whose ancestors came from Kerala. He is a charming, some-what bitter man who fell out with the PM a few years ago when serving as President, a ceremonial role which encouraged Nair's fondness for drink. I asked him whether he still felt Indian. He helped himself to some Indian sweets. My eyes wandered over the Indian art in his living room, mixed with Chinese paintings. He answered that, yes, he still felt Indian, partly because of the anti-colonial struggle. He identified with Gandhi. He read Nehru's books, written, of course, in English. His children, however, were less Indian, and less Malaysian too. "My sons are the cosmopolitans of the future. We have an international culture now. London, L.A., Tokyo. They are all becoming the same."

Can one be truly cosmopolitan? Is there really such a thing as an international culture? Again, as I had done so often in Malaysia, I thought of V. S. Naipaul. I thought of Philip Jey-aratnam. And I thought of myself, my own life. Am I a man of international culture? Or simply a man of several cultures, drifting in and out of them, influenced by upbringing, by travel, by reading, and doomed or blessed—depending on my mood—to be culturally self-conscious. Just as Singaporeans, for lack of a more specific identification, often call themselves "Asians," I am a "European." But I would never wish to be regarded as international. International belongs to no specific culture; it is a low common denominator of modern styles, brand names, slogans on T-shirts. Airport art is international. It describes nothing, belongs nowhere.

Walking along Orchard Road, the main shopping street, with its endless shopping centers and plazas, selling international goods at duty-free prices and offering food from all over the world, some of it very good, none of it authentic, one feels that this is an airport-art city. The few remaining old Chinese shop-houses on Orchard Road have been turned into an airport-art museum of Straits Chinese or Peranakan culture. This hybrid Sino-Malay culture has more or less died out. Its legacy, the food, some of the rituals, its peculiar Malay dialect, is racially harmless, and nostalgia for the *babas* (Peranakan men) and *nyonyas* (the women) is officially encouraged, or at least not resisted, which in Singapore amounts to much the same thing. The Peranakan Corner on Orchard Road offers a Peranakan coffee shop, a photo studio where people can dress up and be photographed in Peranakan costumes, a museum with Peranakan furniture, a Peranakan restaurant, and so-called Peranakan theme parties. A wedding theme party, for example, is advertised as "featuring the colorful *baba* wedding with Chinese, Malay, Indian, and Eurasian guests performing in the most exotic fun party." It is safe and perfectly meaningless, as meaningless as a reconstructed Bugis Street without the raunch.

If Singapore has become a society of digits (as the PM has called his citizens), of statistics, it is perhaps because without a culture to provide myths, ideals, and standards, mathematics is all that is left. The PM's Darwinist social engineering, the PAP's non-ideology called pragmatism, the ideal of the rugged society, constantly on guard against the corrupt and flabby state of other societies, all these are marks of fear, a fear of chaos. Chaos is a variant of a horror vacuum, the horror of inner emptiness.

There is, of course, something Chinese about the idea of the limitless perfectibility of man. Just as there is something Chinese about the moral campaigns, the lecturing by public officials, the ubiquitous slogans. Every taxi has a sticker on the dashboard outlining the Three-S Productivity Plan: "Social responsibility, Social attitude, Skill." Often these exhortations sound like parodies of modern computer language or Pentagonese: "Optimize taxi utilization!" The creation of the perfect gentleman, who exemplifies the perfect social order, is the basis of Confucianism. This idea, combined with social Darwinism and a Cambridge style, is the essence of the PM's pragmatism. It is logical, rational, mathematically precise, and it has resulted in great economic achievements. But it is also sometimes like the rationality of a madman; the logic is there all right, but it is misapplied. And the science is often bogus. To worry about gene pools and the fact that educated Chinese women too often remain single, while uneducated Malays breed large families, may be racist and absurd, but from the PM's point of view, it is logical. To say that if this situation is not shifted quickly, then "disastrous consequences will come in twenty years," as the PM did, is to veer toward paranoia.

Item in the *Straits Times*: "Teenagers now come to the disco only to dance and what is disturbing to some is that dancers tend to pair up with members of the same sex. One by one discos are allowing this trend but the government matchmaking body, the Social Development Unit, is worried by this trend. It has become so widespread that at least one disco—Studio M at the Plaza Hotel—which used to frown on this practice, has dropped its regulation forbidding dancing with friends of the same sex." There is no hint of irony intended in this news story. Talking to students at the National University of Singapore, the PM recalled a young educated woman who came up to him and said, " 'But, Prime Minister, if a man wants to marry me for my genes I don't want to marry him.' And I thought to myself, 'What a silly ass of a girl.' "

There is a character in Philip Jeyaratnam's book called Song Jiang, a young man who wishes he was more Chinese. He is as much a "type" as all the others. The points made through him are not subtle, but they do contain some truth:

I can't remember the lines of Mandarin. I don't have the Mandarin here. I borrowed the book when I read it last year. (Falteringly, but I did read it, struggling with the archaic tones.) So much seems lost today. Impossible to recapture. When I read *Hong Lou Meng* [*The Dream of the Red Chamber*], I do so with a despairing sense of paradise lost. The characters casually quote great lines of poetry. They readily compose their own lines, not great but interesting because the lines are precisely related to each character. And yet today I have to resort to my row of Penguin Classics . . .

That sense of loss—of fallen spring blossoms drenched by summer rain. That yearning and that loss which inspired so many poems

I feel now towards the whole body of poetry. I yearn for it and it
is lost to me.

The irony of all this is obvious: nothing was lost to Song
Jiang, for there was nothing for him to lose. His ancestors,
presumably peasants who arrived dirt poor on overcrowded
boats to work the rubber plantations or tin mines of Malaya,
had never heard of *The Dream of the Red Chamber*. Song
Jiang's China exists in his mind; like his favorite classic novels,
it is a country of the imagination; Song Jiang had to invent
China out of a few fragments left to him: food habits, grand-
parents' tales, a faulty grasp of language, and Penguin Classics.
Similarly, Lee Kuan Yew, or, rather, Harry Lee, had to invent
his China, not for cultural but for political reasons. Lee's great-
grandfather came to Singapore soon after Stamford Raffles got
there in 1819 to establish a base for the British East India Company. Lee's ancestors were Hakkas, whose origins are somewhat mysterious. They are believed to have been northerners
who drifted to southern China, and sometimes further south, to
escape from the Tartar and Mongol invasions. His mother's
family are Straits Chinese. His maternal great-great-grand-
father married a Malay. Most of Harry's school friends were
Malays. His parents admired the British and wanted their son to
be an English gentleman. He obliged but only up to a point.
Like many sharp colonials, he wanted to beat the colonizers at
their own game. "I speak to Harold Macmillan and Duncan
Sandys as equals. At Cambridge I got two firsts and a star for
distinction. Harold Macmillan did not." He can act like an Englishman without being one. He can give brilliant parliamentary speeches in the style of Westminster, even as he consciously
undermines parliamentary politics. He has called himself "an
Anglified Chinaman." He is, in some ways, a caricature of his
Western education, just as his ideas on "Asian" behavior and
thinking are a caricature of what is left of his Chineseness. He
has all the marks of a man who has consciously created himself,
just as he tried to create the perfect Singapore in his own image.

When he entered Singapore politics, he needed the votes of the Chinese, most of whom were educated in Chinese. And so, as a politician, he learned Mandarin and two Chinese dialects. But intellectually, he relied on his coterie of English-educated colleagues. The Chinese community was split between the Chinese- and the English-educated. Lee, as one of his biographers, T. L. S. George, put it, "rode to power on the backs of the first and has increasingly sought to buttress his position with the backing of the second, but he has never won the complete trust of either."

Here the PM's personal life history gets mixed up in the history of Singapore itself. English is regarded as the language of modernity, science, progress, excellence; Chinese represents culture, history, ethnic chauvinism. In principle, this means that the first must be encouraged and the second suppressed. And so it happened at first. The Chinese university was closed down. English education became almost universal. And Singaporeans, more and more, came to speak a hybrid language known as Singlish, an English patois full of Malay and Chinese expressions translated literally: I bring you where you stay, is it? (Shall I take you home?) Modern playwrights like to use Singlish as an assertion of identity. Even when they have been trained in London and speak perfectly good English.

"English expressions are alien to us," said a Chinese sociologist at an elegant dinner party in the flat of a Chinese architect born in Australia. "Feather in his cap, red herring, these things mean nothing to us." Her statement seemed at odds with the surroundings. The flat was decorated in the highest European taste: Victorian lithographs of Renaissance architecture, antique English chests, a nineteenth-century drawing of St. Paul's Cathedral. The architect, who had lived in London for many years, served Italian food. We—the sociologist, the architect, and two Chinese Malaysians—had talked about interior design, restaurants, London, and, after some hesitation, Singapore politics. The sociologist, clearly a woman of great sophistication, was critical of the government. Her criticisms were always followed by a shrug. "Ah, what's the use anyway," she would say. When I repeated some received opinion on the PM's authoritarianism, she suddenly became defensive: "Foreigners are always hostile to Singapore, always judging us by Western standards. Why? Just because we are modern, should we be an open society? Why?" I said that the PM himself set Western standards when he came to power. "Well, why shouldn't he change his mind?"

She had hit upon the essence of the PM's and Singapore's schizophrenia. Which values should prevail? How should Singapore be judged? As the PM said in an interview with the *Straits Times*: "What do we do? One small island which you have to rebuild over and over again. I don't know. But I do know that we face urgent and compelling problems of knowing where we are, how we got there." Lee has called the English-educated a deracinated, devitalized lot. "When I read Nehru . . . I understood him when he said: 'I cry when I think that I cannot speak my own mother tongue as well as I can speak the English language.' " He has expressed the fear that Singaporeans would end up like West Indians, deracinated to the point that race is all that is left. And so the Speak Mandarin campaign was launched in 1979, much to the disgust of Malays and Indians. And Confucian values suddenly needed to be introduced into Singaporean education, not, of course, to foster Chinese chauvinism, but to Look East, to become as successful as Japan, to be their equals, through discipline and excellence, just as Harry Lee had become the equal of Harold Macmillan.

"English is for getting on in life, for practical use. But for moral behavior we must learn Chinese, our own language." Dr. Lau Wai Har, the grandmotherly lady who kindly explained this to me, is the director of the Confucian Ethics (Conthics) Project Team. Conthics is five years old. The idea, according to the *Conthics Newsletter*, is to "inculcate in our pupils Confucian values, using a modern approach." Dr. Lau's office expressed this approach: partly a religious shrine, the walls decorated with pictures of the great sage and calligraphed quotations from his works, and partly a laboratory with the latest equipment. Dr. Lau held out two textbooks for my inspection. One, a Taiwanese social ethics book, one a Singaporean book on Confucianism. "Now, which one looks better? The Singaporean, isn't it?" The Singaporean book certainly was glossier, with nicer pictures. "I am Western-educated," said Dr. Lau, her eyes twinkling behind thick glasses, "so I know all the modern techniques."

I asked her about young Singaporeans, how they were taking to this Confucian education. Well, there had been some problems, she said. The program had been very successful in international circles, but not so with local people. Too abstract. The language was too difficult. The children's Chinese is not good enough. Their English is better. "I fear that some young people are so Westernized that they accept anything Western. They must learn about their own outlook, their own roots." In what way were they Westernized? "They refuse to speak Chinese, they go to discos, eat fast food, listen to pop music. They don't like to read Chinese books. Of course, we only select the Confucian ethics relevant to our times and we only use modern techniques."

I leafed through the textbook, looking at the pictures of ancient bearded sages pointing the way to the perfect moral society. I wondered how this could be revived, be made interesting for the young. Would it really help to teach Confucianism in English as is increasingly done; in other words, to use the language of modernity, of "practical use," to teach "moral behavior" and "their own roots"? I thought of something I read the day before, how the PM described the necessity for Conthics: "No child should leave school . . . without having the 'software' of his culture programmed into his subconscious." I looked up at Dr. Lau, smiling in her grandmotherly way. She held out her hand, ticking off the "software" on her fingers one by one: "We have slides, we have TV, we have cassette tapes, we have video . . ."

"Humbugging" is what Devan Nair, the former President,

called this dabbling in Confucianism. "There is more continuity between the Renaissance, the Reformation, and modern Europe than between Confucianism and modern Singapore. Humbugging, I say, total humbugging."

Devan Nair is an Indian. One cannot expect him to be sympathetic to Confucianist education. And, of course, much of this newly found Chineseness is artificial, culture used as a form of social control. And, yet . . . In some ways, perhaps unconsciously, the PM is very Chinese, or at least a very Chinese ruler. Individual sacrifice for collective ends is extolled as being part of Asian culture. Adversarial politics is not. As the PM said: "That's not the way the Japanese or the Chinese or the Asian cultures do it. That leads to contentiousness and confusion." This, indeed, is how Chinese and Japanese rulers have always justified their power, as guardians of the perfect social order. I am convinced that if Deng Xiaoping had a blueprint for a perfect modern China, it would look rather like Singapore: clean, prosperous, disciplined, pragmatic. One of the outstanding traits of Singapore officials is to use Western tools—parliamentary speeches, newspaper editorials, legalistic arguments, etc.—to put down Western (though not uniquely Western) concepts such as individual freedom or the right to know. What the PM is aiming at is the solution to a Chinese—not to mention Japanese—dilemma that goes back to the dawn of our modern age: how to separate Western science from Western ideas, English as a tool for practical use from English as a conduit for liberalism, Cambridge from Confucianism.

"By switching to English in the past twenty-odd years," said the PM in an interview with *The New York Times*, "we've changed the curriculum, the textbooks, and, with it, the philosophy that is inculcated into the children. They are reading more and more American magazines or British textbooks which instill the belief in the rights of the individual. The supremacy of the individual human being against all else, except in times of war when his individual rights are overcome by the needs of the state. Otherwise the state and the individual are put on a par. This is not acceptable in Confucianist societies."

What the PM, the Straits Chinese from Cambridge, has created is a caricature of the Confucianist society, a microcosm
of a Chinese social order reflected in a distorting mirror, some
parts grossly exaggerated, others rendered invisible. For the
New Singapore Man, the perfect pragmatist, the ideal rational
opportunist, is different from the traditional Confucian Gentleman in one crucial way: the Confucian Gentleman had principles, the pragmatist following nothing but the logic of his
pragmatism has none. But logic ceases to be logical when it is
monopolized by those in power. The one thing the PM will
not tolerate is criticism of what he, in his superior wisdom,
considers to be pragmatic. This is why some New Singaporean
Men, members of a brilliant young elite, mostly Chinese, inev-
itably will be affected by Western ideas, along with Western
science. For people will seek principles that cannot be measured
in statistics or fed into brains like software. They will seek the
right to be critical.

In the spring of 1987, twenty-two young people were de-
tained without trial under the Internal Security Act. They were
accused of organizing a conspiracy to overthrow the government and to establish a Marxist state. The "threat from
within," so often warned against, had to be nipped in the bud.
They got the usual treatment: long hours of interrogation in
cold rooms, a few hard slaps here and there, solitary confine-
ment, followed by edited confessions on TV to prove the government's case and humiliate the accused. In October nine
detainees were released. The point had been made. It was decided that they did not constitute much of a threat anymore.
One of the accused, a businessman named K. C. Chew, ended
his statement by saying: "I shall become like other Singaporeans—eschew politics and pursue wealth."* The idea of a
Marxist revolution in Garden City seemed, on the face of it,

* K. C. Chew was rearrested with several others in 1988.

absurd. But I was intrigued by these young men and women who stuck out. Who were they? What did they think and why?

"I just don't like people to tell me what to do," said a young, soft-spoken lawyer. "We were really just do-gooders. I never expected anything like this to happen," said a human rights activist. "What is lacking here is a sense of pride as a Singaporean involved in the political and creative process," said a businessman educated at Harvard. "When you deal with things in a funny way, you can't help offending the government," said a writer of satirical plays. "The government achieved the opposite effect to what they intended," said a Christian student. "Through education and national service, we felt more Singaporean than our parents. Which is why we wanted more than money—more participation, more responsibility."

In their manners, their way of speaking, their clothes, these alleged revolutionaries were strangely alike: polite, soft-spoken, even timid, neatly dressed in conservative taste, discreetly religious, often Catholic. A priest named Patrick Goh—not one of the detainees—described his task as "calling on the middle class to develop themselves holistically, to be concerned about the plight of the poor, not just to be interested in material life." I had not noticed much serious poverty in Singapore. True, said Father Goh, Singaporeans are quite well-off, but foreign guest workers are exploited. Particularly upsetting was the exploitation of Filipina maids.

One of Philip Jeyaratnam's characters is a Filipina maid, an educated girl, one of hundreds of thousands in the Philippines forced to support her family by working abroad. She is a practical girl, more mature than the Singapore student whose sympathy she arouses.

"My employers are right. They are doing me a favour. I'm worth less to them than their money is worth to me."

"Don't talk like that."

"Then how should I talk? You're just ideals. You sound like a book."

"Maybe if more people had ideals."

"Life would be better. Yes."

"Got to be pragmatic, you know." Ah Leong pulled a face. "Be pragmatic—do anything to stay in power."

The plight of the guest workers. The Filipina maid. These are good causes. But one feels that they are only part of what motivates the Singaporean activist. More important are the ideals, or rather the lack of them. The search for meaning in a pragmatic society. The quest for pride "as a Singaporean." It would be difficult to call the human rights lawyers, the satirical playwrights, the Christian students, dissidents, for it is not at all clear what they dissent from. Pragmatism, the twisted logic of Cambridge, and Confucianism are not really ideas at all; they are tactics, mere methods to maintain order and achieve prosperity. They are not part of any moral universe.

I was talking to two Christian students, a man and a woman, let us call them Timothy and Mary. Timothy had been one of the detainees. He brought me to see his girlfriend, Mary, in her Housing Development Board flat, "so you can see how Singaporeans really live." The flat, in the midst of other, high, clean concrete blocks—no graffiti, plenty of notices about community activities—was large and comfortable. On the wall were Christian images and movie posters. I asked Timothy what got him interested in politics. Has he read Marxist literature? He had, but he was more interested in Singapore history; at school he read biographies of the PM and books on the history of the PAP. Timothy was indeed something his parents were not, a true Singaporean. I was reminded of a human rights lawyer who told me in his office that "most of us feel that we can't go back to China or India. We are here. This is it. Either we deal with the man up there, or we leave." Mary had remained quiet during most of the conversation, only asking the odd question. "You see," she suddenly said, "it is hard for us. If you have a dictatorship or militarism, you have an enemy, something to fight. Here, the struggle is in our own minds—

to conform or not to conform—which is more painful. I see Christianity as a reference. I think of how Jesus Christ would have reacted."

The PM does not seem to understand the rebels he has created. They are outside his frame of reference. They look for values that cannot be scientifically measured, for a faith that cannot be proven. Timothy was philosophical about his prison experience and apologetic about his readiness to compromise with his case officer. To me the most interesting detail of his prison story was the PM's instruction to the case officers to compile psychological profiles of the detainees. The PM was apparently perplexed about these elite students, Harvard businessmen, and bright young lawyers. How was it possible that despite their education and their wealth they could turn out this way? They had been so carefully programmed. What could possibly have gone wrong?

In the first three months of 1987, 1,400 people signed up to join a church. Protestant fundamentalism is the fastest-growing religion in Singapore, where 12 percent of the people are Christians. Every night they gather in stadiums, in church halls, in an old dance hall, famous in the olden days for its "yellow culture"—taxi dancers and the like. American preachers in powder-blue safari suits, frenzied Filipinos, and devout Chinese Singaporeans come together to speak in tongues, cast out demons, and invoke miraculous cures.

We were greeted on Sunday morning at the Calvary Charismatic Center by young Singaporeans in suits and steel-rimmed glasses. They shook our hands warmly, welcomed us, and smiled at us in that beatific way that is disconcerting to the uninitiated. Expensive European cars were parked outside the hall. The members of the congregation were mostly young Chinese, with a few Filipinas. Announcements were made about miracle cures that had taken place at previous gatherings. These were greeted with subdued murmuring. "I'm in a marching mood today," said the Chinese preacher, also in a suit and

steel-rimmed glasses. We sang jaunty American religious songs.
At least I pretended to sing, by miming the words in the song-
book, kindly passed to me by a smiling young man in a business
suit. The girl on my left wore a Snoopy T-shirt and glasses.

There was an atmosphere of good cheer, still fairly subdued.
A Japanese preacher named Dr. Kitano came on and spoke in
good English about Nathan and King David; how Nathan
pointed at the sins of his ruler. Dr. Kitano pointed his long,
pink finger at the congregation and said: "Look at my finger."
Amen! said the congregation, gathering some steam. "Look at
this finger, the finger of Nathan that pointed at his king for
his sins. This is very important, very difficult, especially for us
Asians." Amen, went the congregation, a little quieter this time.
Dr. Kitano spoke about success, its ephemeral nature. "Success
can mean failure, and failure can be success," he said. "This
is very important, especially for us, for me, a Japanese, for you,
Singaporeans." Amen! shouted the man next to me.

The Chinese preacher in the suit and glasses took over again.
He sang a jaunty psalm, then began to pray, as the chorus
behind him faded in and out of the refrain. "Raise your arms,
brothers and sisters!" The man and woman on either side of
me took hold of my hands and held them up. They looked
rapturous. I was getting embarrassed. The preacher kept praying, louder and louder, punctuating his prayers with hallelujahs
and amens. The congregation began to sway, responding to
the preacher, whose prayers over the swelling chorus became
more frenzied. Then, suddenly, it happened: the young Singaporeans in suits, Snoopy T-shirts, and steel-rimmed glasses
were transformed into a hysterical mass. I heard sobbing
sounds, cries to the Lord, amens. The man next to me was
rolling his eyes, babbling; the girl was swaying to and fro,
rocking on her feet. The preacher lost coherence. His prayer
had degenerated into an incomprehensible torrent of sounds.
He was speaking in tongues. All meaning was lost.

4

The Old Japanese Empire

TAIWAN

The young colonel pointed through the window at the coast of China: "There it is, the mainland, bandit territory." He used the official jargon, not much heard these days outside military circles. "And on your left you see Kinmen." You could see most of the island, better known as Quemoy: neat paddy fields and mud-colored villages, with the deeply curved roofs, distinctive of the southern Chinese provinces of Fujian and Taiwan.

Most of the people disembarking from our plane were young women on a day trip. "Dependents of specially deserving soldiers," explained the colonel. There are about 60,000 troops on Quemoy. "Build Up Kinmen, Recover the Mainland," read the large red characters on billboards at the airport. "The Three Principles of the People Unite China," it said on a stone monument, which had a large globe on top with the whole of China painted yellow and the characters for Republic of China written on it. The slogan refers to the three principles—Nationalism, Democracy, and People's Livelihood—laid down by Sun Yat-sen, founder of the Chinese Republic in 1912.

Like most front lines against communism, Quemoy is a little absurd. The last major battle there was in 1958, when the communists launched an artillery attack. After that there have been exchanges of potshots, but even those ended in the late 1970s. Yet there are guards at every intersection or installation—one always wearing a gas mask. The beaches are littered with anti-landing devices and barbed-wire fencing, the waters are said to be mined. There is a huge field hospital dug deep into a granite rock, with empty wards and cavernous operating theaters, part of a network of underground tunnels spanning the whole island. It is extremely expensive and almost entirely symbolic, for the struggle itself is symbolic, waged mostly by the Political Warfare Department.

The symbols are revealing. First the visitor is shown a "folk village," a hamlet, built around 1900, where, so one is told, people live "traditional lives." One is asked to admire the shrine with ancestral tablets, the empty rooms filled with traditional Chinese furniture, the small gallery with archaeological findings. Then you are invited to pose for a picture, sitting on an old palanquin with a young lady in a silk Chinese costume. Texts on the wall inform the visitor about the importance of preserving the heritage of five thousand years of civilization. I asked the guide where the villagers actually lived. "In these houses," she said, gesturing at the empty homes we had just seen. I could not see anybody. "They are all working now," said the guide, impatient to resume the tour. Then I saw the grubby face of a child peering at us around a corner. I peered back, around the corner, and saw a few drab-looking houses with women hanging out the washing, TVs blaring away in the background. "Not so traditional," said the guide, who had a nice sense of humor.

Part of the Chinese heritage is "the largest pottery factory in Taiwan." It is where priceless pieces from the Sung and Ming dynasties are reproduced, to be displayed in the National Palace Museum in Taipei, or exported to America. Hundreds of potters sit in long rows faithfully copying ancient designs and glazes. There are also pottery figures of Sun Yat-sen, "the Father of the Fatherland," and Generalissimo Chiang Kai-shek, who escaped to Taiwan in 1949 and ruled the Republic of China until his death. There was one piece, showing a fortified wall with a soldier standing on top, pointing his rifle at the enemy: "The Kinmen Spirit," it said on the ceramic wall.

In the Political Warfare Museum the visitor is shown badly reproduced photographs of poor peasants on the mainland, toiling en masse, like Egyptian slaves in a Cecil B. De Mille epic. There are pictures of atrocities during the Cultural Revolution. There are displays of everyday items, supposed to indicate the poverty of life on the mainland: filthy old tubes of toothpaste; dusty, rock-hard bars of soap; torn and stained clothes; and so forth.* These are contrasted with evidence of abundance in Taiwan: photos of laughing people at the seaside and nice new apartment buildings; samples of attractive tinned foods, colorful T-shirts, pop music cassettes, and miniature video games. These consumer goods, as well as the pictures of happiness, are packed into helium balloons or plastic floats and dispatched to the mainland as shining symbols of modern prosperity and benevolent rule—proof that the Kuomintang (KMT), the ruling party of the Republic of China, takes better care of its people than the Communist Party. "It is very important that the people on the mainland know this," said the colonel, "for then they will be on our side."

Five thousand years of civilization and modern prosperity. In the orthodoxy of Taiwan, they are linked. That is why visitors are shown the fake traditional village and the classical pottery. Shaw Yu-ming, now the chief government spokesman, explained the official point of view in *Foreign Affairs* (Summer 1985): " 'China' names a country and symbolizes a cultural system of which Confucianism has long been a fundamental ingredient . . . For the last hundred years, China has been trying

---

* These images are particularly anachronistic now that information about mainland China has become freely available in Taiwan.

to reconcile the incoming Western culture with its own . . . On
the mainland, communism, a heresy within Western civilization, has become official dogma and the Chinese communists
have repeatedly tried to destroy traditional Chinese culture. At
the same time, the R.O.C. on Taiwan has implemented modern
and universal education, and succeeded in importing Western
ideas and practices without abandoning its cultural heritage.
From the point of view of many social scientists, the major
reason for Taiwan's successful modernization has been its efforts to preserve the content and form of Chinese culture, while
incorporating elements of Western culture where appropriate
and beneficial. It is my view that Taiwan's experience can serve
as a model for Communist China, and Taiwan's cultural synthesis promises to be the mainstream of the modern Chinese
culture of the future."

Taipei, one of the great nouveau riche cities of East Asia,
shows this cultural synthesis in a concentrated form. In the
first quarter of the century, the old Chinese city was rebuilt by
the Japanese in the image of a European-style colonial capital,
with broad avenues, neat public parks, and pompous public
buildings, many of which still stand. Nationalists with more
zeal than taste constantly talk of pulling them down. "They
are bad buildings," said one government official in Taipei,
"they are not Chinese." After the war, the city was transformed
once more, this time into the temporary capital of the Republic
of China. Today, the economic boom, influenced by America
and following Japan, changed the capital yet again. It still has
an unfinished look, the concrete dust has not yet settled. Colorful billboards—not unlike the ones on the mainland—show
glimpses of the future: high-rise flats, elevated highways, and,
an essential touch this, a small Chinese garden or pagoda in
the foreground. But before that goal is reached, Taipei remains
brash, lively, and in dubious taste, a bit like the clothes worn
by newly rich Taiwanese businessmen: garish pin-striped suits,

loud shirts, and bizarre neckties, like costumes in some prewar
American gangster film. It is as if the crassest aspects of Taiwan's different cultural components—Chinese, Japanese,
American—have been thrown together in a movie studio back
lot: American fast food, Japanese TV culture, and Fujianese
folklore feed a hunger for color and kitsch. Kitsch is endemic
to Taiwan, as almost every image is displaced, borrowed from
another place. Popular culture coexists uneasily with a mori-
bund tradition of Chinese high culture imported from China
in 1949 and officially imposed on Taiwan to give the former
Japanese colony a new Chinese identity. It has lent the place
a schizophrenic quality. It is a society still stuck between different worlds, not just the traditional and the modern, but
worlds of quite varying traditions, some officially propagated,
others ignored. History is both imposed—the five thousand
years and so forth—and denied—the Japanese colonial past—
which reinforces the one-dimensional, fanciful atmosphere.

I met Robert, a professor born in Taiwan but partly educated
in the United States, in a fashionable new bar called Passion.
The interior was white and light gray, as were the tuxedos of
the elegant waitresses. The lights, as in a disco, changed color,
from pink to purple to green. We could have been sitting in
Covent Garden, or Santa Monica, or Tokyo's Roppongi area.
Robert was sipping a poison-green cocktail, called, on the
menu, a Screaming Orgasm. There were a few foreigners in the
bar, but most people were rich, young Chinese in linen suits
and horn-rimmed glasses. Robert was worried that things were
suddenly changing too fast in Taiwan. It had just been announced on the news that school regulations on hair length
would be relaxed. And, for the first time ever, schoolchildren
were allowed to dance. A new opposition party had just been
formed, new newspapers were appearing. New discos were
opening up every day, patronized by teenagers dressed in Japanese fashions—dark, baggy suits, sunglasses, and T-shirts with
garbled English slogans: "UCLA, I Am Yuppie Good Life."

Many of these discos were "illegal," but, like so much that is, strictly speaking, against the law in Taiwan, they operated openly.

Robert, a trim, pensive man, dressed in jeans and a white shirt, was worried because he felt the people at the top, responsible for relaxing the rules, might not know what they were doing. "It is too much, too fast," he said, stirring his cocktail with a mauve plastic prong. "All people think about here is fun, having fun. The Taiwanese don't worry about Japanese or American influence, or whether they are more Taiwanese or Chinese. They don't worry about their identity because they don't have one." Robert's frown became deeper. He clearly disapproved.

He was talking about the descendants of people who fled to Taiwan, mostly from Fujian, several centuries ago, to escape wars and famine on the mainland. These "early-comers," as officials like to call them, make up almost 80 percent of the population. The "late-comers," who came from the mainland with Chiang Kai-shek, and their children are more complicated. "That is not necessarily good," said Robert. "They are also more devious." His frown disappeared. He seemed to approve. Deviousness was a sign of civilization.

Robert's family came from the mainland: "I feel my roots are in China, in Jiangsu province." He spoke fluent American English and prided himself, rightly, on being able to identify regional English and American accents: "You're from somewhere around London, right?" He said he could tell whether somebody was Taiwanese or mainlander almost at a glance. The problem with Taiwan, he said, frowning again, is that "the different cultures, Japanese, Taiwanese, and mainland Chinese exist apart. They don't really mix, to form a whole." I asked him where he would eventually end up. "Oh, the States, I guess."

All they think about is fun. I could see what Robert meant. If commercial sex is conspicuous in Bangkok and Manila, it appears almost obsessive in the rather drab streets of Taipei.

The Taiwanese sex industry, originally a product of poverty and often servicing foreigners—Japanese all-male tours, American GIs—is now flourishing with the new prosperity, catering to Taiwanese. Brand-new hotels, built in the fake-baroque style of Japanese love motels, have brothels on every floor. Certain restaurants and coffee shops offer their waitresses for a price. But of all these establishments the most conspicuous are the barbershops. There are barbershops everywhere, rows and rows of them, whole areas with nothing but barbershops with extraordinary façades: pseudo-Greek columns, chrome and glass, quasi-French. People do not go there for a haircut. They go, as the Chinese say, to rest and feel comfortable. Although the comforts offered—various kinds of massages—include sexual acts, one suspects that sex is not really the point. For the entertainment in barbershops is entirely passive. The point seems to be that the customer, stretched out in a dark room on a reclining barber's chair, is groomed, coddled, patted, caressed, kneaded, whispered to, and generally fussed over, with music playing softly in the background. The customer often finds himself being thus taken care of in the presence of many other men, stretched out in chairs in the same dark room. There is no talk between customers. One becomes a faceless object of the tactile attentions of the masseuse. There is an element of surrender in this, to the passive state of childhood.

The ubiquitous barbershop, offering rest and comfort in anonymous groups, is perhaps not a bad metaphor for a capitalist society ruled by a political party which is organized along Leninist lines but prides itself on its Confucian heritage. The KMT is everywhere, like a benevolent Big Brother, or, in Confucian terms, Superior Man, whose legitimacy lies in his capacity to take care of little people. Singapore's Lee Kuan Yew is a frequent visitor to Taiwan. He is said to feel at home there. In the ideal Confucian state, the little people have no business involving themselves in the affairs of the Superior Men. They are allowed to make money and spend it on fun. In Taiwan, so far, the Superior Men are the mainland elite ruling the Taiwanese people, while trying, as Confucian Superior Men should, to shape them in their own image.

This official image is inescapable. The National Palace Museum, the memorials, statues, and portraits of General Chiang Ka-shek and Sun Yat-sen, the promulgation of Chiang's writings and Sun's Three Principles, the slogans and moral exhortations in public places: "Create Right and Proper Chinese People, Create a Strong and Prosperous State"; "Detect Communist Spies and Smash Their Plots"; "Develop Group Spirit and Moral Righteousness." The official image is conveyed in the national language, Mandarin Chinese, brought over by the mainlanders in 1949. It is the official language on an island where almost 80 percent of the population speaks the Fujian or Hakka dialects, about as different from Mandarin as Italian and Spanish are from French. TV programs, almost all in Mandarin, have to be subtitled so that older people can understand. One still hears stories about children being punished at school for speaking Fujianese. Later in life the Taiwanese sometimes get back at the mainlanders by placing classified ads in the papers insisting on the ability to speak Fujianese; other job applicants need not apply. Most children of mainlanders, especially in Taipei, where the majority of them live, speak no Fujianese or Hakka.

The Memorial Hall for Chiang Kai-shek and the National Palace Museum are both rather splendid examples of classical Chinese architecture, but, like the Japanese colonial buildings, they only add to the stage-set atmosphere of the city. In the entrance hall of the memorial is a huge bronze statue of the Generalissimo, looking like a smiling Buddha. "Ethics, Democracy, Science," it says on the marble wall: the Generalissimo as the Superior Man, bestowing modernity on his little people. Young tourists bow to the statue, take pictures of each other, and giggle, perhaps to break the absurd air of worship in the building. The legendary history of the Generalissimo is presented inside, in the form of pictures, documents, and memorabilia, including large pictures of the Generalissimo's mother. "The Chiang family," so one is informed, "descended from the third son, Duke Ling, of the Duke of Chou, brother of King Wu, founder of the Chou dynasty in 1122 B.C. . . . [He] proved himself an ideal sage ruler, and earned the highest praise from Confucius." About the Generalissimo's mother, Madame Wang, "a great exemplary of Chinese motherhood," we are told that she "brought him up and early instilled in him all the virtues traditional to the Chinese race."

The Palace Museum is not just a museum with the finest collection of classical Chinese art in the world, but, like the memorial, a symbol of the official national identity. Chin Hsiao-yi, the director of the museum, used to be private secretary to the Generalissimo. A senior member of the KMT Central Committee, he is one of the most powerful men in Taiwan. I was allowed to ask him some questions about the museum. A small, neatly dressed man, with a smile that seemed to indicate tolerance and contempt in almost equal measure, he spoke in a way as if everything he said was meant to be recorded. It made conversation a little intimidating. There was also an official photographer, constantly snapping away, as if at a political summit meeting. We met in a large reception room. Professors, curators, and various secretaries sat around in stiff-backed Chinese chairs, silently taking notes and tending tape recorders as Chin explained that the museum demonstrated five thousand years of "cultural homogeneity and continuity."

Would he ever consider showing modern art in the museum—that is, art produced after the Chinese empire came to an end in 1911? Yes, indeed, there was now a gallery devoted to modern Chinese art. Unfortunately, however, "much modern art is so influenced by the West that it is cut off from the great Chinese tradition. Those works cannot be shown in the museum." How would he define what is within or outside the Chinese tradition? "Ah, a Chinese can easily tell, but this is perhaps too subtle for a foreigner. A painting in watercolor, for example, even if the motif is Chinese, would not count as Chinese."

The mystique of being Chinese. It is a kind of racial chauvinism, something to do with an intangible ethnic spirit, closed to outsiders. I had heard expressions of it many times before, sometimes in rather surprising ways. Some years before visiting Taiwan, I met the Chinese-American manager of a first-class hotel in Peking. His name was Peter Sun, as in Sun Yat-sen, his great-uncle. He explained that Overseas Chinese guests in his hotel were treated differently than other tourists by his local staff. Why? "Because we Chinese all feel part of the same family, there is little effort to be especially polite. Many Overseas Chinese find the service here too casual. Foreigners—I mean Caucasians—are treated with more respect." Sun then claimed that Chinese "have a psychological block about expressing themselves in a foreign language." The fact that many Overseas Chinese spoke no Chinese made no difference, said Sun, because they were Chinese at heart. But a Chinese-speaking Caucasian could not break this barrier, because "he would not look Chinese." What about a Chinese-speaking Japanese, who would look Chinese? "No," said Sun, "that would not help, for he is not Chinese."

I heard another variation of the theme from an eminent KMT party historian in Taipei, Professor Li Yun-han. We were sitting in the Generalissimo's old summer palace, a grandly furnished bunker high up in the hills, full of Chiang family memorabilia. Professor Li explained that foreign historians of modern Chinese history produced little work of any worth, because "it is only based on data. They do not really understand Chinese reality, for they did not experience it."

When I asked him how modern academics on Taiwan could produce good work on contemporary China, with only data to rely on, he replied that "because we are still Chinese, we have a better perspective."

I asked him about the tradition of Chinese historiography,

how founders of new dynasties ordered new histories to be written, to legitimize their rule. Was there an element of this in KMT party history? "Absolutely not," said Professor Li, "we are only interested in the facts." I looked around the room, at the large oil paintings of the Generalissimo striking heroic poses, at his calligraphy on the walls, at his old uniforms, lovingly preserved.

There were some fine landscape paintings in the modern gallery of the National Palace Museum, done entirely in the traditional style. There were also some interesting wooden sculptures of shadow boxers and several ceramic pieces. There was not one painting or sculpture depicting anything to do with contemporary Taiwan. The subject matter of classical Chinese art always was rather abstract, like the ideographs in calligraphy; the skill of the brushstrokes counts more than the meaning of the picture or the characters. Nevertheless, in pre-modern China, the subjects of art, however stylized, were still recognizable, they still had a link with reality. Now, painting in the Chinese style means painting an entirely imaginary world frozen in the past. Like the National Palace Museum itself, Chinese art thus purely defined, and however skillfully executed, has become an abstract symbol of the Chinese heritage, cut off from its source, not just geographically, but in time.

The greatest irony about the official images, exemplified by the museum, the memorial, by the KMT historian, is as cinematic as the buildings: it is the strange marriage of science with myth. The bronze deity with family connections all the way back to Confucius, providing science and democracy; the KMT chronicler "only interested in the facts"; the conservation of Chinese mystique at the museum. Modernity and history really are linked in Taiwan; the modern *mission civilisatrice* is based on myth.

" 'China,' " wrote Shaw Yu-ming, "names a country and symbolizes a cultural system . . ." Can the cultural system have any real meaning without the country? How long can the pretense that Taiwan represents the country be held up before the symbol loses all cohesive power? It is a serious political problem for the KMT, for the aim of recovery is one of the main pillars of its legitimacy. It is also a matter of Chinese face, and of an understandable reluctance among mainlanders to be confined to this rich, but parochial little island. To be realistic in Taiwan would mean accepting provinciality.

"What would we be without the aim of recovering the mainland?" asked a government official. "With an independent republic, what would we be? Who knows about Taiwan? People confuse it with Thailand."

But can the idea be sustained? The shared heritage with mainland China, after all, stopped in 1949. The orthodoxy, as usual, finds the answer in Chinese mystique. We Chinese share five thousand years of history and there have been many divisions in the Chinese empire before, always followed by re-unification. According to Chin, the Palace Museum director, "everything, politics, economics, our whole modern culture, is based on the Three Principles. This is a universal idea shared by mankind. The communists have falsified history for thirty years. But the people on the mainland are all aware of that and wait for the day of unification."

It is an illusion, held up officially like a talisman. Like the slogans, the memorials, the statues, the illusion has become part of Taiwanese life; people live with it, without always believing it. But it is an illusion that cuts to the core of an old Chinese problem: the identification of Chinese civilization, which is now scattered all over the globe, with the Chinese state.

" 'China,' " wrote a Chinese-American in a Hong Kong magazine, "is a cultural entity which flows incessantly, like the Yellow River, from its source all the way to the present time, and from there to the boundless future. This is the basic and unshakable belief in the mind of every Chinese. It is also the strongest basis for Chinese nationalism. No matter which government is in power, people will not reject China, for there is always hope for a better future a hundred or more years from now." But Taiwan is not just another Chinatown, it is a modern nation, albeit without official independence. This has created a problem of identity which is quite different in kind from the divisions of many centuries ago: How can a modern Chinese state identify itself with Chinese civilization if it is not "China." The temporary answer is to hold up the illusion that it is. Peking, ironically, is party to this deception. An independent Taiwan would challenge their orthodoxy of One China as much as it would the futile aims of the KMT elders.*

Meanwhile the government has organized a Cultural Council, whose mission, according to one of the councillors, is "to promote Chinese civilization, to raise the national spiritual level"—through the National Palace Museum, but also through "Cultural Gardens" where traditional arts, crafts, dance, and music, normally part of religious festivals, can be performed all the year round and so are deprived of their seasonal significance. With the same goal in mind, fostering an official Chinese identity, the government promotes feature films about the life of Sun Yat-sen, or the Generalissimo, or other aspects of official history.

The Pioneers, made in 1986, dealt with early Taiwanese history—that is, the history of the "early-comers." Schoolchildren were given time off to see the film. It begins with Fujianese families in the seventeenth century, braving the terrible storms over the Taiwan Strait to "open up the land." They are not the rough peasants of real history, but Mandarin-speaking people with elegant manners, schooled in the Confucian classics. Their leader is a traditional patriarch who knows what is best for everyone, including the aboriginal tribes, who were the original inhabitants of the island. His goal is not just to open the land but also to civilize the aborigines, depicted

---

* When President Chiang Ching-kuo, the Generalissimo's son, died in the beginning of 1988, the Peking government commended his efforts to reunify the motherland.

as drunken, head-hunting savages. The aboriginal chief, believing, not without reason, that the land belongs to him, orders
his braves to destroy the new settlement built by the Chinese
pioneers. The tribe is then hit by an epidemic, cured at the last
minute by the Chinese, whose medicine works wonders. This,
after the primitive aboriginal rituals around totem poles failed
miserably. The drunken chief, deeply impressed, allows the
Chinese to teach his people how to till the land. In the last
scene pioneers and aborigines plant the rice, side by side, in
perfect harmony. The civilizing mission had succeeded.

What is interesting is not the distortion of history. In fact,
the Dutch opened the land before the Chinese did, and far from
working the fields in harmony with the tribes, the Fujianese
peasants pushed them into the highlands. But all entertainment
distorts history. The interesting thing is the way superior culture provides its own manifest destiny. It is the modern Taiwanese version of the old American Western, where superior
Europeans killed the bad Indians and made friends with the
loyal ones. The real point of the film is clear: KMT rule over
Taiwan is morally correct because it civilized the country.

I was shown a promotion film at the Government Information Office in Taipei. It made the usual points about preserving the five-thousand-year heritage, the benevolent rule
under the Three Principles, and the remarkable prosperity.
Though part of the official propaganda, these points are not
invalid: the government is relatively benevolent; efforts, however wooden and perhaps futile, are made to preserve the heritage; and the prosperity of Taiwan is remarkable. What is
disingenuous about the film, and indeed about the entire orthodoxy in the ROC, is the idea that, as the narrator of the
film puts it, "after the heroic struggle against the Japanese
warlords" the Generalissimo and his loyalists found Taiwan
as a "backward, undeveloped agricultural society . . . a blank
slate, ideal for carrying out reconstruction based upon the
Three Principles . . . We started with nothing and ended with
an economic miracle." This is what children learn at school,

this is the view given in the official media. Taiwan was a blank slate. The Chinese *mission civilisatrice* began in 1949. As a result, the Taiwanese descendants of the "early-comers" have been deprived of their modern history, their shared sense of past. Instead they are taught to remember a history they never had.

In almost every respect, modern Taiwanese history began in 1895, when China ceded Formosa to Japan after losing a war fought over Korea. Formosans who wished to remain Chinese citizens were allowed to register themselves as such and leave for the mainland. Those who remained became citizens of the Japanese Empire in 1898, when Japan began its own civilizing mission in earnest. Formosa was to become a showcase of superior Japanese colonialism, of Tokyo's manifest destiny. The Japanese, so sensitive themselves to the threat of Western imperialism, preferred not to call it colonialism. They wished to turn their overseas subjects, as much as possible, into Japanese—second-class Japanese, to be sure. They wanted to shape the colony in *their* own image.

An American travel writer, Harry A. Franck, arrived in Taiwan in the 1920s: "Had I come directly from Japan proper to Formosa, instead of by way of several months in China, my impression of its Japaneseness might not have been so acute. But that interim in the quite different, even though neighboring, land of Confucius made the changes which its present rulers have wrought upon the long-Chinese island during the thirty years since they took possession of it stand out in striking relief."

"Un-Japanese" behavior was punished. Elderly people were lectured by Japanese policemen for wearing Chinese jackets and trousers. Their Chinese-style buttons were sometimes ripped off. Traditional, architecture, food, and housing arrangements were criticized as un-Japanese, thus uncivilized. Shinto shrines were built all over the island, and Chinese household gods replaced by Shinto symbols. The Japanese language was taught at schools and in massive adult-education programs.

To this day, some nostalgic Taiwanese parents like to be called *to-chan*, *ka-chan* (mommy, daddy) in Japanese. Everything was Japanized: Confucian ethics were presented in schools as Japanese ideals or, like the Three Principles, as universal ideals, shared by the Chinese. Even the Taiwanese folk deity and Chinese national hero was Japanized: Cheng Ch'eng-kung, better known in the West as Koxinga.

The legend of Koxinga is the supreme symbol of Taiwan's historical confusion. He was born in 1624, near Nagasaki in Japan. His father was a Chinese pirate chief, his mother Japanese. Like his father, he became a maritime adventurer, based on the islands of Amoy and Quemoy, in Fujian province. When the Manchu Ch'ing dynasty drove the Chinese Ming dynasty out of power, Koxinga became a Ming Loyalist. He tried to restore Chinese rule by sailing his fleet up to Nanjing, but was defeated by the Manchu armies at the city gates and had to retreat back to his island bastion. This was too small a base from which to resist the entire might of the Ch'ing empire and so in 1661, he sailed for Taiwan, where he had his finest hour, celebrated in an endless variety of legends, stories, pictures, TV dramas, and movies: he expelled the Dutch from their fort in southern Taiwan and established a Chinese administration. One year later, he died of a mysterious disease.

Like many folk heroes, he became many things to many men. To the Taiwanese people he was a folk deity, blessed with superhuman strength and occult powers. He brought them wisdom and prosperity. In 1875 a temple was built for him in Tainan, where he was cannonized as a Confucian deity for his loyalty and his "great enterprise." His great enterprise was the opening up of Taiwan for the Chinese, and the subjugation of aboriginal tribes—the sort of thing celebrated in the film *The Pioneers*. To the anti-Ch'ing revolutionaries in the early twentieth century, he was an anti-foreign patriot. The Nationalism in Sun Yat-sen's Three Principles refers to Chinese nationalism against the Manchu rulers. After the Nationalists took over Taiwan in 1949, Koxinga became a symbol of defiance against the usurpers on the mainland, while on the mainland he is the heroic freedom fighter against Western imperialism. More to the point, in the 1930s he became a symbol of patriotic resistance against the Japanese.

But the Japanese had already claimed him as one of their own. In a famous eighteenth-century puppet play by Chikamatsu Monzaemon, he became a Japanese hero, whose feats included killing a tiger with his bare hands. A monument was built in Nagasaki and a shrine in Kyoto. The first Japanese colonial governor of Taiwan built a ceremonial gate at the Koxinga temple in Tainan and in 1898 proclaimed it a Shinto shrine. Koxinga's Japanese mother was officially enshrined in Tainan about ten years later and incorporated in the local pantheon of Shinto guardian deities for the island. By robbing the hero of his Chineseness, the Japanese tied him more securely to Taiwan. Koxinga's traditional enemies, in effect, became the Chinese themselves. One Japanese wrote in 1907: "And thus the island, which China had torn from Koxinga's descendants by intrigue, bribery, and brute force, passed again into the hands of the Japanese, in whose veins flows the same blood as filled those of Koxinga." In fact, by divorcing the hero from China, he became as Taiwanese as he was Japanese. Koxinga, in this sense, stood for Taiwan itself, for the Japanese civilizing mission gave Taiwan its first modern political identity, partly following the Japanese model, partly in opposition to it. For the first time there was a common primary school system and a lingua franca, elementary Japanese, in which all clans, tribes, and ethnic groups could communicate.

Knowing Japanese opened up a world to the Taiwanese elite that went well beyond the Japanese empire. Half the books in secondhand book markets in Taipei are Japanese publications of the colonial era. The titles give us an idea of the intellectual life in Taiwan during the 1920s and 1930s: translations of French literature, introductions to German philosophy, English architecture, American politics, Italian art, medicine, economics, science. Although Japanese colonialism was inspired by fear of the West, it introduced the West to the colonies. To be modern was to be Western, and to the Taiwanese, Japan, not China, represented modernity. Harry A. Franck reported in 1924 that "Taipei or Taihoku, Japanese capital of Formosa, is often mentioned as the most modern city in Japan. There was no difficulty in compelling the Chinese or Formosan inhabitants of the island to tear down wherever improvements were desirable, whereas the same thing does not quite apply to the Japanese at home."

Modernization was forced through with a ruthless efficiency—a process repeated by the KMT mainlanders after 1949—and the results counted as proof of political legitimacy. The statistics were impressive: in 1931 Taiwan had 2,857 miles of public and private railroad track; the whole of continental China had fewer than 9,400 miles. Radiotelephone communication between Tokyo and Taipei was opened in 1934. Telegraph and postal services served every town and many villages on the island. And the power plants of Taiwan generated almost as much electric power as the total produced in the whole of China. Education was enormously expanded: Taiwan's first university, now called Taiwan National University, was set up by the Japanese in 1927. (It is typical of Taiwan's confusion between the official past and the actual one that anniversary celebrations of the university result in controversy: should the Japanese years be counted, or did history begin in 1945?) Above all, the Japanese built hospitals. Medicine was the main path to success in the modern world open to the Taiwanese. If they were not allowed to rule themselves, they were at least allowed to cure their own diseases.

In Taipei I spoke to a man whose cosmopolitan style makes him a favored spokesman for the government view. I asked him which country had had the strongest modern influence on Taiwan, Japan or the United States. Without hesitation, he answered in a flawless American accent that Japan's influence was pretty minimal. "The effect of Japanese modernization has only been felt for the last twenty years, while our contacts with the United States go back to the 1920s, in Nanjing, and later Chongqing, the capitals of our government." The man was from the mainland, and it was a typical mainlander's answer; fifty years of Taiwanese history was not only dismissed but completely ignored.

"What about all the Japanese buildings," I asked. "What Japanese buildings?" "Well, for example, almost every government building." "Oh, but they are not Japanese, they are Western."

Herein lies part of the confusion: Since the modernity introduced by the Japanese was inspired by the West, it need no longer be recognized as Japanese. It is telling that the Japanese words still commonly used today are mostly of European origin: *autobi* (motorbike), *biru* (beer), *rajo* (radio), *saku* (condom—"sack"). In his book on the colonial period, George Kerr describes how "Japanese and Formosans alike found a useful area of compromise by adopting Western ways, modified by either Formosan or Japanese taste. Very prosperous Formosans often chose to live in Western-style houses, with one or two Japanese-style mat-floored rooms in the living quarters and perhaps a Japanese-style garden on the grounds. Prosperous Japanese, on the other hand, lived in Japanese-style houses with a Western-style room attached, in which stood an upright piano, a table covered with tasseled green baize, and Western chairs."

"We Chinese are not like the Japanese," said the scholar in Taipei. "They accept Western culture totally. We still maintain our own way of life." For many years Japanese films were not allowed to be shown in Taiwan. Even now the number of films is restricted to about five a year. In 1985, none were shown; in 1986, six, while two hundred American films were released. "We don't want them to influence our filmmakers too much," said a man from the Motion Picture Association. What about American films? "We are not worried about those, because people are used to them." Films about Japanese militarism, said the man, are especially sensitive: "We cannot allow those."

I told him I had seen billboards in town advertising just such a Japanese film, about the attack on Pearl Harbor. "Oh, that does not concern the Chinese, it is only about the Americans."

I was told something closer to the real nature of the problem later, by a candid civil servant. "We must be very careful," he said, "for older Taiwanese feel nostalgia for Japanese culture. They miss it. But others hate the Japanese, so we must be careful." What he was really saying is that Japanese entertainment threatens the official Chinese image of Taiwan.

But Japanese culture is everywhere, in a Western guise, its origins blurred, suppressed, or forgotten. This is what makes the surface of modern Taiwan look so familiar to anyone who knows Japan. What to call it? The coffee shops, with their quasi-baroque, partly French château, partly alpine Swiss interiors, where teenaged girls eat spaghetti and chocolate parfaits. The sing-along, *karaoke* bars, where customers sing Japanese songs through microphones, accompanied by taped background music and video pictures of lonely Japanese women in evening dresses staring romantically at the harbor lights of Yokohama. (They even have *karaoke* taxis now, where you can take a mike in the back seat.) The TV variety shows, with their endless parade of mediocre teenage singers, clumsy dancers, and screeching MCs in tuxedos performing in clouds of dry ice and banks of flashing disco lights. Like the colonial buildings, they are Japanese fantasies of Europe and America transferred to Taiwan. They are forms of modern kitsch twice removed from their source, and thus they almost defy interpretation. What to call it? Japanese modern? Asian baroque?

Next to the Farmers Association in a small town in southern Taiwan we ate hamburger steaks in a *karaoke* restaurant called Boston. It was dimly lit, the walls were covered with wood paneling, the ceiling with fake black leather, the tables with tartan cloths. The waiters wore bow ties, the disc jockey a tuxedo. There were not many people there—a raucous festival was going on at the local temple nearby, dedicated to the worship of Matsu, the mother goddess of Taiwan. A few young couples were eating spaghetti in silence, flipping through a large, leather-bound book filled with song titles and their corresponding numbers, which they would scribble on a piece of paper and hand to the waiter. Occasionally one of them would get up, after requesting a number, walk to the spotlit stage, take the microphone, and, accompanied by the *karaoke*, sing a song, with lamentable skill, and no visible joy, mimicking the coy motions of TV performers. There was no laughter or applause. Just flashing disco lights and the steady drone of the *karaoke* machine. The singer would then shuffle back to his or her table, where the silent partner was already selecting another number in the book. It was like a parody of modern ennui, a world of joyless gimmicks, a world with no known past.

It is a world described wonderfully by Edward Yang, one of the best young Taiwanese filmmakers. Yang grew up in Taiwan, but studied in America. His subject is Taipei, the hybrid city, filled with people who have cut themselves loose from the past, from the traditional family with its well-defined limits, without yet having found new limits, new values, new definitions. The heroine in *That Day on the Beach* is a young woman who grew up in a traditional Taiwanese (not mainlander) family. Her father is a Japanophile doctor who behaves like a prewar Japanese patriarch. The house is Japanese, the children have Japanese names. The patriarch decides whom his children will marry. The girl runs away to marry the man she thinks she loves and settles in Taipei. He has to devote himself to corporate life; she stays at home and struggles against boredom by taking classes in Japanese flower arranging. Her best friend drifts from man to man. Her husband comes home drunk most nights. The marriage breaks down. He takes a lover, then disappears, probably—we are never shown—by committing suicide. What is interesting about the film is not so much the theme; old, small-town values collapsing in the big city is a trusted old theme in Asian films. The interest lies in the complete absence of moralizing and sentimentality. The life of the heroine is confused, sad even, but not to be condemned. Her choice to leave the old world behind is shown as inevitable. The hybrid city, so often depicted as the symbol of modern evil, actually looks alluring. The neon advertisements of Japanese products, the streets at dusk clogged with traffic, the office interiors, the TV commercials, have, or are shown to have, a compelling beauty. Yang's camera is nervous, probing, never still, as if it is trying to make sense out of the absurd images of modern life by picking them all up for scrutiny.

The camera, that quintessentially modern invention with its voracious and promiscuous eye, is perhaps the best artistic tool with which to describe a place like Taiwan. Filmmakers escape the burden of having to be "Chinese," which bears down so heavily on the talents of other artists. The camera is too new, too neutral to be specifically Chinese, and the Chinese film tradition hardly exists, especially on Taiwan, where films from the mainland cannot be seen—post-revolutionary ones for obvious reasons, and many pre-revolutionary ones because they were made by leftists. I met Yang at the Sheraton Hotel coffee shop, together with an equally brilliant Taiwanese filmmaker named Hou Hsiao-hsien. If Yang, in his fashionable clothes, his American English, his horn-rimmed glasses, is of the city, Hou has the earthy look and manners of the village. I asked them whether they did not miss a tradition to be inspired by or to react against. Hou then made the point that European directors were always looking over their shoulders at old masters, which made them self-conscious. "We are the first generation, the pioneers," said Yang. "We can try anything we like."

Hou plays the hero in one of Yang's films, entitled *Taipei Story*. Should he move to America? Should he marry his girlfriend? Should she be more like her younger sister, dancing in discos, watching Japanese commercials on video, changing lovers? He still believes in family loyalty, the values of the old world; she no longer does. They are stuck in between worlds. They try anything. "We are still waiting for the dust to settle," said Yang. "That is what my films are about."

*   *   *

For ten years Antonio Chiang edited a magazine called *The Eighties*, opposed to the KMT government, published by Kang Ning-hsiang, one of the most prominent opposition politicians. *The Eighties* was often banned, but somehow Chiang always managed to stay out of jail and remain in print. Both Kang and Chiang are classified as moderates in the fractious world of Taiwanese opposition politics. Chiang is the kind of intellectual that radical idealists like to hate, in revolutionary terms, a Danton as opposed to a Robespierre. He takes pride in being Taiwanese, but is too cosmopolitan, too sophisticated, too well-read to be comfortable in the narrow world of Taiwanese nationalism. Indeed, he is somewhat contemptuous of it. His new magazine, *The Journalist*, attempts to stay away from opposition politics altogether. Although he has a wide following among the Taiwanese, and his views are constantly sought by foreigners, he cuts a somewhat sad figure. He, more than anyone else I met in Taiwan, exemplified the man trapped in between worlds. Cut off from China, and too Chinese (or Taiwanese) to choose a life of comfortable obscurity in America, Chiang is confined to the insularity of Taiwan.

He invited me to a friend's house in Beitou, a hot-spring resort near Taipei. The house, built by the owner himself, a well-known Taiwanese artist sympathetic to the opposition, had a large communal bath, Japanese style—conservative Chinese prefer to take baths in private and most old Japanese baths in Taiwan have been divided into narrow cubicles. We slipped into the scalding sulphurous water which smelled of rotten eggs. I asked Chiang whether forty years of KMT education had worked. Were young Taiwanese losing their Taiwaneseness, were they really identifying with the official image of mainland China? No, he said, it had not worked. "Inside Taiwan we see ourselves as Chinese, but as soon as we step outside the island, we are Taiwanese."

It was, perhaps, a typically Taiwanese answer. I had asked a Taiwanese girl in a disco the same question. She wanted to leave, to live in America. "This place is too small, too narrow. But I was born as a Taiwanese, so I will always have a home. Mainlanders are different, they always want to send their children away. They don't care about this place. It is not their home." Her friends, one of whom was a mainlander, giggled: "Don't listen to her, she is prejudiced."

At a lunch party organized by the Government Information Office, I sat next to an elegant lady just back from a trip to Paris. She wore an expensive fur coat and talked incessantly about "creativity," "exciting experiments," "audience reactions." She worked in the theater. "We are so free here," she said, bubbling over in excitement, "we can do anything we like." She was a mainlander. I asked her whether the complicated relationship between mainlanders and Taiwanese was too sensitive a subject for drama or literature. Not at all, she answered, but it is simply not an issue here. "Nobody even thinks about it."

"Well," said a government bureaucrat, in the smiling manner of a tactful host trying to ease his guests into another subject, "we Chinese all have regional feelings. Taiwan is no exception. But it is not an issue anyway." He conceded that thirty years ago it might have been a problem, but not with young people today, "it is not an issue."

I pressed the point again, which was rude; Chinese banquets are like diplomatic functions: occasions for polite small talk. Were there any plays or books about prejudice or discrimination among Taiwanese and mainlanders? No, said the lady, echoed by the bureaucrat, "but it is not an issue." Another government official who had been listening with an air of irritation, then broke into the conversation, his face red with anger. He was half Taiwanese, half mainlander, he said, and thoroughly sick of talking to foreigners about the subject. "Only foreign journalists are interested in it," he shouted. "Sure, it is a good story. But here only a minority is conscious of it. It is purely political." The artistic lady agreed. "Politicians are always looking for controversy, it is more fun." She giggled into her kid glove at her own sarcasm. But is it too sensitive a subject for the theater? The government man was shaking with rage. "Yes, it is political and very sensitive and I would certainly not want any books or plays on this issue."

It is sensitive because it reveals an elementary truth about Taiwanese society. Although by no means all Taiwanese are opposed to the KMT,* almost everybody involved in the opposition is Taiwanese. There is more to it than a struggle between democracy and authoritarian rule. It is a matter of identity. This includes a shared sense of the past. Modernity and prosperity can only legitimize political rule when the ruling elite is demonstrably superior, more modern, more prosperous. That is the principle of colonialism. On Taiwan, due to the very success of the KMT government the principle has broken down. This is one reason why recovering the mainland must stay part of the orthodoxy, and why talk of Taiwanese independence is officially banned. In an independent Taiwan, the KMT mainlander elite could no longer justify its monopoly over political power.

Both the Japanese and the KMT tried to either co-opt or destroy the Taiwanese elite. One of the most painful events in postwar Taiwan, carefully deleted from the public memory, was the massacre of Taiwanese on April 28, 1947, by Nationalist troops commanded by Ch'en Yi, a notorious governor of Fujian during the war. The Taiwanese elite, having struggled for so long to get Home Rule under the Japanese, resented the way the island was taken over and plundered by the Nationalist regime on the mainland. Resentment boiled over into rebellion, Nationalist troops were shipped in, and thousands—some say tens of thousands—of Taiwanese civilians were killed. The message was clear to generations of Taiwanese: politics is a dangerous business; it is safer to get rich instead. The Tai-

---

* The majority of KMT members are in fact Taiwanese, as is the current President, Lee Teng-hui. But mainlanders still control such vital institutions as the armed forces and the Central Bank and remain the guardians of KMT orthodoxy.

wanese were offered the same deal as the Chinese in Malaysia.

Ch'en Yi, having made a fortune by collaborating as provincial governor with the Japanese, and having served as a henchman for the Nationalists, tried to come to an arrangement with the Chinese communists when things were clearly going their way. He was arrested and executed. To appease the Taiwanese, he was given the sole blame for the April 28 massacre, which then became a taboo subject. It is not taught at school, and many parents prefer not to tell their children.

Hong Chi-chang, an assemblyman and prominent member of the opposition party, the DPP, hopes to revive the memory. He wants to make April 28 a National Day of Reconciliation. The government is asked to formally apologize for the massacre. Hong's "April 28 Movement" also wishes the government to abolish the "place of origin" on identity cards. "Taiwanese," he says, "must be identified by residency, not family background." The ultimate aim is an independent Taiwan, a Taiwan for the Taiwanese. This was bound to come. Having become prosperous and modern, the Taiwanese have ceased to be little people. A new elite has grown up to challenge the old one, clinging to its refuge with no hope of recovering the mainland. And a hopeless dream is not enough to hold out against provincial nationalism.

This is what gives many young Taiwanese their spark. A journalist working for an opposition journal asked me to meet him in a Japanese restaurant. He got so excited as he talked about the future of Taiwan that he forgot to eat his raw fish. He felt a sense of crisis about the future, after President Chiang Ching-kuo dies. But he was optimistic. He wanted to stay in Taiwan. "Of course, we can spend our time on fun, in barbershops. Or we can have a comfortable life in America. But we face challenges here. We can fight for a better life, better politics, a better society. We will be very important, maybe take over from Hong Kong as a financial center. You should come and live here." His enthusiasm was infectious and stood in marked contrast to some of the mainlanders I had met. I asked him about that. His explanation was quite simple. That is because mainlanders are depressed about the smallness of the island. "And the KMT cannot go on giving them power, nor can they recover the mainland, so they will face a real crisis after the fall of the Chiang dynasty."* I felt some sympathy for the mainlanders—for the ex-soldiers driving taxis in Taipei or running mom-and-pop stores in small towns.

"Love and Care for Taiwan, Support the Opposition" is the slogan on the cover of one of the more radical journals supporting Taiwan independence. Inside the cover is a picture of a nightclub hostess. The accompanying text gives one a fair idea of what the Taiwanese nationalism is all about. It begins with the words of a popular song: "She wears pretty clothes and has seductive manners. She sits with her clients, who pull her this way and that. The red neon lights bring out the sadness in her heart. Ah, ah, ah . . . who really understands the tragedy and bitter tears hidden behind her professional smile . . ." And then comes the message of the song. "During the last four hundred years, Taiwan was like this hostess. First she went with the Dutch, then with Koxinga, then with the Manchus of the Ch'ing empire, then with the Japanese, and finally with the KMT. Always she was pulled this way and then that way, fighting back her tears, putting on a smile, looking longingly in all directions, into the misty darkness. When will we be able to look up to the sky again? When can we be our own true masters?"

In Taipei I went to see a new film about aboriginal girls sold as prostitutes to the shabby low-class brothels of Huahsi, an area of Taipei known to tourists as Snake Alley. It was not a good film, at once sensational, titillating, and sentimental. The depiction of aborigines as drunk, corrupt, and addicted to drugs

* Chiang Ching-kuo died on January 13, 1988. Any potential crisis was averted by a remarkable show of flexibility. A Taiwanese President was appointed; opposition parties recognized; and visits to mainland China allowed for the first time since 1949.

was patronizing, to say the least. The audience was invited to enjoy, vicariously, their degradation, but morally let off the hook by getting a sermon about social injustice. It was like a cheap Victorian morality play. One felt manipulated in a rather nasty manner. I saw the film with an aboriginal couple, Mr. and Mrs. Chen. I felt embarrassed for them and assumed that they hated it as much as I did. I was wrong. Mr. Chen liked it. "It was a good film," he said. "It was about my people."

Mr. Chen is a civil servant. He belongs to the Tayal tribe from central Taiwan. According to Harry A. Franck, "the ferocious Tayals, who tattoo themselves blue in the face, are the fiercest, the most persistent, and the most successful head-hunters." This was in the 1920s. Most of the aboriginal prostitutes in Snake Alley are Tayal. Mr. Chen, a slim, dark man, who could have been anything from a Nepali to a native Filipino, is one of the few aborigines with a university degree. After studying in America for several years, he worked as a journalist in central Taiwan. But he was hindered in his work because he speaks little Taiwanese. He only speaks the official Mandarin Chinese. His father hardly even speaks that. He is more comfortable with Japanese and his tribal language. The Taiwanese would not trust Mr. Chen, so he had trouble getting stories. And so he decided to join the government.

I asked him what he said when people in America inquired about his nationality. "Of course, Chinese." But did he feel Chinese? "My tribal identity is still very strong. But I feel honored to be part of the Chinese family. We were taught about the great Chinese civilization. I would like to visit China one day. Even so, some people don't respect us. They think we are barbarians." Which people? "Difficult to say. Well, the Taiwanese. They call themselves native Taiwanese, but they are not. We are. If they would take over our government, I don't know how we would be treated." He said he believed in the aim to recover the mainland, because he did not want to stay on the island. "I have a global vision."

It is a common pattern: The oppressed minority identifies

with the ruling outsiders to keep the oppressive majority at a distance. It was the story of the montagnards in Indochina, who first helped the French and then the Americans against the Vietnamese. The Ambonese did the same for the Dutch during their rule in the Dutch East Indies. And it was the story of the Taiwanese tribes under the Japanese, despite some violent uprisings and bloody massacres.

"We mountain people are very obedient to authority," said an aboriginal mayor of a village on the east coast. He was a jovial fat man in a silk shirt, with the features and skin color of a Malay. "Is that a good thing?" I asked. Yes, that was a good thing. But were they always so obedient? Had not the Japanese enforced obedience by terrorizing them? "No, not at all, the Japanese were good to us." What about the rebellions? "That was not our doing. Other people pushed us."

Mr. Chen's father remembered one of the bloodiest rebellions, which happened in 1930, in a place called Wushe, in central Taiwan. When the Japanese provincial governor arrived with his retinue one autumn day to open new administrative buildings, hundreds of tribesmen swooped down on them from the surrounding mountains and 197 Japanese were killed. Japanese troops massacred a large number of aborigines in return. They burned the villages down, because, so the Japanese troops said, women and children committed suicide by hanging themselves in their huts. There were many reasons for the uprising: low pay, bullying policemen, compulsory labor. What rankled most, however, was the way Japanese demanded the services of attractive local girls.

Mr. Chen's father, then called by his Japanese name, Tanaka, was still at school. His Japanese became good enough for him to be employed as a Japanese teacher. He was allowed to wear a Japanese police uniform, which, I was told by his son, "gave him a lot of face in the village."

He now owns a hot-spring hotel in the mountains near Wushe and plants tea on the mountain slopes. He calls his children by their Japanese names and has fond memories of their last family holiday in Japan. On the way to his old village, entirely populated by aborigines, I asked him about the Japanese period. Yes, he said, mountain people were oppressed by the Japanese, but when they left, we felt sad. "We mountain people bear no grudges. We mountain people have warm hearts." The Taiwanese, or "lowlanders," on the other hand, are vindictive. He shared his son's misgivings about what would happen if they gained political control. "Now the mainlanders are in power, so we are doing better."

The village was little more than a few narrow streets with wooden shacks. The only modern buildings were a Presbyterian and a Catholic church. A loudspeaker from the Presbyterian church urged people to send their children to Sunday school. The announcement was made in Mandarin and the tribal language. Young men raced up and down the main street on motorbikes, swerving dangerously. "Better get out of the way," said Mr. Tanaka. "We mountain people drink a lot." We visited a family friend in his wooden hut. It was simply furnished with a wooden table and an old sofa. There was a large television set and a calendar on the wall with Japanese girls posing in bikinis on a beach in Hawaii. Apart from us, there were two men in the room. The TV was tuned to a Peking opera. One of the men switched channels to an American cop show. The friend, quite drunk, began to sing an old Japanese song. The other man was convulsed in giggles, hiding his face in his right arm. After a while, Mr. Tanaka got up. "We'd better go," he said. "They are drunk." It was seven o'clock in the evening.

There are 320,000 aborigines in Taiwan, about 1.8 percent of the total population. About 70,000 are members of the Presbyterian church. There is an almost equal number of Catholics. Most were converted after the war. A young aboriginal social worker called Ziro, who lives in a mountain village near the east coast, said the "Christianity stopped us from being headhunters. It didn't force us, like the Japanese did, but it gave us a moral brake." Christianity, he said, was the faith of the supermen, of our liberators from the Chinese who exploited us and the Japanese who oppressed us.

The foreign missionary saving native souls seems an anachronism now. And to those who believe in reviving, or preserving, minority cultures, he may even be repugnant, the arrogant white man imposing his values on the economically dispossessed. But what if the minority culture is so weak, so fragmented, so demoralized that it cannot survive in the modern world, except in cultural reservations, where it becomes a fake culture catering to the tourist trade? Older aborigines are afraid to let their children go to the cities, because life there is "too complicated." Yet the children run away. "They do not have the education to compete as equals with the majority," said the village mayor, "but they want the material goods."

A Canadian missionary named Michael took me to Lanyu, or Orchid Island, off the southeast coast. Lanyu is the home of the Yami, the least modernized tribe in Taiwan. They were considered to be so exotic by the Japanese during the colonial period that Lanyu was designated a closed anthropological park, a kind of human zoo for Japanese scholars. There are about three thousand Yami people on the island. They make a meager living by fishing and planting taro root. The older men still wear loincloths; the women wear shells around their necks and chew betel nut. Next to Lanyu lies Little Lanyu, where the spirits of the dead live, so children are not allowed to go there.

The only evidence of the modern world on Lanyu is a large nuclear waste dump, completed in 1982, after much local protest. The Taiwan Power Company compensates for its unwelcome presence by sponsoring island projects, such as boat races or scholarships to vocational schools. The Yami wanted the company to buy them a TV transmitter, so they could get better reception in their huts. The company, according to a spokesman, "considered whether watching TV was really socially desirable, whether it was good for people's eyes." The Yami got their transmitter.

Some Taiwanese from the "mainland" encouraged the Yami to improve their lives by starting a cooperative store to sell tropical fish. It has not been a success. Yami fishermen are not used to catching more fish than necessary for feeding their families. And there were problems about fishing during taboo seasons. An aquarium was built in the co-op, to attract tourists, but the first time a group arrived, the co-op was closed. The aquariums are virtually empty now and the co-op is a sad place, with rotting fish tails hanging from the ceiling.

Michael, a lanky man wearing a T-shirt and a baseball cap, handed out copies of *National Geographic* to a group of young men lying on a wooden platform next to a concrete hut. The platform on stilts, a traditional feature of Yami housing, was built by the men, the concrete hut by the government. Most of the men appeared bored by the magazines, except for one boy about fourteen, who was fascinated and asked Michael questions about Vancouver, the Cotswolds, Botswana, or whatever happened to catch his eye. He told us in fluent Mandarin that he had failed to get into middle school. Instead he entered a special government school, where he was taught the necessary skills to work in a fish-processing plant. The plant was still in its planning stage. He had run away from home once, to Taipei, where he was picked up by agents for a sweat-shop. There he was confined virtually as a slave, until he ran away one night, pursued by thugs employed by the boss. "Taipei was fun," he said.

When it was time to say goodbye to the boy at the small airport, his parents turned up, both barefoot, the father wearing a loincloth. Michael lined the three of them up for a photo-graph. They were peering intently into the lens when there was a sudden commotion in the airport lounge. A Taiwanese tourist was handing out chocolates from a paper bag. He was im-mediately surrounded by elderly Yami people frantically stretching their hands. The boy's parents joined the fray. The boy looked embarrassed. "Their thinking is very different from ours," he said.

He is an extreme example of the Taiwanese conundrum, of a man stuck between worlds shaped by others. He has outgrown the world of his parents, with its spirits and taboos, but is not yet ready for the "complicated" society of the Taiwanese cities. His thinking is shaped by the official images of the mainland Chinese. He was taught the geography of China at school, not that of Taiwan. He was taught the Three Principles and the heroic struggles of Sun Yat-sen and the Generalissimo. Then there are the images brought by the missionaries.

Three North American spinsters live on the island working on a translation into Yami of the New Testament. They must first learn Yami themselves and teach the Yami how to read romanized script. But eventually, they hope to reach "maybe hundreds of people." It might not be quite as absurd as it seems. At least it preserves the language, and Christianity is perhaps the only way for losing tribes to recover self-esteem. "The Church," said Ziro, the social worker, "helps us think about our identity. It might not solve our problems, but it is better than disappearing without a trace."

The cruel dilemma of the Taiwanese aborigines is that they have to accept an alien world, based on alien myths, to survive. The boy educated at the fish-processing school has reached a point of no return. Any attempt to force him to return to the world of his ancestors is not only futile but cruel.

One of the Yami community leaders is not a Yami, but a Taiwanese called Lin Mao-an. A small man in jeans and glasses, he looked like a graduate student or a bookish social worker. Lin's first visit to Lanyu was on a student excursion. A year or so later, still a student, Lin had a religious vision: "I thought I could see God, and I cried and cried. Then I asked God about my future, for I was very confused at the time. I cried again and suddenly my future was revealed. I had to do something for the Yami." He moved to Lanyu, married a Yami, and set up a kindergarten. It is a small wooden building in the main village, with children's drawings, Christian symbols, as well as the obligatory pictures of the Generalissimo and Sun Yat-sen on the walls.

Lin does not speak Yami, but believes Yami culture is "very good." He established a committee to promote Yami culture, because he thinks the Yami people "should learn more about their culture." The problem is that there is no consensus among the Yami themselves about what Yami culture is. So, says Lin, "we must define it first." I asked Lin what he thought about his own past, the culture and traditions of the Taiwanese. He was never much interested in that: "Perhaps I was anesthetized by my education, but I don't feel deprived." Did the Yami feel deprived? No, he said, not much. An attempt was made to get youth groups together to discuss Yami culture, but only four or five people turned up. So why was Lin so interested? He thought for a moment, smiled, and said: "Well, it is like this. Why do foreigners come to Taiwan to tell us how to be Chinese?" It was a very Taiwanese answer.

KOREA

On a cold day in November 1986, Colonel Schreuders returned to the spot where Chinese troops killed some of his men one early morning in 1951. Schreuders belonged to the Dutch battalion defending a bridge in Hungsong, a small town about eighty miles from Seoul. The battle, forgotten by almost everybody but the survivors and Dutch diplomats required to pay their periodic respects to the dead, cost seventeen lives, and the town was destroyed. Hungsong is now a prosperous-looking place with supermarkets, cinemas, and fashion shops. The memorial to the Dutch commander who was killed by a hand grenade minutes after his guard shouted, "The Chinks are coming, look out!" lies in a playground. The colonel tried to find familiar landmarks with his old army map. He found none, except for the lone steeple of an old church which had been pulled down only days before he arrived. A Korean veteran of the battalion made the motions of firing an imaginary gun. "I shot a lot of enemies here," he said with a smile to the colonel, who did not appear to remember the man. A priest rang the bell in the steeple. Small boys played with a plastic machine gun in the playground. A U.S. army tank battalion rolled through the town for regular maneuvers, and helicopters made dives for the riverbank.

The colonel made a short speech in the town hall. It was platitudinous but oddly moving, because it obviously meant much to him. He told the town dignitaries how happy he was to see how well South Koreans had used "the freedom we all fought for." I wondered what was going through the minds of the Koreans. I thought of some statistics I had jotted down in my notebook that week: half a million North Korean soldiers just across the border; nearly 40,000 American troops in South Korea; $6.5 million worth of tear gas used by South Korean riot police against students during the last nine months.

Some 1,200 students were arrested that week after a fierce battle with the police at Konkuk University in Seoul. Many of them had shouted North Korean propaganda slogans and claimed that the Korean War had been a national struggle for reunification crushed by Yankee imperialists. They set fire to effigies of Nakasone and Reagan. Most students expressed sympathy for the demonstrators' feelings if not always for their most extreme aims. Tear gas hung in the air of virtually every campus in Seoul.

I was driven back to Seoul by the Korean veteran who shot many enemies. He was an animated man who spoke fluent Malay—not a good sign for a Korean of his age, for it probably meant he served as a camp guard in Malaya or Indonesia under the Japanese. I did not press the point. He expressed a great disgust for Americans. "They are very stupid people," he said. "They should have won the Korean War. They had nuclear arms but were too soft to use them." He clenched his fist and banged the steering wheel as he spoke. The Americans could not fight because they were afraid of dying and because they ate candy. "They are soft, soft, soft!" he said, and spat out of the window. He then shifted to more familiar ground: how Korea had a culture superior to Japan's; how the Japanese had tried to rob Koreans of their unique and superior culture; and how during bad times he had often asked God why he had to be born a Korean. He expressed an even greater disgust for his ancestors than for Americans. "I hate my ancestors. They did nothing but fight among themselves and let the big powers take over our country."

It is something one hears a lot in South Korea, this complex and sometimes explosive mixture of shame and chauvinism. The one, of course, stokes the flames of the other. There is a Korean term for pandering to foreign powers: *sadae chuui*. And Koreans are forever accusing one another of it. These accusations are not without reason, for Koreans have a long history of using outside powers to fight opponents at home. In the seventh century the Korean peninsula was unified for the first time, when the kingdom of Silla defeated the kingdoms of Koguryo and Paekche with the help of Chinese troops (according to a history book published in North Korea, this treacherous act "cost the progess of Korean history very dearly"— Silla was in the South, Koguryo in the North).

In the 1890s Chinese and Japanese troops helped the Korean government put down a peasant rebellion, which was inspired by a popular religion called Tonghak, or Eastern Learning, a syncretic creed that mixed local shamanism with Buddhism, Confucianism, and Taoism. It was also influenced by Catholicism, even though Eastern Learning was a reaction against Christian ideas, known as Western Learning. The rebels believed that man and God were the same, that all human beings were equal, and that the day would come when a perfectly egalitarian society would be established. To this end they struggled against exploitation by the Korean gentry, or *yangban*, and the intrusion of foreign merchants. The founder of the religion, Choi Jae Woo, had been sentenced to death as a heretic in 1864. He was tied to a tree by his hair and had his throat cut.

"The Tonghak rebellion was bigger than the French Revolution," said Mr. Hong, a spokesman for the Tonghak religion today—renamed Chondogyo in the early part of this century. The faith is described in an English-language pamphlet as "the guiding light of the Orient, a native and unique Korean religion." "Chondogyo," the pamphlet explained, "reveals valuable new concepts in concert with the creation of a new era in a new world order to replace the passing away of an old fashioned and irrational world." Many nationalist heroes, who believed in Chondogyo, had died for the nation, said Mr. Hong. Syngman Rhee, the first President of the Republic of Korea, regarded Chondogyo believers as communists, because they were for equal income distribution. In the summer of 1987, believers held a demonstration in Seoul. They wanted the spirit of Tonghak incorporated in the preamble of the new constitution. "Tonghak," said Mr. Kim, who had joined the conversation, "is the mother of democracy. Please believe in our religion, it's a good religion, a world religion." Mr. Hong nodded off to sleep. Mr. Kim had alcohol on his breath. The Chondogyo headquarters looked shabby, clearly a sign that the religion is no longer a flourishing concern. But its spirit can still be detected in the rhetoric of most Korean rebels: The search for universal values, the fear of foreign power and influence, the millenarian faith in an egalitarian society; these ideals are constantly invoked, like a kind of national mantra.

The line between "pandering to" foreigners and depending on them simply to survive is, of course, a thin one, given Korea's precarious geographical position between three major powers—China, Russia, and Japan. For much of its history the survival of a unified Korean state depended on the patronage of one power—China. By the same token, shifts in the power balance around the Korean peninsula led to divisions inside the country. In the late nineteenth century there were pro-Russian factions in Korea, pro-Chinese factions, and pro-Japanese factions, all accusing each other of selling out the country.

Today, North Korea calls the South a toadying puppet of the United States. In the late 1940s leftists accused rightists of having been Japanese collaborators during the colonial period. North Korea claimed to be the legitimate heir of Korean destiny by pointing to their Beloved Leader Kim Il Sung, a former anti-Japanese guerrilla fighter. The South, whose government, army, and police force were indeed full of former Japanese collaborators, said the Beloved Leader himself owed his exalted position to his mentors in the Soviet Union. Critics of Park Chung Hee used to delight in using the Japanese name—Matsumoto—which he adopted as an officer in the Japanese Imperial Army. People who dislike the oppositionist Kim Dae Jung were appalled when he turned up in Seoul in 1985 shielded by American congressmen and reporters, ostensibly to avoid the same fate as "Ninoy" Aquino.

Kim Dae Jung himself put the *sadae chuui* syndrome rather well in his *Prison Writings*: "How can we avoid the sin of those who led this nation to destruction when the Yi dynasty was losing to the Japanese aggressors or the sin of our ancestors who lent cowardly cooperation by simply looking on? Let us remind ourselves that liberation from Japanese colonialism was not attained by our own strength and that there were many pro-Japanese elements at that time. After liberation, did our national spirit stand on solid ground, cleansing itself of pro-Japanese elements and pushing the patriots to the fore? The sin of this kind of betrayal of the legitimacy of our nation has since become the karma that suppresses all the regions of this country. It has made empty slogans of conscience, justice, and patriotism and has made the country a playground for those who would use any means to attain their ends, those motivated by devilish and selfish intents. How can we escape punishment for these sins? We should gladly accept it."

The national spirit, the sin of betrayal, the legitimacy of our nation. These are the moral themes of Kim's writings and speeches; they are themes that obsess Koreans. After the student riots in July 1987 forced the government to concede to presi-

dential elections and restore Kim's freedom, Kim called for a
confederation to promote peaceful coexistence of the South
and North and "restore the homogeneity of the Korean people." In a speech on August 15, Liberation Day, he said: "Since
the liberation from the Japanese colonial yoke forty-two years
ago, our national history has been marred by illegitimate and
dictatorial governments. Thus we are ashamed of ourselves in
front of our ancestors who died for the cause of national liberation." Kim is not only an outraged nationalist but also a
devout Catholic, with a highly personal interpretation of Liberation Theology. Again and again in his prison letters he compares his plight to that of Jesus Christ. He sees himself as much
more than just a politician; he is the true patriot bearing the
cross put on his shoulders by treacherous toadies, which should
make him the only legitimate leader of his country.

Because of the deep division running through the Korean
peninsula, legitimacy is a particularly acute problem. Both
halves of the divided country wish to be recognized as the only
legitimate Korea. The battle for legitimacy is not just a military
one but also one of symbols. Each side presents itself as more
independent from foreign powers, culturally, economically,
and politically, than the other. To cope with the crisis of national identity Koreans on both sides have turned it into a cult.
A patriotic scholar named Kim Young Soo wrote in a book,
The Identity of the Korean People, that "it is a well-known
fact that the North Korean communists have obliterated the
national identity." It is the argument one hears in Taiwan from
KMT historians when discussing mainland China. Kim cites
the uprising against the Japanese on March 1, 1919, led by
Christians and Chondogyo believers who were spurred on by
patriotic students, as the "formation of new national sovereignty." Though quickly crushed by the Japanese, it formed
the basis of modern nation building, "the mobilization of a
modern people."

The only true national flag, says Kim, is the flag of South
Korea, the Taeguk Ki. "The North Korean communists, like

the militaristic Japanese policemen, dealt out heavy punishment whenever they found any North Korean carrying Taeguk Ki. This fact eloquently points out that North Korea did not have any intention to succeed to the history of the Korean people." The only true national anthem is the South Korean "Aeguk Ka," which "symbolizes the national consciousness of the Korean people." The "Aeguk Ka" was composed at the beginning of the century. In the days of Japanese colonialism it was sung to the tune of "Auld Lang Syne." "After the division of Korea, the Republic of Korea has respected 'Aeguk Ka' cherished in the heart of the Koreans, while North Koreans adopted a new song having nothing to do with the Koreans. The legitimate national anthem of Korea, therefore, cannot be any other than 'Aeguk Ka' . . ." And so the argument goes on, including the only legitimate national flower, the rose of Sharon, as opposed to the *yulan*, a kind of magnolia Kim Il Sung is supposed to favor. The battle of symbols would seem a little absurd if it were not backed up with such awesome military might.

One can tell just by looking at a map, and yet it comes as a shock when you actually hear the North Korean loudspeakers blaring martial music and propaganda one hour's drive away from Seoul. The Demilitarized Zone (DMZ) is very close indeed. The standard tour took us to the Anti-Communism Exhibition Hall, where we saw tanks, planes, pictures of parades in Pyongyang, and grizzly life-sized models of North Korean soldiers hacking a mother and child to death. We saw the old train that used to go all the way to the Yalu River. It is still "waiting for the peninsula to be united," said the sign. We crossed Freedom Bridge, on each side of which guards of the 1st Battalion, 9th Infantry, saluted and screamed their motto: "Keep Up the Fire!" We were briefed at Camp Kitty Hawk by a corporal who expressed pride in being "In Front of Them All at the Edge of Freedom." We were driven to the Joint Security Area, where North Korean soldiers peered at us through binoculars, picking up every word we said with sensitive microphones and taking our pictures for their files. We peered back at them from Freedom House. We saw the MAC building, where North and South Koreans had held a battle of flags: the national flags on the conference table got bigger and bigger, until the North Korean flag would no longer fit in the building and a compromise was enforced. We saw the Bridge of No Return, where the last prisoners were exchanged after the end of the Korean War, and where two American officers were axed to death in 1976 by North Korean guards when they tried to prune a poplar.

The military hardware and the pictures of atrocities are not the eeriest things about the place. Far stranger are the two villages on either side of the border. In North Korea lies Kijong-dong, better known as Propaganda Village. It has a huge flag-pole, 500 feet tall, and an immense North Korean flag. It also has a number of what look like high-rise apartment buildings, not designed in very good taste, but quite luxurious looking nonetheless. The odd thing is, however, that nobody lives in them: They are for show, a fake village built only to impress. A solitary man arrives every day to hoist and lower the monstrous flag.

In South Korea lies Taesong-dong, or Freedom Village (in fact, literally translated, it means Attaining Success Village). The flagpole is only 300 feet tall, but, so the U.S. corporal told us, the $1,500 South Korean flag is bigger than theirs. People do live in Attaining Success Village: government-supported farmers, who have to abide by a strict curfew. They are surrounded by some of the most formidable armies in the world and subject to a continuous blast of propaganda, most of all from the loudspeakers of Propaganda Village. They make about $25,000 a year. They are the bit-part actors in an elaborate struggle for national legitimacy.

If South Korea claims historical continuity as proof of its legitimacy as the only true Korea, North Korea stresses egalitarianism and national independence. Kim Il Sung's "Juche Philosophy," calling for absolute self-reliance, is expounded in an endless series of books, articles, speeches, films, in fact in everything emanating from North Korea. Just as it is expected of official foreign visitors to don a yarmulke at the Wailing Wall of Jerusalem, visitors to Pyongyang are supposed to pay obeisance to the Juche Philosophy. It may be an economic disaster, but it is part of the national cult, represented by the Great Leader.

In South Korea, Park Chung Hee came up with his own version of the Juche Philosophy: the Spirit of Jaju. "Through a renewed awareness of our own identity," he wrote in a book entitled *In Search of Our Identity*, "we are on the way to rediscovering our values inherent in our own culture and tradition . . . Among the many legacies left behind by our forefathers, the spirit of Jaju is the most priceless. Succinctly speaking, Jaju means we should be master of our own house. It is also a way of saying that we, the Korean people, inhabit this beautiful land and that it is Koreans who shaped an ancient history that goes back over five thousand years."

Other historical legacies used by Park to support the legitimacy of his republic, and the legitimacy of his own rule, were the unique spirit of Hwa (harmony) and the Philosophy of Beneficial Man, "aimed at instilling in both people and government a resolve to do good and to benefit all mankind." The unique spirit of harmony, says Park, was cultivated by the Hwarang, literally the Flower of Youth. These were teenage warriors of the Silla kingdom, who fought the warriors of Paekche and Koguryo, the other Korean kingdoms, during the seventh century. Silla was located in the part of Korea where Park was born, and which he built up as the industrial and historical heart of South Korea.

The old capital of Silla is a place called Kyongju, now a tourist center surrounded by reconstructed Buddhist temples and traditional Korean houses made of concrete. The capital of Koguryo was Pyongyang, while Paekche was located in what is now the province of Cholla, the birthplace and political stronghold of Kim Dae Jung.

The Philosophy of Beneficial Man was, so Park tells us, "the

supreme ideology of the nation's foundation by Tangun." Tangun, a divine figure, whose father was a god-king and mother
a bear-woman, is supposed to have founded the first Korean
state in 2333 B.C. His philosophy, says Park, "has served as a
basic principle of politics and religion throughout Korea's five
thousand years of history." Park, naturally, acted according to
these politics of harmony and benevolence. History in East Asia
always was an instrument of politics, but in the battle for
Korean legitimacy this ancient custom has truly reached its
pinnacle.

Park's answer to Kim Il Sung's propaganda of egalitarianism
was rapid modernization. According to Mr. Hong and Mr.
Kim, the Chondogyo spokesmen, Park was better then Syngman Rhee, because he developed the economy for the people.
And by and large the people agreed. They were willing to
sacrifice political freedoms for order and prosperity. Few countries in Asia look as relentlessly modern as South Korea. And
in few developing countries is wealth as evenly distributed. But
this is not enough. It is never enough.

"Are you American?" asked a youngish man in a tweed
jacket as we were both sneezing and crying during a tear-gas
battle on a Seoul campus. I indicated that I was not. "Good,"
he said, "I don't like Americans." He introduced himself as a
professor of "media communications." He knew all about the
student radicals and expressed great sympathy for their aims.
This country may look rich to a casual visitor, but he assured
me this was not so. In fact, many people were very, very poor.
He wished to show me what he meant. He would take me to
the worst slum of Seoul, a place called Kuro-dong.

We took the subway, which turned into an elevated railway.
We entered a dreary industrial suburb which seemed densely
populated. Was this it? "No, no, it gets much worse. You will
not believe how poor it is. It is unbelievable, unbelievable." He
shook his head and affected a look of disbelief. The industrial
suburb seemed to go on endlessly, the streets got narrower,
more packed with small dwellings. Was this it? "No, much

worse, unbelievable." Finally he signaled that we should get
off the train. We walked through a rubbish dump, took a taxi,
walked a bit more. The professor shook his head a few more
times in anticipatory astonishment at the injustice of it all.
Finally we found our destination: a maze of narrow streets,
lined with small but neat houses. There were shops which
seemed well stocked and children playing around the great
brown pots containing kimchi, cabbage pickled in red pepper.
The people looked neither prosperous nor especially poor. This
must be it, said my friend. "What do you think?" I told him
what I thought, that compared with most slums in Asia it did
not seem too bad. He thought for a bit, then shook his head
again and said it must have changed since the last time he was
there. "They must have painted the houses."

This is not to suggest that poverty does not exist in South
Korea, that labor has not been exploited, or that living in Kuro-
dong is not hard. It does show how strongly Koreans feel about
equality. The professor had been genuinely outraged. It was
my lukewarm response that embarrassed him into finding an
excuse for his feelings: It must have changed.

Korea is both hierarchical and egalitarian. Kim Myong Dong,
a sociologist at Seoul National University, calls it popularized
elitism. The elites of Korean society, by collaborating with the
Japanese, by benefiting from the Americans, by, in the case of
the military elite, brutally crushing student rebellions, have
been discredited. Rising prosperity created new potential elites,
who lacked political power. The political tensions in South
Korea resulted not from poverty but from new wealth. "The
concept of equality in the West," says Kim Myong Dong, "is
equality before God. Here it means the same social status and
wealth." Colonialism, war, and military rule broke down the
hierarchy of the old society. Now, says Kim, everybody wants
to be on top. This is partly what brought the students out into
the streets, and why they were supported by much of the middle
class. Rapid modernization, Park's claim to legitimacy, no

longer solved the problem; indeed, it made it worse. Which is why Park's successor, Chun Doo Hwan, a former general and head of the KCIA, who grabbed power in 1980 and put down the student rebels in Kwangju, shifted his claim to legitimacy. His goal was a highly symbolic one—the Olympic Games of 1988—which was to be another milestone in the cult of nationhood. Finally, South Korea would stand up and be recognized as the truly legitimate heir to the five thousand years of history.

"See you in Seoul in 1988" was the most common slogan in town. The Asian Games held in 1986 served as a warm-up for things to come. "The Asian Games," said Chun, revealing all the traditional insecurites, "have shown that we are vigorously surging ahead in the world after having shaken off age-old poverty and stagnation . . . It was a national festival that enhanced the self-dignity and pride of the Korean people." Far more than sports was involved in the games: it put Seoul ahead of Pyongyang in the battle of symbols and South Korea won more medals than Japan. An account appeared in *The Journal of Cultural Information*, a free paper handed out in South Korean tourist hotels, which conveyed the almost hysterical mood of the event: "Triumphant results of the Korean athletes created the ecstacy [sic] among the public and promoted national prestige at home and abroad. Japan's crumbling sports empire was shaken." An exhibition was set up next to the new National Museum (the old Japanese capitol building) ceaselessly replaying videotapes of the Korean triumphs, often against a backdrop of the national flag. It brought to mind the obsessive repetition of the February Revolt on Philippine TV.

The extraordinary opening ceremony featured martial arts, paratroopers falling from the sky, thousands of schoolchildren doing rhythmic gymnastics, and fifteen thousand dancers "in an explosion of color and sound featuring 5,000 years of Korean heritage" (*The Journal of Cultural Information*). A writer from mainland China, Li Yu, made a shrewd comment in a

South Korean paper: "This grand ceremony was not a festival of Korean culture, but a symbol of the efforts of the Korean people to resist foreign invasions."

In an article published in the *International Review of Mission*, a Presbyterian minister named Park Hyung Kyu wrote: "The history of the Korean people may be looked at from two aspects: the *self-identity* of the Korean people and *liberation* from the ideological, political and economic domination of foreign powers." The problem is that the quest for identity so often drives Koreans into the embrace of foreign ideologies. In other words, Koreans often can only define themselves in terms of a foreign civilization.

The most conspicuous sight in Korean towns at night is the large number of neon-lit crosses on top of churches, chapels, and cathedrals. Apart from the Philippines, Korea is the most Christian country in Asia. Hundreds of thousands, often from rural areas, seek salvation every Sunday in the stadiumlike churches of messianic preachers like Paul Cho, whose professed goal is to convert the Japanese, so they can be forgiven for their national sins. The Pope, on his visit to Korea, drew crowds in the millions. Billy Graham is a folk idol. There is one crucial difference with the Philippines, however: the Koreans converted themselves.

Korean Christianity began in the eighteenth century as a scholarly exercise by Korean students in Peking who wished to acquire Western learning, and ended as a kind of talismanic vehicle for political change. This beginning is significant, because, for once, it was not foreign missionaries but native scholars who spread the gospel. The town where Kim Dae Jung grew up, a port called Mokpo on the south coast, is said to be 60 percent Catholic. Mokpo lies in Cholla province, an area with a long history of opposition to the central power in Seoul (there has never been a President from Cholla; the military strongmen all came from Kyongsangdo, the industrialized southeast). Christianity did well in Korea since the late eighteenth century precisely because it offered an alternative to the stultified Confucianism—itself originally a borrowed ideology—of the governing class. It offered a new system of values which transcended those of the rulers; it promised social equality. Catholicism appealed first to scholars deprived of official rank and thus of political power and then to the poor.

Christianity was also the main force of modernization. Here foreigners did play a vital role. Through the work of foreign missionaries, especially Protestants, Christianity became the vehicle for modern education, medicine, liberal politics, and nationalism. A proper grammatical system for Hangul, the much-revered Korean phonetic script ("the most scientific and best writing system in the world," one is often told), was first worked out when the Bible was translated.

When the Koreans rebelled against the Japanese on March 1, 1919, fifteen of the thirty-three signatories of the independence declaration were Protestants. A Protestant political activist, who spent a long time in jail, once told me that "our government has sold out to foreign domination. We can only regain our national freedom and sovereignty through the gospel."

The poet Kim Chi Ha was an inspiring figure in several student revolts during the 1960s and 1970s. His political poems were directed against the *sadae chuui* of South Korean leaders: "You political bandits! Confess how you sold out our country! When those imperialist Japanese bastards crushed the independence of our people, you joined their army. When the American bastards came, you followed them . . ." (*The Voice of the People*, 1974).

Kim became a Catholic in 1971. He explained why in a pamphlet smuggled out of prison in 1974: "I was desperate to find a way to overcome the fear of death, as well as the material poverty of our people and the spiritual dehumanization that threatens Korean society." He thought of the Tonghak rebellion and followed the nineteenth-century example of linking the word of God with an inner call to become a political activist. The next and logical step led to Catholic Liberation Theology.

"Through my own participation since 1971 in the vigorous development of the human rights movement of Korean Christians, I became convinced that Koreans could offer a golden example to the world, especially the Third World. In our tradition of strong resistance and revolt, resulting from the deep contradictions in our society, a new principle of human liberation was born: the identification of God with revolution."

Kim now lives with his family in a traditional Korean house in southern Cholla province. Instead of leather jackets and black turtleneck sweaters, he now wears traditional Korean clothes. He no longer writes revolutionary diatribes. Instead, he composes long poems in the form of *pansori*, a kind of rhythmic storytelling, which has a long popular tradition, especially in Cholla. His themes are earthier, less political, closer to the life of the masses, or *minjung*, in whom he still expresses great faith. He is no longer a Catholic; he has turned to the philosophy of Tonghak to find the spiritual answers to the ravages of what he calls "American modernization." The poet-revolutionary has turned into a scholar of national mythology.

The two are not so far apart. Korean scholarship is often a way of finding moral sustenance. And a new morality, dogmatically upheld, forms the basis of the revolutionary spirit. A remarkable aspect of Kim Dae Jung's *Prison Writings* is the way he forages through the classics of mostly Western literature, apparently at random, to come up with spiritually uplifting mottoes—rather like a Confucian scholar delving into the *Analects*. His reading lists typically range from Nietzsche's *Ecce Homo* to E. H. Carr's *What Is History?* to Tolstoy's *War and Peace*. "Good literary works relieve our emotions and serve as an inspiration that makes our spirit vigorous and resilient," he writes to his family.

Learning results in higher status, both social and moral. Koreans seem to have an almost unlimited faith in learning, as if culture rubs off on the soul. Seoul probably has the highest concentration of academies, colleges, and universities of any capital in the world. There is even a Korean Academy for

Democracy. The campuses of the better schools are huge and well equipped. Lavish universities are to Seoul what palatial railway stations were to Victorian London: monuments of national progress. They are also a mark of Korean egalitarianism; status is decided by examination. University students represent the highest expectations of Korean families. Those dedicated to learning have the license to be the moral guardians of the nation.

The demonstrations usually started around noon. First the students shouted slogans through megaphones. Key phrases like "Reunification," "Justice," "Kill Chun Doo Hwan," "Kill the Yankee Imperialists," "Democracy," were repeated in unison by the crowds. Then rocks and gasoline bombs were thrown at the riot police hiding behind their shields in modern samurai armor. Tear-gas canisters were fired back at the students. More rocks and bombs flew through the air. Armored cars rode up to the front gate and more tear gas was released. When the students ran out of rocks and bombs, they sang revolutionary songs—sounding rather like wartime Japanese military marches. The police retreated. The demo of the day was over.

There was something almost medieval about these violent campus rituals. Both sides knew the rules of battle and tended to stick to them, as if engaged in a kind of blood sport. The ceremonial atmosphere was heightened by the odd air of normality surrounding them. Students with tennis rackets under their arms picked their way through the debris of broken glass and torn posters. Sophomores holding handkerchiefs to their mouths against the tear gas went off to volleyball courts or English classes. Professors strolled to their offices looking suitably absentminded.

The main point of the demos was to make a point. The extreme slogans, the martial songs, the bursts of predictable violence, displayed a position of moral purity. I asked a student watching a demo at a Seoul university what he thought. He said he did not agree with the slogans but admired the students' sincerity. This kind of sincerity, untainted by political compromise, has been remarkably effective. Students were responsible for the fall of Syngman Rhee in 1960. They seriously challenged President Park in 1979. And in 1987, backed by a sympathetic middle class, they made Chun Doo Hwan's government agree to presidential elections and many reforms. This was accomplished in several weeks of spectacular demonstrations across the country. On TV, South Korea looked like a war zone. The extraordinary thing was, however, that normal life had hardly been disrupted. Driving into Seoul on the day after the students' demands were met, there was not a broken window to be seen. The violence, like that of the campus riots of the year before, was ritualized to a remarkable degree, a huge show of moral sincerity.

When asked what the intellectual basis of the protest movement was, whether there was some philosophy, ideology, even faith, propagated by charismatic mentors, Korean counterparts of Marcuse or Angela Davis, people gave vague answers. Some mentioned the economic "dependency theory," others mentioned articles by purged Korean professors who had studied in the United States. Radio Pyongyang broadcasts were apparently listened to and copied. But the most pervasive influence appears to have come from Japan: Marxist texts, often written by Japanese intellectuals in the early 1930s, and handbooks compiled by the Japanese student movement in the 1960s offering instructions on how to build barricades and what to say under police interrogation. It was another example of foreign ideas—secondhand at that—to oppose the government at home. The ultimate aim was also originally a foreign idea: democracy.

Alien creeds—Confucianism, Christianity, democracy—often come to mean something different once they are transplanted in Korean soil. They tend to be, as it were, purified and infused with uncompromising sincerity. It is as though Koreans are always at pains to prove their worth, indeed their legitimacy as a culture, by pushing ideas that trickled down from outside civilizations to their extremes. Democracy, instead of being, as the Thai human rights lawyer put it, "the right to think critically before accepting things," becomes an expression of dogmatic faith with Korean radicals. Christ, it seems, is always reborn in Korea. (The members of the Unification Church, or "Moonies," believe this to be literally true. To them the Rev. Moon Sun Myong is the Messiah. Though perhaps more popular abroad than in South Korea itself, Moonie-ism is a peculiarly Korean faith.)

Radical students refuse to compromise on principles of democracy, as they see them, for that would sully the moral purity which legitimizes their rule as the conscience of the nation. Just how they define those principles is less clear than their almost talismanic adherence to the word itself: "democracy." Chun Doo Hwan's government claimed to believe in democracy too, but the official concept of the word was often as vague and as uncompromising as that of the students: anybody who spoke out against the government was regarded as "undemocratic," if not "communist."

Kim Dae Jung talked about democracy constantly, but one searched his prison letters in vain for a definition beyond moral platitudes: "Democracy is government by the people . . . It is the politics in which people grow." In fact, everything in Kim's writings points to a very Korean concept of politics. The right to rule belongs to the man of virtue: his legitimacy, his Mandate of Heaven, so to speak, lies in his benevolence. This is, of course, precisely what Park Chung Hee saw as the "basic principle of politics and religion throughout Korea's five thousand years of history."

"I hate America," said one campus activist. Why? "Because America stops democracy in Korea." Why would America want to do that? "I don't know." One is often told —by Kim Dae Jung, among others—that only with true democracy in South Korea can the Korean peninsula be reunified. A variation of this is that real democracy can only come once reunification is achieved. This is presumably what the man who hates America means: With reunification the Americans can go home and democracy will no longer be stopped.

Gregory Henderson wrote in his *The Politics of the Vortex* that Korean student protest, based upon purist interpretations of foreign ideas, goes back to the fifteenth century. Students at the National Academy, sons of the administrative elite, regarded Buddhism, with its emphasis on religious merit, as hopelessly outdated, and favored Confucianism as a state ideology stressing public morals. They supported "the extreme Confucianist reforms of the young official Cho Kwang-jo, and when he fell in the purge of 1519, they 'forced their way through the gates of the palace compound and carried to the very door of the king's residence their lamentations and protestations that the accused was innocent.' "*

It would be a dangerous historicism simply to substitute "democracy" for neo-Confucianism, and Kim Dae Jung for Cho Kwang-jo, but the principle of student protest is similar: in the fifteenth century (Henderson writes) "students played active political roles in supporting 'justice', often in terms of the theory and dogma of a political system artificially adopted from a 'superior' nation."

The feeling that Korea is inferior because it does not match up to the abstract ideals acquired through foreign learning is made worse by the officially encouraged practice of constantly comparing South Korea with the most advanced countries of the world, particulary Japan and the United States. It is an old habit, formed over centuries of being a small culture on the borders of Chinese civilization. This is combined with an equally official antidote: a continuous campaign to be patriotic, to be proud of the unique Korean culture, the most scientific and best writing system in the world, the dubious five thousand years of history, the unique Korean spirit, and so on and so forth. This is hammered home in the newspapers, where earnest

---

* Henderson quotes from an unpublished dissertation by Edward W. Wagner.

students win official approval by expressing such sentiments as this: "Now is the time to see the renaissance of our own spirit among college students who have blindly sought Western styles for a long time. Should a thought like mine occur in every student's mind, we could succeed in achieving the spirit of our ancestors. When these traditional values once again take form, the development of our nation will be realized."

Roughly the same message is propagated through institutions like the Academy of Korean Studies. And it is celebrated in folk custom contests, held in baseball stadiums, where people dress up as farmers or fishermen, are transported in fake fishing boats on wheels, and perform folk dances en masse. One such folk dance, the Sodongpae, was traditionally performed by young boys. It is now practiced by a group of old men, the only ones who remember how to do it.

The traditional spirit is promoted in an artificial folk village outside Seoul, where men and women in traditional costumes apply themselves to traditional crafts and stage traditional wedding parades and perform traditional dances. Much of this folk revivalism was initiated by Park Chung Hee for political reasons. He liked to foster the "particular ethics of the Korean people, who have never quite separated the idea of the individual and the state." It was his way of defining Korean democracy.

One of Park's supporters in the attempt to restore Korean ethics was Dr. Ahn Hosang, the first Minister of Education of the South Korean republic. He studied philosophy in Germany and Japan before the war and wrote many books on Korean history. We had tea at his house in Seoul. We spoke in a mixture of German, Japanese, and Korean. Dr. Ahn would leap up every so often to find a book or article of his to illustrate a point. All his writings, it seems, seek to prove one thing: Koreans, far from being a peripheral culture on the edge of Chinese civilization, were actually the original race of East Asia and the founders of China. "Confucius, he was Korean. We Koreans built the Great Wall. *Alles war koreanisch.*" Dr. Ahn, like other nationalist scholars, wishes to purge Korean history of colonial Japanese influence. The point here is racial homogeneity. "We Koreans have 5,000 years of history. The Japanese said it was only 2,190 years old, while they claim that their own history goes back 2,600 years. So if we believe, as they do, that we have common ancestors, they would be our elder brothers. *Das ist ja Unsinn*. Our ancestry goes back to Tangun, who established our country on October 3, 2333 B.C." There was a picture of Tangun on the professor's wall: a hirsute figure in a Chinese robe.

Tangun is still venerated as a god by a fair number of Koreans, who believe that Tangun's message of peace will one day unite the world. It is yet another instance of the Korean desire to seek universal values in their own uniqueness. In this way, they are very much like their Japanese mentors before the war. Whether Tangun really existed has been a matter of great and acrimonious debate among Korean scholars. The Tangunists, encouraged by the government, won a battle, if not the war. In new Korean textbooks the divine bear-man is no longer called mythical, but "legendary, based on fact."

"This is not good enough," said another historian, Park Song Su, a researcher at the Academy of Korean Studies. I asked him how he could possibly prove the existence of a prehistorical figure first documented in Chinese in the thirteenth century as a mythical king. There is plenty of proof, he said, and he produced a sheaf of newspaper articles, all by Professor Park himself. He pointed at the pictures of ancient rocks, shards, holy trees, and other relics. "All Korean," he explained, "all uniquely Korean." He had found similar relics in Japan, which proved that Japanese culture came from Korea. And all this started before Tangun. But did Tangun exist? Of course Tangun existed: "We Koreans know it is true." Why was it so important to prove this point? "Why, because the Japanese tried to deny it." Then the conversation turned to homogeneity again. "The Japanese say that we Koreans are mixed with Chinese and Japanese. What would you, as a Dutchman, think if people said the Dutch were mixed with Negroes? We must prove that the Japanese are wrong. We are not mixed. We are not bastards."

I wondered what my interpreter, a young Korean woman working for an American advertising company, made of this. She was cosmopolitan, spoke good English, believed in democracy; she had expressed sympathy for the student demonstrators. But she thought Professor Park had a point. "Our history is distorted by Christian academics who deny that Tangun was real," she told me later.

I was reminded of a discussion I had had with another young Korean woman, a highly "Westernized" intellectual, fluent in English and French, who had lived in Paris. We were driving through the countryside of Cholla province, its lush hills dotted with tombstones, when she suddenly announced that her family line could be traced all the way back to the Chinese sage Mencius, who lived in the third century before Christ. I thought she was joking and laughed, whereupon she flew into a hurt rage: Westerners may not understand these things, but, she could assure me, Koreans attach great importance to bloodlines, and her connection to Mencius could be proven by family documents. Having a long trip ahead of us, I elected to say no more.

There are Koreans who see all this as nonsense. The disturbing thing is that they are finding it difficult to say so in public. In the political climate of intense nationalism, in conservative government circles as well as among the radicalized students, liberal skepticism is quickly branded as unpatriotic. It is not surprising that, according to a liberal historian in Seoul, Dr. Ahn's ideas find a ready audience among left-wing students as well as among reactionary extremists.

Some people get so carried away with folkishness that it dominates their daily lives. Han Chang Gi, a sophisticated magazine editor in Seoul, known as a liberal and a friend of the radical poet Kim Chi Ha, pointed his steel chopstick at a bowl of fish on the table of a traditional Korean restaurant.

The bowl was not Korean enough for him: it was influenced by the Japanese style. He explained how he grew up in a small village in the 1940s. He worshipped modern Japanese houses with electric lights. He was ashamed of thatched Korean roofs. His schoolteacher, playing Western songs taught by the Japanese on a brand-new organ, seemed like a deity. He was ashamed of hearing his family sing Korean songs. But when he grew up he saw the error he had made. And "as a form of repentance for my shame, I revived folk songs and I edit a magazine which is truly Korean, with Korean subjects written in a Korean style." He lives in a Korean house, with nothing but Korean antique furniture, where he eats Korean food and drinks Korean tea in the old Korean manner of a Cholla peasant. Dressed in slacks and an elegant tweed jacket, he crouched on his floor, fussing about with wooden utensils and bamboo tubes. I couldn't read his magazine, so I asked the descendant of Mencius what she thought of it. She said it was "not sincere."

As with everything else, from democracy to religion, the Korean spirit must be upheld with sincerity. The spoon-fed nationalism promoted for decades by the country's rulers has not led to a more cosmopolitan outlook among their critics: on the contrary, radicals have become more intensely, more sincerely nationalistic.

What about the tens of thousands of students sitting in coffee shops, flipping through Japanese fashion magazines, discussing American films, listening to melancholy Korean songs on the jukebox? The official Korean spirit can hardly seem convincing to them. The gap between their intellectual ideals and the spiritual straitjacket of government propaganda is too painfully obvious.* Official exhortations, gold medals, and folk dances are inadequate to mask the gulf between rising expectations and reality. How to define and channel those expectations?

---

* The gap is no longer so acute in the more liberal climate of South Korea today. The press is relatively free and the arts are flourishing. But extreme nationalism still sets the tone, perhaps especially in "progressive" circles.

How to bridge the gap? A Confucian educational system stressing rote learning of "correct" facts makes students singularly ill equipped to deal with the dilemma. The facts disseminated by the government as the correct line are so widely disbelieved that student radicals look with some sympathy to the opposite extreme.

In their zeal for purity, students can be as Confucian as government bureaucrats: something is either absolutely correct or absolutely false. If one decides that the government is the purveyor of falsehood, then the opposite must be true. Hence the North Korean slogans. Hence the student who said, in all seriousness: "We have tried capitalism, why can't we try communism, so we know what it is like?" Moderate professors, who do not like authoritarianism any more than their students, complain that they can no longer reason with the radicals. In the words of one professor: "I am often asked by my students whether violence is justified. If I say no, they think I am being paid by the government. If I say yes, I lose my job.* What can I do? Talk about Jesus?"

A female student wrote in her English-language school newspaper: "In reality it is a really difficult task for us to keep and cultivate truth and purity in our heart. The distance between the real and the ideal worlds puts ourselves in embarrassment. Modern mechanized civilization urges us to be skeptical about the significance of our existence. Hypocrisy and corruption in our inner world lay us in exasperation and discouragement."

It is the kind of exasperation that leads to neurotic forms of rebellion. The tension between shame and chauvinism explodes in Molotov cocktails and extremist fantasies. It is one way of salvaging self-esteem. The government's response in 1986 was, in the words of a senior Education Ministry bureaucrat, to promise "more moral and anti-communist education for students attending elementary and secondary schools . . . This intensified anti-communist education will help students acquire

* Not likely to happen anymore.

correct knowledge and information about North Korean communism."

The psychological flip side of *sadae chuui* is another emotion Koreans like to claim as uniquely theirs, called *han*. Like all words supposed to define the essence of national character, people love to argue endlessly over its exact definition. There is, of course, no foreign word that quite conveys what only Koreans feel, or so one is told. The literal translation of *han* would be "resentment" or "grudge." But that is not quite it. The literary scholar Yi O Ryong, in his book about the subject, entitled (in translation) *The Korean Heart: Essay on the Culture of Han*, describes *han* as a lingering frustration about distant ideals. "The *han* culture," he writes, coming to his definition of the Korean identity, "is a culture which is tortured and downtrodden, but which nevertheless aims at establishing a world of beauty and calm—a spiritual world which might always be out of reach." He goes on to explain that "the day when Koreans are released from their *han*, on that day the world will overflow with pure peace." Again Christ is reborn in Korea. Again the millennium springs from the unique Korean identity.

A more political definition of the word comes from another scholar, the late Suh Nam Dong: "*Han* is a deep awareness of the contradictions in a situation and of the unjust treatment meted out to the people or a person by the powerful. And this feeling of *han* is not just a one-time psychological response to a situation but is an accumulation of such feelings and experiences."

The main focus of *han* is, of course, Japan. It is made quite clear in Korea why. Most historical sites, especially Buddhist temples, bear a conspicuous sign telling the visitor how soldiers of Hideyoshi's invasion army destroyed the original building in 1592. The results of the second wave of Japanese domination of Korea, which began in the last decade of the nineteenth century and was consolidated by formal annexation in 1910,

are even more apparent. Japanese colonialism in Korea was a
mixture of brutal military rule and a *mission civilisatrice*, of
callous exploitation and remarkably efficient economic modernization. Of these elements it was the civilizing mission that
hurt the Koreans most. Being forced to adopt Japanese names,
bow to the emperor, worship at Shinto shrines, learn Japanese,
they rightly saw as assaults on the Korean cultural identity.
Centuries of learning to be more civilized than the Japanese by
being "purer" adherents of Chinese civilization were undone.

Most painful of all was that much of the Korean elite was
recruited by the Japanese rulers and, within strict limits, benefited from Japanese modernization. This aspect of the past is
being deleted from the national memory: there is little mention
in South Korean textbooks of the extensive pro-Japanese movement, the Ilchinhoe, in the first decade of this century, described
by Gregory Henderson as "Korea's first successful political
party." Instead there are many pages emphasizing "National
Suffering." The literary critic Ahn Woo Sik wrote in a Japanese
weekly journal that the colonial period was almost completely
ignored in Korean novels until the late 1960s. The common
explanation is that Korean writers did not wish to remember
that nightmarish period. The real reason, says Ahn, is more
subtle: "It was also because of our feelings of shame at not
having been able to resist the Japanese invaders."

When a Japanese brings up the subject of Korean ambivalence and collaboration, it is met with outrage in South Korea.
When a Korean pop song became a hit in Japan some years
ago, Korean newspapers saw this as a plot to unleash a Japanese
cultural invasion of the Korean peninsula. A newspaper editor
named Kim Dae Jung (no relation to the politician) wrote that
"to dominate the world in the next century, Japan must first
dominate Asia. To do this, it must patch up relations with
South Korea. However, in this day and age, the old imperialist
methods will not wash. Instead, Japan will laugh with us, sing
with us, and make us assimilate their culture." Japanese education has left such a mark on educated Koreans now in their

fifties and sixties that hating the Japanese seems also to mean hating part of themselves. To wipe out the national shame, young South Koreans must oppose their fathers and grandfathers, who compromised their sincerity.

A schoolmaster of about sixty kindly offered to help as my interpreter in Kwangju. We spoke in Japanese. I am always a little embarrassed to have to communicate with Koreans in Japanese; it is like using Russian to get around in Poland. But he did not seem to mind. He told me how he had been dragged off to Japan in 1941 to work in a factory in Nagoya. Koreans were treated like animals, he said. When the factory was bombed by the Americans, Japanese got clothes and rice rations, while Koreans were left to fend for themselves. He ended up in a camp, where he was half starved and regularly beaten by guards. There were tears in his eyes as he told his story, but after a moment of silence he cheered up and asked about a Japanese film star popular during the war. He had loved her films. Was she still alive? And what about Hasegawa Kazuo or Iriye Takako or Tanaka Kinuyo? He complained about the price of subscribing to Japanese periodicals these days. He loved Japanese literature, which he preferred to Korean books. He apologized profusely to me, a European, for his rusty Japanese.

Koreans try to hide or blot out the Japanese past in a number of symbolic ways. The old Japanese capitol building, built in the shape of the first of two Chinese characters that mean "Japan," was erected by the Japanese smack in front of the royal palace in Seoul, much of which had to be destroyed to make space. After the Japanese left, an old Korean gate was put up in front of the capitol, to obscure it from the public view. After much debate over whether the capitol should be pulled down it was decided to turn it into the National Museum instead. This seemed sensible until the next controversy: One of the murals in the building depicts an old Japanese legend. It would have to be deleted somehow, just as a number of handsome cherry-blossom trees had to be uprooted from a

palace garden when it became known that they were planted
by the Japanese.

But no matter how hard Koreans try to blot it out, Japan
keeps on reappearing. Modern Seoul looks more like Tokyo
every day, with its coffee shops, its bric-a-brac modern buildings, and its neon-lit pleasure areas tucked away behind the
steel and glass. Like Tokyo, Seoul is an odd mixture of the
rigidly regimental and the utterly random. Not only are the
police force, the military, and the bureaucracy modeled after
the prewar Japanese system, but Japanese modernity is to be
seen in magazine and newspaper layouts and in TV programs
and films, despite the fact that Japanese films and TV are effectively banned in South Korea.

Japanese books, on the other hand, are available. The president of a Seoul university was quoted in a newspaper article
as saying that some of the books, "imbued with potentially
dangerous ideas refuting traditional values and thoughts, could,
if fully blown, jeopardize the sovereignty and basic nationalistic
views of the Korean people . . . Under any circumstances, when
rationale and self-control are uprooted, dire consequences visit
upon a society, making the public bewildered and confused."

Japanese culture is especially bewildering and confusing, say
the moral guardians of the people, whether of the right or the
left, because it appeals to the masses, while Western culture
influences the elite. Some members of the elite like to point out
how much closer educated Koreans are to Western culture than
the Japanese. They point to the brilliant Korean soloists in
classical European music, to the influence of Western literature,
and so on. I was taken to a restaurant by a well-known Korean
novelist in his sixties. We ate steaks and drank French wine.
He asked the waiter to turn up the music. It was a Korean
violinist playing a Bartók violin concerto. The author closed
his eyes in rapture. "Ah," he whispered, "the Korean spirit."

But even the various forms of popular "Westernization" are
often filtered through Japan: the coffee shops, fashion, baseball,
popular music, TV variety shows. The only two habits that are

recognizably American in Korea are the chewing of gum and the regrettable use of mayonnaise on salad—and even that may have come from Japan. There can be few peoples in the world so influenced by a country they profess to hate so much. The Japanese have a huge cultural center in Seoul. Many Koreans make use of its facilities. But it must be guarded day and night, lest feelings of *han* get out of control.

This sense of historical victimhood, the constant undercurrent of resentment, quickly leads to neurotic xenophobia. There is a book widely read by students, written by Paek Ki Won, entitled (literally translated) *Essay on the People's Anti-Japanese Struggle*. It is, as the title implies, mostly an anti-Japanese diatribe. But in the chapter on reunification of the Korean peninsula the discussion becomes anti-foreign in a much wider sense. The chapter is addressed, in true Korean style, to the author's mother, who was separated from him during the Korean War: "Mother, why did we have to suffer for so long? We went out to buy a pair of football boots and never saw each other again. Why did this happen? Our simple love has been smashed. Mother, who is our common enemy? It is those damned foreigners! . . . When the life of our country is cut in two, our race will cease to exist. Our race can no longer contribute to the development of world history. On the contrary, our country will be like a nail stuck into the flow of history. Mother, who will be happiest about this and use it to their advantage? Those damned foreigners!"

During a campus riot at Korea University in Seoul I asked a student whether he spoke English. "This is Korea, you must speak Korean!" he screamed, and stomped off. Some of his friends were more forthcoming. They explained why they thought reunification was not just desirable but inevitable. The Vietnamese did it, so why can't we? I pointed out the sad plight of southern Vietnamese today. "That won't happen to us. We are a strong people." How can the two economic and political systems be reconciled? "Nationalism!"

*   *   *

I arrived in Pusan, the port city of the southeast, in August 1987. My fellow passengers on the ferry from Japan were mostly Korean nationals living in Japan; the older ones still spoke Japanese with Korean accents, while the younger ones, born in Japan, spoke perfect Japanese but appeared not to understand any Korean; all were treated brusquely by the Korean customs officers, as if they were traitors to their race.

The customs people were polite to me and showed a great interest in my books. They opened a Japanese weekly magazine which featured photographs of a young Japanese woman novelist whose main subject is sex with black men. The pictures showed her nude, in the company of several black GIs, frolicking on a beach in Okinawa. "This is not our custom," said the customs officer, and he threw the magazine into a tray, from where it was swiftly retrieved by another customs man, who disappeared with it into his office. A Japanese book entitled *Anti-Japanese Thought in South Korea* then became the object of close scrutiny. Was this anti-government? I was asked. Is it pro-North Korea? Who invited me to come to South Korea? Would I please wait until the book was thoroughly checked? After half an hour the officer returned with the book. His verdict came with a smile: "It is anti-Japanese book. It is very good book."

The book, in fact, was a collection of articles published in the 1970s by academics, critics, and left-wing student radicals concerned with the "national identity." One contributor, speaking for the National Students League, wrote that now (in 1971) "our country is losing its anti-Japanese spirit, a priceless jewel earned through the endless suffering during our unspeakably dark history. This loss will shake the foundation of our national soul."

I had returned to South Korea to see a new monument to this "priceless jewel," indeed to the national soul: the Independence Hall. The *Korea Times* called it a "national shrine." It was opened by President Chun Doo Hwan on August 15, the anniversary of Korean liberation from Japan. It ought to have been opened the year before, in time for the Asian Games, but only eleven days before the ceremony the main hall burned down because of faulty wiring (Japanese wiring, rumor had it). Several high government officials resigned in disgrace. This time, the opening took place without a hitch, except for the absence of Kim Dae Jung. He had been invited to the ceremony, but refused to come, because he was to be seated in the benches for cabinet members and lawmakers, which he thought quite inappropriate. He wanted to be seated in the royal box allotted to the presidential couple and the heads of political parties.

I approached the national shrine several days later, the only foreigner, as far as I could see, in the midst of busloads of people, old and young, many of them sunburned country folk, streaming toward the hall from all directions, leaving a trail of soft-drink cans, plastic bags, and chewing-gum wrappers. Two Buddhist monks prostrated themselves in the direction of the shrine, banging little drums. Hawkers sold snacks and Korean flags.

The main building, a huge edifice in the shape of a Chinese temple—"1.2 times larger than Peking's famed Tiananmen Gate," said the brochure—was called the Grand Hall of the Nation. Inside this hall was a large sculpture of nine nude human figures pointing at what one assumes is the glorious future. According to the official news release, it was entitled "The Indomitable Koreans." The *Korean Times* called it "Koreans, the Unyielding Spirit." The sculpture was illuminated by twenty-four colored spotlights that revolved to the accompaniment of Wagnerian music, mixed with the recorded sounds of cheering crowds, banging drums, and neighing horses.

The Independence Hall was inspired by a controversy in 1982 over Japanese textbooks, which glossed over—"distorted," say the Koreans—colonial history. A national campaign was launched to collect money to build the hall. The idea was to set the historical record straight.

At almost every step the visitor is reminded of Korean martyrdom at the hands of foreigners, especially the Japanese.

There are huge blown-up photographs of mutilated corpses of Korean freedom fighters, close-up pictures of wounds inflicted by Japanese floggings, displays of Japanese torture instruments, and—the most popular item in the permanent exhibition—a waxworks diorama of Japanese torture chambers, with bloody effigies enduring water treatment or having their fingernails pulled out. The crowds jostled each other to get a closer look. Children shrieked and laughed. An old woman in Korean dress shouted at me: "Japan did this! Japan did this!"

"We will continue to collect the historical relics," said the Minister of Culture and Information, "to supplement the structure and make it a training ground for the education of national spirit." Or as the editorial of the *Korean Herald* put it: "The Independence Hall should stand tall and long to inspire Koreans with a keen sense of national identity."

The Independence Hall seemed a melancholy monument and, insofar as all national cults are abhorrent, rather appalling. Not only does it present history as myth—all national cults do that—but it is largely a negative myth. It is truly as if Koreans will stop feeling Korean if they lose the "precious jewel" of hatred for the Japanese; as if they cannot define their national uniqueness in terms other than institutionalized xenophobia. The Independence Hall is less an expression of independence than of *sadae chuui* and *han*—the one being a natural concomitant of the other.

Then there is the style: the classical columns spouting eternal flames, the heroes draped in flags, the monumental scale, reminding one of masses packed in football stadiums forming pictures of great leaders and national symbols by holding up colored cards in unison. In front of the Grand Hall of the Nation, said a news release, "is a stone-faced plaza where up to 120,000 people can assemble." It is a nauseating thought.

It is interesting how in their respective cults of national identity Pyongyang and Seoul end up expressing it in similar ways. It is an international style called Socialist Realism in the Soviet Union; it is the style of Mussolini's Rome, Albert Speer's Berlin,

Sukarno's Jakarta. Joseph Goebbels described it as "steely romanticism," the aesthetic of "healthy SA man." It is pure kitsch, as the forms of religious worship are used to express a political concept. It appears modern; it is in fact a product of the modern age, but it is at the same time a regression. To a European today, the worship of nationhood seems absurd, a nineteenth-century anachronism. To many Koreans it seems normal, which explains, perhaps, why the architects could take the Independence Hall seriously, why they appeared to miss the obvious stylistic parallels with countries they are supposed to abhor. But then again, this may be appropriate. Korea's fate is to always resemble the powers that threaten her.

5

Searching for Soul

JAPAN

The blinking TV sets in every corner, emitting loud game shows or commercials; the long queues in front of the green lights that say "Aliens"; the coy twittering voices from hidden loudspeakers imploring the travelers to be careful, to hold on to the rails, to keep on moving, not to forget anything; the neatly uniformed young porters, like discotheque soldiers, going about their business with rigorous efficiency; the squat provincials with golden teeth, white patent-leather shoes and golfing pants, loaded with Napoleon and VSOP; the South Korean tourists and Filipina girls abused by officious immigration officers; the unrelenting Muzak, occasionally interrupted by Vivaldi's *Four Seasons* . . . Japan.

Arriving in Japan always fills me with feelings of ambivalence. It is like coming home to a country which, to me, can never be home. I spent my twenties in Tokyo. Everything is familiar: the language, the manners, the advertisements, the TV programs. Japan is part of me, yet I can never feel part of it. This may have something to do with me. But it is also in the nature of that most insular of nations. It fills me with love and horror, which alternate and sometimes even coincide, the one sometimes, in a perverse way, feeding on the other. Japan looks the most modern society in Asia, politically, culturally, aesthetically. It is also among the most archaic. It is one of the most open societies—foreigners can go there, live there, marry, and prosper. But it remains in many ways as exclusive as Burma. Japan is "Westernized," yet, somehow, the country in East Asia least touched by the West. I am never sorry to leave, yet I always yearn to go back.

We were in a tiny bar in Tokyo with room for about eight people. The bar, named La Getee, after a French avant-garde movie, was in a ramshackle, charmingly decayed area of Shinjuku called Golden Gai, which, in the early postwar years, used to be on the fringes of a large black-market and red-light district. Shinjuku, once the raffish meeting place of Tokyo bohemia, is now a shining symbol of Japanese consumerism: block after block of luxurious department stores, high-rise hotels, fashion shops, and discotheques. The raffishness of the old back streets, where I used to go drinking as a student in the 1970s, has been transformed into a commercialized travesty of their former bohemian charm: small porno shops and peep-show parlors and luxurious massage establishments, called "soaplands"—named thus after the Turkish embassy objected to their former name, *toruko*, denoting the usually nonexistent Turkish baths. It has been decided that Golden Gai, too, must make way for progress, and is to be replaced by more office blocks, or fashion boutiques, or possibly a multistory car park.

I had a drink with Yanagimachi Mitsuo, one of the best young filmmakers in Japan. With his bespectacled moon face and his fashionable clothes that never quite suit his chunky frame, Yanagimachi looks like an intellectual country boy. He is still unaffected by the cynicism that pervades the entertainment industry. Mediocrity still angers him. "How can we make films here anymore?" he said after a few glasses of whiskey. "What can I say about all these salarymen and their boring lives? I love Japan. I really do. But there is something rotten

about it now. Just look around you." I looked around, somewhat blurry-eyed myself, and saw the "mama-san." She nodded
and said he was quite right. She was used to hearing the
Weltschmerz of her regulars. "I look at myself in the mirror
and I can see I look silly in a suit. What can we do? Start
wearing kimono again? That would be ridiculous." Mama-san
poured him another whiskey and water.

His last film, called *Fire Festival*, was about a hunter living
in a small village threatened by corporate men from the city
who wish to turn the area into a holiday resort. The hunter
clings to a kind of mystical communion with nature, praying
to ancient, half-forgotten gods. In the last scene he murders his
entire family in a fit of rage—against what? "He retained something we have lost," said Yanagimachi.

We are not really asked to admire the murderous hunter.
We are made to feel ambivalent. The killings are not glorified
in any way, but the film does express a certain empathy with
the hunter's somewhat ill-defined motives. Something we lost.
Mishima Yukio elicits such emotions in many Japanese. Few
admired his theatrical suicide. Indeed, his final deed was ridiculed as a flamboyant anachronism. Yet he made—still
makes—many Japanese feel uneasy. His implied motives—not
his ranting on about the emperor and the samurai ethic—no,
his implied motives struck a chord; namely, the feeling that
something was lost in modern, commercialized Japan, something that past heroes thought was worth dying for. Exactly
what is lost remains vague, something to do with "sincerity,"
"spirit," a "pure" Japan without foreigners, in short, a pristine
Japanese identity.

There is certainly nothing pristine about Tokyo, which was
almost entirely destroyed twice in this century, once by an
earthquake in 1923, which struck just as people were cooking
their lunches in houses still made of wood, and once by incen-
diary bombs in 1945.

Tokyo is not the real Japan, one is often told. Well, maybe
not. But it is not foreign or even cosmopolitan either. It *is*

fashionable, though. There is something neurotic about the speed of Tokyo fashions. A new ice-cream parlor from California opens up. For a month or so, people queue around the block. After that the place is virtually abandoned. It is the same with clothes, films, writers. Monthly and even weekly magazines specialize in information on the latest fads in Western capitals. Not in the form of reviews or even descriptions, but simply lists: boutiques in London, cafés in Paris, discotheques in Los Angeles, restaurants in New York. Like Alice Through the Looking Glass, fashionable Japanese are admonished to run faster, faster, ever faster to keep up with the outside metropole. This is also true of intellectual styles. The cultural critic Kato Shuichi wrote that "imported Western ideologies have long deprived many Japanese of the ability to think. New thoughts have been imported one after another, made popular, and then forgotten without leaving any trace of influence. Those who run around in pursuit of the imported thoughts have had the illusion that running around is thinking."

It is perhaps the neurosis of a country always stuck on the periphery of a great civilization. Koreans and Japanese, when China was still the metropole, often engaged in a game of one-upmanship as to which was closer, more clued in to the latest trends in Changan or Nanjing. The winner would be considered the more sophisticated. The conservative politician and novelist Ishihara Shintaro once called it "the hunger mentality": "The whole Japanese nation seems to become one vast mirror receiving and reflecting the light from another civilization. The pattern shows a psychological tendency to grab for all possible information from the outside and greedily absorb it."

And yet Japan is hardly nondescript. Its character is overwhelming. On the surface the Japanese have achieved what all non-Western nations strive for: they are modern without being fake Westerners. The image of modern Japan, or rather the kaleidoscope of images appears unmistakably Japanese even when patterned after alien models. This Japanese modern style is not just exported to the former members of the Japanese empire, but is swiftly replacing American influence in Hong Kong, Bangkok, and other parts of Asia. I saw pinups of Japanese TV stars in Rangoon and Peking. This is partly because of economic strength, but also because the Japanese style—the baggy clothes, the sugary pop songs, the lachrymose dramas, the stylized TV variety shows—seems more congenial. The style is usually glossier than its Western models, more predictable, and in the case of pop music, less aggressive. But this doesn't compensate for the Japanese sense of loss. For none of this modern pop culture originated in Japan. As one can see so clearly in Taipei and Seoul, Tokyo acts as a conduit for Western fashion, relaying it to the rest of Asia, after filtering it through an Oriental sensibility. It would perhaps be more accurate to say that the Japanese re-create Western fashions according to their own taste. They Japanize what they begin by mimicking.

The popular Japanese press likes to measure time in "booms." The latest fashion, relentlessly pushed on TV, slavishly followed by millions, almost always develops into a boom. A "Mona Lisa" boom, when the painting was exhibited in Tokyo, prompted at least one young woman to pay a plastic surgeon to fix her face to resemble Da Vinci's model. The gourmet boom saw countless young people, dressed to the nines, stiffly wielding knives and forks to eat exorbitantly expensive European food in restaurants decorated with Toulouse-Lautrec posters and plastic stag heads on the walls.

The American writer Donald Richie, who has lived in Japan since the war, wondered in one of his essays "why the Japanese went to all the trouble of franchising a Disneyland in the suburbs when the capital itself is so superior a version." Re-creating foreign forms, often stripping them of their content, or intended meaning, has lent to Tokyo that air of jerry-built fantasy that marks most capitals of Southeast and East Asia, only more so. (The same might be said, with some mischievous exaggeration, of all foreign influences in Japan, from Chinese Buddhism to European political institutions: façades, gutted of their original meaning, serving purely indigenous purposes.)

Tokyo is a city of façades, of plaster Trevi fountains, concrete medieval castles and Olde English pubs. My favorite coffee shop in Tokyo is a baroque French ballroom, built under a railway station, with plastic cherubs and wall paintings of Greek gods and Napoleon's coronation. This is more than mere imitation. Rather, it is taking the visual essence—in Japanese eyes, that is—and re-creating it in miniature. (The Japanese, unlike the Americans, do not go in for oversized kitsch; "the biggest . . . in the world" is not for them, while "the smallest . . . " often is.)

One of the most extraordinary pieces of re-creation can be seen in Kagoshima, the city in southern Kyushu where Zero fighters trained for their attack on Pearl Harbor. A right-wing logging millionaire from that city, who had made a fortune supplying sleepers for the Manchurian Railroad, expressed the desire after the war to build a paradise on earth. And so he had a hot-spring resort built on the beach of Kagoshima in the form of a tropical arcadia. It is a bizarre microcosm of Hawaii. The hotel is staffed by Hawaiian dancers in hula skirts who greet the guests, all identically decked out in uniforms with palm-tree motifs, with loud "alohas." There is a Hawaiian dance hall, a Hawaiian restaurant, where the waiters dance around the fire after dinner, hollering like banshees; there is also a quasi-Hawaiian jungle, filled with trees and jungle foliage that hide plaster animals staring at the frolicking couples taking their hot baths in a space the size of a large aircraft hangar. One suspects that many people prefer this artificial paradise to the real thing. The synthetic is traditionally favored over the organic, the miniature considered more beautiful than the original model.

What is most remarkable, however, is that what booms and fashions have done to foreign forms also applies to Japanese traditions. Recently there has been a spate of Japanese booms: a hot-spring boom, especially popular with young single women, a Kabuki boom, an Old Tokyo boom, a Japanese restaurant boom. The effect is often curious. Traditions are revamped and given a theme-park gloss. The Japanese form often appears as fake as the French gourmet restaurant. This is not a uniquely Japanese phenomenon, of course; mock Tudor and Ye Olde English tea shops in Britain are much the same thing. But it is not so much the modern vulgarization of traditional forms that is disturbing, but the idea of tradition as just another transient fashion, another form without substance. One sometimes wonders whether anything in modern Japan has lasting value, whether anything substantial can visibly last. There is a rootlessness, a constant evanescence about Japanese sophistication which explains, perhaps, both the melancholy Japanese love for fleeting beauty, for visible decay, and the anxiety about cultural and spiritual loss.

In 1942, just three months after the attack on Pearl Harbor, a famous young writer, Ango Sakaguchi, wrote a startling essay entitled "A Personal View of Japanese Culture." He began by quoting foreigners extolling the beauty of "traditional" Japan and lamenting modern vulgarity. Jean Cocteau, on a visit to Japan, had asked why Japanese no longer wore kimonos. "What is tradition?" countered Ango. "What is national character? Is there something inherent in our character that gave the Japanese a definite predisposition to invent the kimono and wear it? . . . What the hell is the kimono anyway? We came across Western clothes a thousand years late, that's all." Ango observed that he was not the only one in Japan who favored modern change. "Most Japanese, when they see the old look of their native places destroyed and new Western-style buildings appear, are happy, not sad. We need new transport facilities and elevators. A more convenient life is surely more important than traditional beauty . . . All we want are the necessities of life. Even if our ancient culture disappeared entirely, there would still be life. As long as there is life, our distinctive character will remain in good shape."

Ango's essay is all the more remarkable if one considers the time it was written. In 1942, the cult of the unique and ancient Japanese spirit was at its hysterical peak. Western influence, officially regarded as spiritual pollution, was proscribed, as far as that was still possible (German culture, however, as long as it was "healthy," Richard Wagner, say, was permitted). And far from being in good shape, the distinctive character of the Japanese had been the focus of anguished debate and soul-searching among intellectuals for at least a century. Japan, alone among Asian nations, had been so quickly and successfully modernized that she could match many Western powers in military might. But the price for this was a permanent crisis of identity, manifested in wild swings from worshipful, indeed humiliating, emulation to violent rejection of the Western world. The more Japan imitated the West, the more national pride had to be saved by a mythology of pure national spirit.

In the second half of the nineteenth century Japanese rulers were faced with two choices: they could "throw out the barbarians," as many nationalists proposed, and risk a military conflict with enemies who were much better armed; or they could keep the barbarians at bay by emulating them. The latter course was eventually decided upon and the Japanese went about it with characteristic zeal. One writer argued that English should replace the Japanese language; an ambassador to the United States, later to become Minister of Education, wanted Japanese to marry American women to improve the racial stock. The Japanese emperor, hitherto a virtual recluse in the court of Kyoto, posed for a photograph in a splendid French-style military uniform, an ostrich-plumed hat by his side. To compete with the imperialists, Japan built her own empire, complete with railways, factories, and imposing imperial buildings. Surplus energy was unleashed in continental wars, where Japanese soldiers fought in Hungarian cavalry uniforms. The Sino-Japanese war in 1895 was described by the Japanese Foreign Minister as "a collision between the new civilization of the West and the old civilization of East Asia."

> Never, since the country was founded, has our national glory shone so brightly as it does today;

Never, since the country was founded, has the fame of our countrymen been so lofty and grand as today.

How fortunate, how happy we are to be Japanese, alive in such
glorious times.

[1895, Toyama Chuzan, trans. Donald Keene, in *Dawn to the
West*]

Asia's youngest imperialists posed for pictures in topees and
white suits. Traditional arts gradually froze in their pre-modern
styles. Intellectuals tried to replace the values of a disowned
past with political or religious values—Christianity and, later,
Marxism—which promised universal validity. These values
were not only "modern"; they were a link to wider civilization
beyond the narrow Japanese borders. In 1907, the writer Ari-
shima Takeo met Kropotkin in London: "I forgot that I was
in England, that I was a Japanese, and even where in space his
study might be situated. I listened like a docile little child sitting
by the knee of an aged parent to his tranquil and compassionate
words" (trans. Donald Keene, in *Dawn to the West*). Educators
turned to Samuel Smiles's *Self-Help* or Johann Friedrich Herbart's *sittliche Ideen* (moral ideas). "Ah, Herbart!" wrote one
enthusiastic pedagogue. "Awake or asleep, we cannot forget
the name of Herbart. Ah, Herbart! Day and night we do not
fail to propound the theories of Herbart."

Basil Hall Chamberlain, the British scholar of things Japanese, noted in 1891: "Whatever you do, do not expatiate, in
the presence of Japanese of the new school, on those old, quaint
and beautiful things Japanese which rouse our most genuine
admiration . . . generally speaking, the educated Japanese have
done with their own past. They want to be somebody else and
something else other than what they have been and still partly
are."

But it never really worked. Many of the writers who agonized
over their souls, Westernized but not Western, ended up committing suicide. Cultural conflict may not have been the only
reason, but it certainly did not help. The confusion was bound

to result in a nativist reaction, often in the minds of the very
same people who had promoted Western civilization before.
And no matter how much Japanese tried to separate Western
technique from Japanese spirit, the break with the past could
never be papered over.

> *Blow, come on, blow,*
> *Cold wind down from Chichibu,*
> *Blow, rolling down the mountains!*
> *The world's at its last gasp, come on, blow!*
> *Blow on my back!*
> *A cat is yowling in my head.*
> *Somewhere somebody is serving up Rodin for bait.*
> *Coca-Cola THANK YOU VERY MUCH*
> *Ginza Second Ward, Third Ward, and Owari Street,*
> *Electric car, electric light, electric wires, electric power . . .*
> ["Madman's Poem," 1914, Takamura Kotaro, trans.
> Donald Keene, in *Dawn to the West*]

One wonders what Sakaguchi Ango would have thought of
Tokyo today. He died in 1955, ravaged by drugs and alcohol.
He never saw the Economic Miracle. Now the Japanese have
far more than necessities. They have the world's fastest trains,
the largest department stores, an average of two TV sets per
household, artificial singing birds in underground shopping
malls, nouvelle cuisine, giant video screens blasting rock music
over broad avenues lined with so-called fashion buildings filled
with the latest products from St.-Germain and Santa Monica;
they have high-tech restaurants, Colonel Sanders, Häagen-
Dazs, and Maxim's. They have Disneyland.

According to a poll in 1986, more than 80 percent of the
inhabitants of two Tokyo neighborhoods (one middle-class and
one working-class) thought the Japanese were "one of the
greatest races in the world." More than 70 percent thought
that Japanese society was among the best in the world. Echoing
Ango's words, the critic Kato Shuichi wrote that "the mass of

people accept our hybrid culture just as it is . . . They never think of purifying this hybrid culture . . . It is only the intellectuals who have that ambition.

I wonder if he is right. To be sure, one finds little resistance to the physical mishmash of Japanese modernity, the film-set architecture, the raw concrete, the billions of TV screens following you about like blinking eyes. And Japanese intellectuals often seem marginal figures, writing for one another, respected as men of learning, but not taken very seriously by the world at large. Nevertheless, the ambivalence toward the West, toward the mythical Japanese past, the modern anguish articulated by intellectuals, these, I think, are felt by many Japanese, even though they cannot easily express it. The sense of spiritual loss, the question of what it means to be Japanese—what is the essence of Japaneseness?—is probed like a bad tooth, on TV, in popular magazines, as well as in scholarly journals.

In the 1890s, the writer Tokutomi Soho argued that Western science and Eastern morals were fundamentally incompatible, and that Japan's only choice was complete identification with Western modernity. In the same period members of another school of intellectuals believed that Japan had a mission to protect Asian values against a hostile Western world. The frequency with which one still hears echoes of both these opinions today suggests that the debate is far from over.

When I first arrived in Japan I supplemented my student's stipend by teaching English. One of my pupils, called Sato, was a man in his late twenties, an employee of a well-known electronics firm. As far as I knew, he was conventional in every way: married with two small children, educated at a decent private university, on his way to middle management. He was always affable, not a great linguist, but intelligent. After lessons he would take me out drinking. He liked singing, so we would go to places where he could stand on a podium with a microphone.

After a few drinks, still quite affable, he would start to bait me. My Japanese was by no means perfect and there were many

words I did not know. "I bet you don't know what . . . means,"
he would say. When indeed I had to confess my ignorance, a
happy smile would appear on his face. "Ah, I thought not."
An alternative would be to ask for the exact equivalent in
English of some Japanese word believed to express a uniquely
Japanese quality. "I bet you have no word in English for *kokoro*." Well, I would say, there are a few words that come
close to describing it, words like "soul," "spirit," "heart." "No,
no, no, one word which means exactly the same." Yes, well,
perhaps that would be difficult. "Ah-ha, I thought so, those
Japanese nuances, no foreigner can ever understand." After
this had gone on for some time, going down the list of unique
Japanese words, he would fall into a morose silence. "This
country is no good," he suddenly blurted out after a long pause.
Oh, why not? "No future for my children here. Please take me
with you, to your country." Yes, but why? "We Japanese are
just economic animals." What about the Japanese spirit I had
heard so much about? He waved his hands dismissively. "Economic animals, sex animals, economic animals, sex animals."
This was usually about the time he asked for the bill. When
he turned up for his next lesson, he was his affable self again,
telling me how he had no desire to go abroad. "We Japanese
have nothing to learn from foreigners anymore."

The Japanese spirit. It is a subject of almost obsessive anxiety.
The national soul—how it must be revived, defended, even held
up as a model to the outside world—this nebulous soul is
endlessly discussed by politicians, journalists, and scholars. *Nihonjinron*, or defining Japaneseness, has grown into a huge
intellectual enterprise, responsible for hundreds of books, thousands of articles, TV programs and radio shows. The key word
is "uniqueness"; the uniqueness of Japaneseness which is beyond understanding in terms of Western logic, even though it
can serve as the premise for scientific research. A neurologist
made a name for himself by writing a book about the uniqueness of the Japanese brain, which was uniquely sensitive to the
sounds of temple bells, waterfalls, cicadas, and other natural

vibrations. Again, one wonders how many Japanese take this kind of thing seriously. Whether they do or not, Dr. Tsunoda's book *was* a best-seller. The intense narcissism of *Nihonjinron* is like a national neurosis—and like most neuroses, it is often irrational.

The career of Professor Umehara Takeshi is only a slightly eccentric example. Umehara, a jolly, smiling man with a shock of unkempt hair, often appears on TV or in popular magazines expounding upon the roots of Japaneseness. To add drama to his often mystical points, he likes to be photographed in mystical poses, examining ancient rocks at country shrines, lit by the first beams of dawn or the red glow of sunset.

According to his own account, published in the *Chuo Koron*, a leading intellectual journal, Umehara began as a student of Western philosophy. "Like many cultured Japanese, I turned my back on my native soil and moved to Tokyo, where I cast an admiring eye on Western culture." Then, thirty-five years old, he had a "crisis." He realized that his beloved Western culture was leading mankind to destruction, that the "philosophy underlying modern European culture is basically flawed." The thought struck him that "the only true solution to the impasse of modern civilization, for which European culture is responsible, is to be found in the thinking of Oriental culture, especially Japanese culture."

At the core of Japanese culture is the unique Japanese spirit. To find this spirit in its purest form, Umehara looks back to a kind of Ur Japan, long before it was influenced by China or Korea, back to the earliest stages of the Jomon earthenware culture, about 12,000 years ago. Although Jomon culture lagged behind other civilizations materially, Umehara claims it had a very high "spiritual culture." He admits that it is difficult to know quite what this spiritual culture was, but by studying the ways of the few remaining Ainu people of the far north of Japan, and of the Okinawans down south toward Taiwan, one can find an approximation of the Ur Japanese spirit. (To the intense annoyance of Okinawans, "mainland" Japanese scholars often seek their roots in what they regard as the more primitive pockets of the Japanese isles.) This native spirit, then, still lives on in the hearts of Japanese today. It is merely a matter of stripping off the superficial layers of foreign influence, accumulated over thousands of years, for the Jomon Man to emerge in his pristine spiritual state.

I later asked Professor Park, the Korean academic who found proof for Korean uniqueness in shards he discovered in Okinawa, about Umehara. "A most interesting man," he said. "I agree with most of his ideas, except for one basic misconception." What was that? "The original spirit was not Japanese, but Korean."

Because the earthenware culture had not yet evolved into the next stage, the hunter-gatherer society, the Jomon spirit was unfettered by class divisions, such as plagued Western and Indian civilizations. Instead it was infused with a unique sense of social harmony, a sense with which the Japanese are still uniquely imbued. This prehistoric sense, expressed in the worship of nature, symbolized by sacred mountains, trees, rocks, the sun, and the Japanese emperor, can save the world from the "disease of Western thought which puts man in the center of the universe." (Umehara therefore proposed that the Japanese emperor system was the answer to the world's ecological problems.) Umehara believes that a "reevaluation of Jomon culture is vital, not only for Japan but for the rest of the world, indeed for the sake of mankind."

By an old sleight of hand Umehara has found proof for both Japanese uniqueness and its universality. By turning to the spirit of an undocumented period, Umehara and his fellow believers can reject Western civilization (apart from its useful science and technology) and remain the heirs of universal values. It is a variation of what a far more sophisticated thinker—the novelist Natsume Soseki—said in 1902, when he was living in London, feeling lonely and rejected by the indifferent Western world: "Europe is not the only model. We can be a model too." To claim universality for Japanese mysticism, men like Ume-

hara must have a sense of mission. The world must be converted, for otherwise Japan would not be a civilization, but
simply a culture on the periphery of China or, more to the
point today, the modern Western world.

I am always a bit suspicious when people tell me the real
Japan (or wherever) is in the countryside, the proverbial Village. In some ways I prefer the attitude of Kuma, an artist born
in a village in northern Hokkaido. I traveled with him in a
minibus along the coast of the Inland Sea. We passed through
some of the most spectacularly beautiful scenery in the country,
but Kuma, dressed in his usual dark kimono, would turn his
back to the window and with a note of defiance in his voice
declare the landscape to be a bore. It was perverse, a little
childish, ridiculous even, but I think I understand what he was
trying to say. Japanese love to be nostalgic about the Village,
the real Japan, before "foreign" industrialization ruined it. The
same Japanese, singing childhood songs about rural beauty,
will happily litter the landscape with cans, plastic bags, and
bottles, but to condemn this as hypocrisy is to miss the point;
the songs belong to a world of the imagination, where Coca-
Cola bottles and beer cans do not exist.

In the early 1980s Japanese viewers were enthralled by a TV
soap opera called *Oshin*, which also became enormously popular in China, Hong Kong, and Southeast Asia, especially Singapore. When the then Prime Minister Nakasone visited
Singapore, he commented on the program: "This is, as you
know, the fictionalized story of a woman who steadfastly refused to be daunted by her harsh circumstances and, ever cheer-
ful, turned adversity to advantage as she grew to be a pillar of
strength and compassion. It is no accident that this drama has
been so popular with the peoples of our two countries, for it
is both a testament to the way we must live and a parable of
our capacity to succeed."

Oshin was a well-made, lowbrow counterpart to Edgar
Reitz's *Heimat*, the eleven-part series about the history of a

German village. Reitz's film was a highly sophisticated celebration of the Village, and all its solid rural values. It was also
a not so sophisticated attack on postwar American materialism,
the City, which came to destroy all those healthy country ways.
Oshin followed the same pattern. In the beginning we saw the
poor country girl struggling through the 1920s. Then she suffered patriotically through the war, doing her bit, like everybody else. Then she suffered even more during the American
occupation, with rough GIs walking all over her tatami floors
in their boots. And finally, in the 1960s, she became a rich
businesswoman. But something, naturally, is lost, as, in the last
frame of the long series, she stares into the sunset with an
expression almost of despair. It was a moralistic story, holding
up good, old-fashioned Japanese ethics—"the way we must
live"—as a model for the pampered young. And like *Heimat*,
it was elegiac in tone, lamenting the spiritual loss wrought by
modern materialism.

The ideal, pristine Village always was a fantasy. In the real
world, traditional village life was dirt poor and fraught with
cruel social discrimination. But it is a potent fantasy. Nativist
scholars and politicians identify such half-mythical rural values
as mutual trust, social harmony, communion with nature, sen-
sitivity to the four seasons, temple bells, waterfalls, and cicadas
with Japaneseness. The rule of law, contracts, rationalism, individualism, in short, the City, are Western. The harsh, brutal,
aggressive West, with its single angry God, was born in the dry
desert; the soft, feminine, peaceful East, with its many, sometimes impish, but always pacific gods, was born in the wet rice
fields. This cultural bias, this hankering after *Gemeinschaft*,
can be held by people who in other ways are not especially
anti-urban. Christian love, said former Prime Minister Nakasone Yasuhiro at a political convention, must have come from
Asia, for "how can it have been born in a world which depends
on contracts? The Ten Commandments are a product of desert
life, where 'eye for eye, tooth for tooth' principles prevail."

In a curious dialogue, published as part of a book, Nakasone, the politician, and Umehara, the scholar, seated in front of a golden screen, discussed the role of Japanese culture in the modern world. They tried to reconcile the "wet," harmonious Japanese spirit with modernity: Oriental ethics and Western techniques—"the parable of our capacity to succeed." Western civilization, they both agreed, was a danger to world peace, because of its divisiveness, its pluralism, its dependence on contracts instead of trust. Moreover, said Umehara, the worship of one God had brought tension to the world and could easily lead to war. What was needed was harmony and integration. Only Japan was in the unique position to achieve this aim, as only Japan could boast two thousand years of civilization, while retaining a primeval, harmonious spirit. Indeed, said Nakasone, this spirit is also shaped by our warm and humid climate, and our being blessed with natural forests.

Thus it is that Umehara blames the creation of deserts in Africa and Asia, as well as pollution of air and ocean, on Christianity and Western civilization, "which claims the human right to control nature." And thus we find a professor of art, Takashina Shuji, identifying the unique nature of Japanese avant-garde art with "lyricism," which is "intimately tied to the attitude toward nature that permeates Japanese art as a whole." Most Japanese avant-garde painting (unlike graphic arts, sculpture, architecture, or theater) is not avant-garde at all, but derivative of Western models. But what makes it different, indeed unique in Takashina's eyes, is this communion with nature. "It is because nature for the Japanese is not something which can be reduced to the logic of rules and compasses. Like the human heart, it has its own logic that rationality does not know . . ."

Blessed with natural forests; sacred mountains; the primeval spirit; the celebration of the irrational. These are familiar concepts to anyone with some knowledge of modern European history. They bring to mind German mysticism, Wandervogel communing with nature on mountaintops, the angst-ridden Wagnerian soul recoiling from French Enlightenment, *Runen* signs, the exaltation of Nietzsche's Superman; the lamented "loss of natural good sense" and the "psychic bastardization of our people" (Alfred Rosenberg). "Today a *new* faith is stirring: the myth of blood, the faith that along with blood we are defending the divine nature of man as a whole." Alfred Rosenberg wrote this in his *Myth of the Twentieth Century*, published in the 1930s.

Nakasone and like-minded politicians believe in the superiority of the "mono-racial state." Umehara and like-minded scholars believe in the pure Japanese spirit. They may differ in terms of political aims or terminology, but the ideal of a pure *minzoku* is rarely in doubt. *Minzoku*, unlike *minshu* (masses) or *kokumin* (national populace), is somewhat akin to the Nazi use of the word *Volk*. It implies blood purity and spiritual unity. It is the kind of national mysticism that appeals to people still deeply anxious about their place in the world, and who, periodically, seek to retreat from modern confusion into the security of the "mono-racial state." The late Terayama Shuji, playwright, novelist, filmmaker, once likened his country to a glass dome, transparent but impenetrable to outsiders. The glass wall is the mystique that envelops the Japanese *Volk*, or, as nationalists like Nakasone prefer to call it, the Yamato *minzoku*, after the ancient clan that unified Japan as a kingdom around the fifth century, a period associated with pristine Japanese values (not by Umehara, though; to him, a Jomonist, the Yamato people were already tainted by foreign influence). As a collective term for these *völkisch* nationalists, the American scholar William Wetherall coined the phrase "Yamatoists."

Watanabe Shoichi is a Yamatoist. He is also a professor of English literature. No doubt he has written about his subject, but I have never seen anything. He is much better known as a prolific writer on matters of the national soul. Watanabe is a Christian, teaching at a Christian university, where I met him. He is middle-aged, and has a smiling baby face, with a boyish lock of hair that falls into his right eye. He was dressed in a turtleneck sweater. He believes in racial purity. Why, I asked, was this necessary? "Perhaps not necessary," he said with a smile, "but beautiful."

Watanabe insisted on speaking in English, which is rare in Japan. He spoke it well, which is even rarer. "Yes, quite beautiful, quite good . . ." He stared out of the window, at the students playing baseball below, and then reconsidered. "No, no. That's not right. A mystical view of blood purity is necessary to preserve national unity and identity."

Even after many years in Japan, when I should know better, I still find such statements hard to take. He must have seen my expression change. "But," he said, "Japan is an open society." What about the Vietnamese refugees? I said, spoiling for an argument. Why does Japan refuse to take more than a token number, and then only under pressure? "We are an open society. But our culture is hard for foreigners to understand. Those refugees can't get used to our way of life, that is why we refuse them."

I was reminded of a Japanese politician who once said that Switzerland, in terms of culture and climate, was more congenial to the Vietnamese than Japan. I asked Watanabe, whose smile first froze and then faded into an obstinate pout, whether it wasn't up to the refugees to decide whether they could get used to Japan? "This is an open society." Pouting myself, I said that I did not think so. "This is an open society," he shouted. No, it's not. "Yes, it is!" No, it's not! I looked at my watch and decided it was time to leave. Watanabe's smile reappeared. "It was a great pleasure talking to you," he said.

"Since the Meiji Restoration in 1868," wrote Kishida Shu, a Freudian psychologist, "the Japanese went through a very fast process of modernization. Despite high-speed change, we were able to maintain our Japanese identity, not because it was based on firm principles, but because it was based on . . . the illusion that all Japanese are connected by blood. Muslims stop

being Muslims when they lose their faith in Allah . . . The
Japanese identity is threatened when foreigners are to be as-
similated in our midst . . ."

It is a shocking realization to a European, raised in the
shadow of the Holocaust, that blood-and-soil mythology still
exists in a state of innocence, that it exists among a people for
whom it lacks the associations with Auschwitz and Treblinka.
Indeed, one realizes that references to Auschwitz are meaningless to the people of one of the most powerful nations in the
world. The mono-racial ideal: it seems so incongruous in the
modern world, so utterly contrary to the cosmopolitanism of
contemporary urban life. It cuts to the quick of a vital question:
Is there room in the modern world for a blood-and-soil society?
Or is the cosmopolitanism of the modern world doomed to
fail, to get bogged down in the mud of nativist reaction?

When some years ago, the mayor of Hiroshima suggested
building an Auschwitz Museum in his city, implying that the
Japanese and the Jews were the main victims of World War II,
nobody in Japan thought it inappropriate, or even in bad taste.
Just as nobody seems to care about the recent Japanese best-
sellers explaining how the world is dominated by a Jewish
conspiracy. One popular writer, Uno Masami, explains Japan's
strained economic relations with the outside world entirely in
terms of a Jewish plutocracy trying to keep the Japanese down.
If only Hiroshima had been left in its ruinous state, he wrote
in one of his books, just as the Jews made sure that Auschwitz
was preserved. The Jews turned their victimhood into a "racial
strength"; the Japanese, by covering up the results of the atom
bomb—designed and planned by Jews—and by believing the
Tokyo Trials verdict—delivered by Jewish judges—that Japan
was responsible for the war, "lost their racial confidence."

It is not that the Japanese are especially anti-Semitic. Most
Japanese have only a very hazy idea of Jews or Jewish history.
The point is rather that racism is only understood to be an
issue when Japanese are the victims. A popular novel and TV
soap opera of the 1980s concerned the internment of Japanese-

Americans during the war. There is an art gallery and a library in the Peace Memorial Museum in Hiroshima, designed to warn new generations of Japanese about the horrors of war. The library is stocked with books on Hiroshima and Nagasaki, on the bombing of Tokyo, on the Vietnam and Korean wars, on the Nazi death camps, but almost nothing on the war in Asia that resulted in the dropping of the nuclear bombs. All the paintings and drawings in the art gallery were of the Hiroshima bombing, except two, which showed the suffering of Japanese-Americans in American internment camps. Contrary to Uno Masami's impression of postwar Japan, Japanese victimhood looms very large in literature and popular arts. Which is why in Yamatoist writings, the loss of Japanese soul, national identity, Yamato spirit, or whatever one wishes to call it, is blamed on foreigners, specifically Americans. Americans occupied Japan, imposed the "Peace Constitution," a new educational system, and, through the Tokyo Trials, a view of the recent past which condemned Japan's military adventures in Asia and the Pacific.

This is what Eto Jun, a literary critic, means when he says that the American occupation destroyed the continuity of Japanese culture. It is what former Education Minister Fujio Masayuki means when he calls the occupation period an act of "racial revenge." It is the point of Muramatsu Takeshi, a professor of French literature, when he claims that "spiritually, the postwar identity crisis is much more serious than the anti-Western allergy of the 1930s and '40s, because our postwar identity was created by foreigners."

Muramatsu, a thin, long-haired intellectual, whose movements have a nervous, somewhat sinister elegance, made this point in his pleasantly cluttered Tokyo flat, which bore the marks of a Japanese Francophile: baroque bric-a-brac, dusty Greek sculptures, French novels, and chintz curtains. I was reminded of photographs I had seen of the house of Mishima, a close friend of Muramatsu's. Mishima, too, dreamed of a pristine Japan, while living in the midst of French antiques and

Greek sculpture. In his garden was a large statue of Apollo on a plinth. "My despicable symbol of the rational," he told his biographer, Henry Scott Stokes. "My ideal is to live in a house where I sit on a rococo chair wearing an aloha shirt and blue jeans," he told reporters. According to people who knew Mishima well, his statements were never entirely facetious. It is the tragic fate of Japanese intellectuals that the more they are drawn to the West, the more they wish to be Japanese. As did Mishima, they sometimes end up as caricatures of both.

Like the Meiji emperor in his French uniform, dispensing a European Constitution on the same day as praying to his divine ancestors, nothing in modern Japan is purely Japanese or purely foreign. Everything is a mixture, a hybrid, as Kato Shuichi said. The cultural critic Unno Hiroshi calls the contemporary fashion for things Japanese "japonesque," a mimicry of Western taste for japonaiserie. Young Japanese see Kabuki through the eyes of David Bowie. "We can only look at Japanese tradition after looking at the West first," writes Unno. "I look at Japanese culture through a whiskey glass."

This might explain why the noisiest Yamatoists began as intellectuals who looked at the West first. Professors of French or English are especially common. They often feel rejected, or worse, ignored by the Western world they tried to enter through study, and turn away in disgust—a disgust also aimed at their own countrymen lacking in both Western sophistication and the pure Yamato spirit. Yamatoism, like all fundamentalist creeds, is an expression of the déclassé, in this case Japanese intellectuals at a loss how to cope with "internationalization." They look through the whiskey glass and hope to find pure blood.

In a student area of Tokyo called Takadanobaba, behind a sculpture of a nude Marilyn Monroe about to pounce on a sumo wrestler, is the office of Suzuki Kunio, leader of a "spiritual movement" called Issuikai. The movement publishes a monthly paper called *Reconquista*. Their stated aim is to reconquer what Suzuki thinks has been lost: the pure Japanese spirit. On the wall of his small and shabby office hang pictures of Emperor Hirohito in military uniform, taken during the 1930s, and of Mishima.

The *Asahi* newspaper published an interview with several members of Suzuki's movement. They were all in their early twenties. One young man called Kimura explained his motives for becoming a right-wing nationalist: "My father was a soldier. At school I joined a study group interested in military songs. There I met an older boy involved in the right-wing movement, so I decided to join, too. Soon I discovered that there are higher values than simply preserving one's own life—namely, the values of the nation, the race, the emperor." A former law student named Matsubara welcomed the freedom of speech that came with postwar democracy. "I also have no great dislike for Western culture. It's just that our country lacks cohesion. We are not really conscious of our Japaneseness and this gives me a feeling of loneliness."

Suzuki looks like the sort of man people with feelings of loneliness can turn to. He is quite unlike most right-wing activists: short-cropped, husky bumpkins with the cruel and ignorant faces of camp guards. Suzuki is a quiet-spoken man in his early forties, casually dressed, more like a research fellow than a right-wing activist. He receives many fan letters from young women, who profess to admire his romantic spirit.

Suzuki offered us tea, asked us if we wanted to take any pictures of him, and when we declined, began to explain his position. When he was still at school, his mother interested him in joining a new religious group called Seicho no Ie, a Japanese version of Christian Science with strong nationalist leanings. His new faith did not match what he learned at school, however. "I felt depressed reading about modern Japanese history. We were supposed to feel that we lived in a bad country." And because of these biased textbooks, he said, many people of his generation felt guilty about the Japanese role in World War II, and "people who did better than I did at school all joined the left-wing student movement." He concluded there had to be something wrong with Japanese education. "It must be changed, it is too depressing." He used the word *kurai*, which literally means "dark."

A young member of the spiritual group, who had been engrossed in a book on international terrorism, suddenly broke his silence to exclaim that it was all America's doing: "They wanted us to be weak. That is why they rigged our education system. To stop Japan from being a major power." He got more and more agitated and followed us into the street: "Marcos. The Americans got rid of him to save their military bases, which are there to threaten Japan. We want to be independent, but America won't let us!"

Far from being unconscious of their Japaneseness, these young Japanese appear to be suffering from the reverse problem: they are so acutely and permanently conscious of their Japaneseness that personal anxiety gets mixed up in the nation, the race, the emperor. The loneliness, one feels, stems from a weak sense of self, independent of Japaneseness, not from a lack of Japanese consciousness.

Suzuki resents being called a right-winger. He sees himself as a realist. But filling his postwar void with the prewar spirit poses problems: the national symbols—and what else is there to express something as vague as national spirit?—are tainted by the war. Moreover, they are largely bogus. And not just bogus, but alien. The intellectual fathers of the postwar Yamatoists are such scholars as Nishida Kitaro and Watsuji Tetsuro. These highly respected academics, trying to reconcile traditional Japanese thought—or anti-thought, like Zen Buddhism—with the European terminology they had acquired, propagated a mystical view of the Japanese state. This view, in turn, was the heir of nationalist ideas devised around the middle of the nineteenth century by quixotic philosophers who hoped to purge Japanese culture of Chinese influence. According to prewar nativist orthodoxy, the Japanese "race" congealed around the sacred emperor into something usually translated as "the national polity." Individuals in this scheme of things were mere extensions of the benevolent imperial will, hence the automatic sense of social harmony, communion with nature, and so forth. It is this religious surrender that attracts the young Yamatoists. It is this state of mind, so to speak, that Suzuki seeks to reconquer. Nishida, like Umehara some forty years later, believed in exporting these ideas: "A principle for the whole world will be born from our historical spirit; the way of the emperor must be applied to all countries." Japanese uniqueness is elevated to a universal principle. If Christ was reborn in Korea, God was born in Japan.

Umehara has written that prewar emperor worship and State Shinto were devised in imitation of European institutions, a kind of Bonapartism grafted onto Japanese traditions. He may well be right, hence his quest for Japanese values 12,000 years ago. But Germany rather than France was the main source of ideas. Nishida was deeply influenced by Hegel and Watsuji studied in Germany with Heidegger. Japanese thinkers in the first half of this century recognized that Germany was struggling with similar problems of cultural and political identity, and they found German Romanticism, with its celebration of the irrational and its national mysticism, congenial; it was both "modern"—because it was European—and, translated into Japanese terms, useful as an antidote to the politically disturbing effects of modernity, such as socialism, individualism, materialism, urbanization—in short, the old nationalist bugbear: the pluralist City. Before the war a group of extreme Japanese nationalists even called themselves the Nihon Roman-na, the Japanese Romantic School, and they were an early influence on the young Mishima. Marxism, the arch-foe of reactionary Romantics, appealed to Japanese intellectuals for analogous but also for opposite reasons: although it had the seeds of anti-Western nationalism (seeds that sprouted in China and Vietnam), it was a modern rejection of Japanese tradition. Marxists tried to apply universal values to Japan.

Having failed to conquer the world for their causes, Germany and Japan have had to redefine themselves yet again after the war. This is why both the Marxists and the Yamatoists have attached such importance to education, which is like the rope in an endless tug-of-war. Former Education Minister Fujio Masayuki caused such a furor by saying out loud what many people think that he had to be sacked by his Prime Minister, Nakasone. He stated in an interview that the Koreans were partly responsible for Japanese colonial rule. This deeply upset the Koreans. But it was only a sideline to his main theme, which was to "restore the spirit of our race through history and tradition."

Fujio is a stocky man of the old school, who likes to speak his mind frankly, with none of the shifty nervousness often displayed by officials when interviewed by a foreigner. In fact, there is something rather sympathetic about Fujio. He comes across as a proud, stubborn, reactionary, but rather jovial old farmer. His manner of speaking is informal to the point of sounding gangsterish.

"The problem is quite clear," he said, clenching and unclenching his large fists: "We were robbed of our Japaneseness by the Americans during the occupation. Our heroes, the shining examples of Japanese loyalty, heroes like General Nogi or Admiral Togo, they were rubbed out of our history books. Napoleon, he conquered Europe, but he's a hero. Admiral Nelson invaded half the world, he's a hero. So why can't we have heroes?" He spread his fingers on his desk and jutted his chin toward me, his small, shrewd eyes challenging me to contradict him. "Our history books must reflect our pride as a nation."

I reminded him of his remark about Korean responsibility for being invaded by the Japanese. "Ah, those Koreans. Well, they're immature, you know. They must face the reality of their own history."

What about Japanese history? I asked. Is the use of history to inspire national pride the best way to face reality? "We're not like the Koreans, you know. We do it scientifically." He raised his chin so high, his eyes seemed to disappear.

It was the answer I got from the Kuomintang historian in

Taipei; "scientific"—as if the modern jargon could hide the traditional purpose. But surely, I said, Japan, like any country, has its share of shameful episodes in history. "Well, maybe," he conceded, "but in our modern history there are no shameful episodes. Anyway, we can't say we Japanese were bad just because foreigners say so."

Here he exposed the raw Yamatoist nerve. Because foreigners say so; foreigners made our postwar history; foreigners robbed us of our identity. I thought of something Watanabe had said: "If the Tokyo Trials hadn't taken place, there would have been no neo-nationalism."

"Finally," said Fujio in the published interview that cost him his job, "we must die as Japanese. Our children will always be Japanese and the core of our education should be to make them Japanese. Now, what is the root of our Japaneseness? What makes us aware of our shared Japaneseness? Surely, the Japanese flag and the national anthem. Singing 'Kimigayo' and raising the flag, we feel that we have a common consciousness . . . This should be the nucleus of our education."

It is a legitimate concern. Nations need symbols. But here the Japanese, whose symbols have been distorted and abused for so long, have a harder problem than the Germans. Nazi symbols, though often derived from Germanic traditions, were artificial aberrations associated exclusively with one outlandish regime. Germans can abolish the swastika without feeling deprived of an expression of their national identity. And whatever revisionist historians may say, Germans cannot claim innocence of the Holocaust. The Japanese case is not so simple. For Japanese militarism and mystical nationalism were part of a continuous process. Unlike in Germany, there was no clear dividing line between the past and a criminal regime. The symbols— the flag, the national anthem, the martial songs still blasted out in pinball parlors and bars—have remained the same. And whatever atrocities Japanese soldiers might have committed in Asia, there was no equivalent of the Holocaust. Yamatoism never led to systematic genocide. State Shintoism, emperor wor-

ship, the "national polity," and so forth may have been to a
large extent nineteenth-century ideas, but they were so tangled
up with older Japanese traditions that they have become virtually indistinguishable in the modern Japanese mind. Which
means that one should either condemn the entire Japanese past,
as many Marxists do, or pretend that Yamatoism had nothing
to do with the war. "Until 1941, Japan was a completely normal country," said Watanabe, "an open society, in fact." The
fact that foreigners and Japanese leftists condemn Yamatoism
only causes more confusion. It makes it easy for Yamatoists to
argue that the Japanese are dupes of foreign or communist
propaganda.

We had no shameful episodes; bombing Hiroshima was a
worse crime than the Nanjing Massacre; the annexation of
Korea was legal; the Great East Asia War was waged in self-
defense and to liberate fellow Asians; the Yasukuni shrine is
simply the resting place of brave souls who died for their country. This is what Fujio says. It is the line held by Japanese
revisionist historians. If only we could believe it, Japanese children can respect the flag and sing the national anthem without
a pang in anybody's conscience.

The Yasukuni shrine remains a problem, however, for the
brave spirits resting there include those of war criminals, such
as Tojo Hideki—war criminals, that is, according to the verdict
at the Tokyo Trials. Worship at the shrine is one way of de-
criminalizing the wartime leaders; a way of cocking a snook
at the "Tokyo Trials view of Japanese history." Should a Japanese Prime Minister be seen to do this in his official capacity?
Yamatoists think he should. Koreans, Chinese, and Japanese
Christians and liberals think he should not. Most Japanese
appear to be indifferent. But as long as the postwar "Peace
Constitution" forbids any link between state and religion, it
will remain a matter of controversy.

The shrine is a curious place, with its peaceful doves fluttering
about the trees, festooned with names of old Japanese battle-

ships and regiments; the displays of cannon, a Zero fighter, and the first train to use the Burma railroad, built by foreign slave labor; the bronze reliefs of battles in China and the memorial to the Kempeitai, the Japanese equivalent of the SS. Every morning there is a parade of sound trucks at the shrine, filled with right-wing thugs in paramilitary gear. They sing wartime military songs and shout anti-communist slogans. They bow in the direction of the emperor's palace and line up to listen to uniformed men with grim faces holding forth about the Japanese spirit. After that they set off in their trucks to scream abuse at the enemy in the labor union offices and the liberal newspapers; confused, crew-cut country boys yelling through their loudspeakers at the big city buildings.

The Yasukuni shrine was built in 1869 as a home for the spirits of those who died for the emperor during the battles against the shogun's government in Tokyo (then still called Edo). Before the Meiji Restoration in 1868, the country was divided into pro-emperor and pro-shogunate factions. When the emperor faction won, the imperial household became the focus of Yamatoist mythology concocted to give an identity to the new Japanese state, or, more accurately, to lend legitimacy to the new rulers, who were country samurai from the south. This involved military adventures abroad, worship of the national soul, and spiritual union between the emperor, identified with the state, and his subjects. To give all this religious significance, a travesty of ancient animist rituals was made into the official Japanese creed and called State Shintoism. The Yasukuni shrine was the supreme symbol of this new religion. Which is why the American occupation forces, in their ham-fisted but not wrongheaded way, severed the link between Shinto and the state. And this is why modern Yamatoists say that the continuity of the Japanese identity was broken by ignorant foreigners; and also why they say that Shinto should be restored to its former position as the national religion. It is their answer to the cri de coeur of Ishihara Shintaro, the novelist and politician: "Japanese have lost the heart of their ideological and spiritual frame of reference, and nothing has been found to substitute . . ."

Yamatoism is basically a religious issue with political consequences—or, to put it differently, a religious issue manipulated by politicians: Nishida's philosophy was used by the militarist leaders of the 1930s and 1940s; the theories of Umehara and others are useful to Nakasone and his nationalist friends. Yamatoists are like fundamentalists elsewhere: Jerry Falwell's born-again Christians, Muslim revivalists in Malaysia, reactionary Buddhists in Thailand, Tangun worshippers in South Korea. They share the idealistic rebellion against modern materialism, the "vices" that so many fundamentalists talk about. They seek to revive what has been "lost." The Thais turn to Buddhism and the Malays to Islam. The Japanese fundamentalists, after the failure of Marxism and Christianity, do not usually seek what is lost in any universal religion. There are religious groups based on Buddhism, it is true, but even they—the Sokagakkai, the Risho Koseikai—often end up as variations of Yamatoism. To escape from the Disneyland they created themselves, Japanese tend to turn inward, to a defensive national solipsism.

The fascinating thing is that this mental process, starting with a tentative search for universal principles and ending in cultural narcissism, can take place in great liberal minds. One of the most brilliant figures of the Meiji period was Uchimura Kanzo (1861–1930). He had the courage in 1890, when the Imperial Rescript on Education was promulgated, to challenge the state's manipulation of ethics and religion. He resigned as newspaper editor in protest against the impending Russo-Japanese war. Uchimura, clearly, was a man who stood up for his principles, who dared, in an authoritarian age, to stick his neck out. He was a pacifist and a Christian who saw Puritan New England as his spiritual home. This same man, however, came to believe that "our involvement with our nation is so deep that we cannot think of our salvation apart from Japan."

He also wrote that "my Christianity is patriotic . . . Patriotism means that one believes in the divine mission of the nation and devotes one's entire self in behalf of the mission . . ." He ended up sounding like Nishida and Umehara: "Now that Christianity is dying in Europe and America because of their materialism, they cannot revive it; God is calling upon Japan to contribute its best to his service." God, to this essentially liberal man, became a kind of Japanese emperor. Far from helping the individual transcend his society, Uchimura's faith was an attempt to dissolve modern alienation by identifying his religion with the society.

Uchimura's ideal, a Christianized Japan, never even got off the ground. But the yearning for a spiritual *Kultur*, something uniquely Japanese to protect the soul from foreign materialism, is still there. Now that the Japanese are admonished by their leaders to "internationalize," the key word of the 1980s, the yearning is stronger than ever. The internationalization of Japan is, of course, a meaningless concept. When asked in frequent polls what they think it means, ordinary citizens will say what they think the pollster wants to hear, that we all want peace. "We want world peace," said Fujio, "but as Japanese, not as cosmopolitans."

In 1977 I joined a modern Japanese theater group for a tour of Japan. I was the only foreigner in the group, led by the playwright and director Kara Juro. Kara prided himself on his Japaneseness. Though influenced by the European absurdists, as well as, curiously, by Tennessee Williams, his brand of commedia dell'arte was a conscious attempt to revive a Japanese spirit, without rehashing traditional forms. By no means militaristic or right-wing, Kara's Japaneseness, rather, was a nostalgia for the dark undercurrents of his native soil: the world of riverside vagrants, prostitutes, gangsters, striptease artists, and itinerant entertainers. During the nightly drinking sessions with his tight-knit band of actors and friends, he would often express a certain envy for people born in villages. He would play a record over and over again by a folk singer who sang about the cold north in his thick country dialect. Kara, a small, chunky man, born in a bombed Tokyo slum, would open his eyes wide, screech like a child, and wipe tears from his cheeks with the back of his hands. His *nostalgie de la boue* (quite literally) was an instinctive anti-modernism, or, rather, anti-rationalism. His obsession with mud, blood, and the *Sturm und Drang* of Japanese surrealism was his way to re-create Nietzsche's Superman.

He wrote a part for me in one of his absurdist plays. I was to be Midnight Cowboy disguised as a Russian spy. "To be in our play, you really have to become a Japanese," said one of the actors. "You have to think, eat, move, and talk like a Japanese." Much, on the other hand, was made of the one token foreigner. "Hey," visitors to the rehearsal room would invariably say to Kara, "you've gone international."

I did my best to play up to the role expected of me, the international man, who ate, drank, and talked like a Japanese. To make others laugh and to preserve a certain ironic distance from my role, I would overdo it; I became a foreign caricature of a Japanese, deliberately exaggerating Japanese mannerisms. After a while this became a strain. I got mildly hysterical.

Then, one night, the role exploded. It began after our last performance in Kyoto. A well-known film actor was in the audience. He went drinking with us afterward, and as was usual on these occasions we drank a lot. The visitor began to needle Kara, making mildly disparaging remarks about the theater. Surely TV was a better way to make a living, he said. Kara lost his temper and tried to bash the actor over the head with a sake bottle. He only managed to hit the nose, from which blood began to gush forth. At this the entire troupe, growling like a pack of hunting dogs, threw themselves on the hapless actor, punching and kicking and clawing, until the victim had to be carried out, a bloody mess. It was a rather shocking spectacle, this rugby scrum of all against one. I had watched it happen, without stirring, feeling rather cowardly. Kara's wife, an actress with a fiery Korean temper, then berated her husband for his violent behavior. Kara's eyes bulged in anger. "Shut up, woman!" he screamed, and threw a heavy glass ashtray at her head. Fortunately he missed. It went crashing through the paper door.

Without quite knowing what I was doing, I stood up and shouted, in an absurd surge of European chivalry: "Don't throw things at women!" There was a stunned silence, followed by embarrassed looks through corners of eyes. The foreigner, the international man, had gone berserk. Kara was speechless with rage, white-faced, puffy-cheeked, shaking. After a minute or so, he managed to shout: "How dare you say such a thing?"

"I am free to say what I want," I said, my bottled-up frustrations spilling out in petulant anger.

"Free, free, we all want to be free," Kara whined. "But I thought you were with us, part of the group." He looked wounded and genuinely perplexed, his round face a bewildering blob of red and white flushes.

Then, suddenly, the final word was delivered, in a tone of renewed rage: "You're nothing but an ordinary foreigner after all!"

Kara never forgave me. I had betrayed his expectations. By breaking the code of expected behavior, by challenging the leader to his face, by standing up, however absurdly, as an individual, by claiming to speak out for higher principles, by suddenly behaving like a Westerner, I had betrayed Kara, betrayed the group. Just an ordinary foreigner after all. I had been given the chance to be Japanese and I blew it.

"What do you think of peace?" I was asked this question in Hiroshima Peace Park by a young girl in a sailor suit, her school uniform. A Snoopy pen was held at the ready to jot down this foreigner's answer on her pad. A woman in glasses, in her early thirties, probably the girl's teacher, stood behind her, beaming at me. I did not want to give the expected platitudinous answer. But for lack of another answer, I asked the girl what she thought. She giggled, covering her mouth, casting a glance at her teacher, who nodded encouragement. "We think peace is good," said the girl.

Hiroshima Peace Park, with its Peace Memorial, the Flame of Peace, the Children's Peace Monument, the Peace Bell, the Peace Clock Tower, the Peace Cairn, the Peace Fountain, the Statue of a Prayer for Peace, the Peace Tower, the Statue of Peace, the Monument for the "Woods of Peace," the Pond of Peace, the Peace Bridge and the West Peace Bridge, the Monument Commemorating Pope John Paul II's Appeal for Peace, the Peace Hall, the Peace Museum. What do I think of peace, or, rather, Peace?

"Hiroshima," says a booklet called *Hiroshima Peace Reader*, published by the Hiroshima Peace Culture Foundation, "is no longer merely a Japanese city. It has become recognized throughout the world as a Mecca of world peace."

"The world is still controlled by the 'philosophy of power.' We must convert the world to the Hiroshima spirit." —the mayor of Hiroshima, August 6, 1987.

"We love Peace City Hiroshima in our peaceful heart," said the slogan on a T-shirt sold at the Peace Museum.

"I would like to interweave dream and reality in harmony and enrich the citizens' lives," said the novelist Ota Yoko when discussing the future of Hiroshima in 1946.

Hiroshima is the center of a new religion. As with some Buddhist sects, which promise salvation to those who repeat one prayer over and over again, Peace is the mantra of the Hiroshima spirit. Like all religious centers, there is something unreal, even a little spooky about Peace Park, indeed a place where dream and reality are interwoven. I find it difficult not to take an ironic distance from it all. From the slogans, the trinkets, the wreaths donated by East German labor unions, or from the young American dressed as a Buddhist monk, praying in front of the Peace Fountain. As in all modern religious centers, the faith in Hiroshima is often expressed in kitsch, inappropriate images that stand for displaced emotions.

As in many religions, these images are often horrific: the ghastly tableaux of victims running away from moving plastic flames, their wax fingers dripping wax flesh. And as with so many, if not all religions, this one absolves the believers from personal responsibility, for which faith is a substitute.

"Let all souls here rest in peace, for the error will not be repeated." So says the famous inscription on the black stone coffin under the cenotaph. Which error? Who won't repeat what?

I was met by an old friend on my first visit to Hiroshima. He took me straight to his university, where I was ushered into a common room. A number of young Japanese sat around the room in a silent circle, as an elderly woman showed a middle-aged American a series of large photographs. The American was bald and dressed in a loud plaid suit. Slowly, one by one, as in a magic lantern show, the pictures of burned corpses, skin diseases, blinded eyes, and bloody, hairless scalps were laid out for his inspection. The woman spoke softly about Japanese suffering and about peace. All of a sudden, the American crumpled, like a large broken doll, and fell to his knees. He clutched the woman's hands and begged for her forgiveness, his voice choking, his eyes filled with tears. The people around the room stared blankly, showing no emotion at all. I looked away in embarrassment. The woman stroked the man's hand, smiled, and softly forgave him.

Forgave him for what, though? He looked in genuine distress. But what sin, in Japanese eyes, did he commit? Guilt by association, because Americans dropped the bomb? I thought of an article I had read by a Japanese academic, a woman called Hasegawa Michiko, who was too young to have experienced the war. She wrote that Japan had embarked on its war in Asia because the Japanese "began to subscribe to the characteristically Western worldview of dividing nations into friends and foes, and of recognizing foes as enemies, and of behaving antagonistically toward enemies." After the war, said Miss Hasegawa, "the Japanese determined never again to take up residence in the violent Western-style community . . ." Was the American guilty, then, of imposing "internationalization" on an unwilling people?

Who was responsible? The Americans, the Japanese emperor, the military leaders and their Yamatoist idealogues, who attempted, as they put it, "to overcome modernity" and to restore rural values? Was it Robert Oppenheimer, the Jews, modern technology, or Japanese culture, the samurai spirit, and all that? The faith remains mute.

The paradox of Hiroshima is that in a way it is like a city without a past. A Japanese novelist once used the term "crystal" to describe the shiny, fashionable, stylish surface of modern Japan, the country of boutiques, fashion centers, and Disneyland architecture. Hiroshima is the consummate crystal city: chic, but oddly devoid of character. It is a city that thrives on materialism. The people of Hiroshima appear to take little notice of the peace pilgrims. Nor do they seem to care much about the pure Japanese spirit. They are too busy buying, eating, drinking, following the Hiroshima Carps baseball team. Hiroshima does have a past, of course, as a military city, built as a base for Asian conquest. Hiroshima was the center for men who wanted to overcome modernity.

I watched the young Japanese in their fashionable "international" clothes, going to Hollywood movies, eating American ice cream, dancing at discos, buying videos, appearing on TV in game shows and spaghetti-eating contests. Perhaps they seem a little mindless. But they can read the books they want. They have the freedom to define themselves. They have the right to think critically before accepting things. No doubt something has been lost. Something always is.

What do I think of Peace? I hope the City will never burn again.

Bibliography

I decided not to clutter the text of this book with footnotes. Instead I would like to express my debt to the following authors, whose works have been indispensable. Some are more scholarly than others, but all have added to what knowledge of Asia I might have.

BURMA

One of the best general histories of Southeast Asia remains D. G. E. Hall's *A History of South-East Asia*, first published in 1955. I used the Macmillan Student Editions paperback, reprinted in 1977.

G. E. Harvey's *History of Burma* (London, 1925) is an excellent standard source.

I also used E. Tennyson Jesse's *The Story of Burma* (London, 1946), H. Fielding Hall's *The Soul of a People* (London, 1906), and B. R. Pearn's *History of Rangoon* (Rangoon, 1939).

On modern Burma I recommend the stimulating, though controversial *Politics, Personality and Nation Building*, by Lucian W. Pye (MIT, 1963), and the equally stimulating, though even more controversial *Buddhist Backgrounds of the Burmese Revolution*, by E. Sarkisyanz (The Hague, 1965). A sober analysis of contemporary Burma is offered by Josef Silverstein in his *Burma: Military Rule and the Politics of Stagnation* (Cornell, 1977).

THAILAND

For the history I turned extensively to David K. Wyett's *Thailand: A Short History* (Yale, 1982).

The translation of Khamsing Srinawk's story is by Domnern Garden. The story was published in Khamsing Srinawk's *The Politician and Other Stories* (Oxford, 1973).

Sulak Sivaraksa's books, from which I quoted his polemical and always interesting ideas, are *Siam in Crisis* (Bangkok, 1980) and *Siamese Resurgence* (Bangkok, 1985).

Niels Mulder, the Dutch anthropologist quoted in the text, wrote *Everyday Life in Thailand: An Interpretation* (Bangkok, 1985). He has the rare ability to be both scholarly and entertaining.

Those interested in modern Thai literature should get *In the Mirror* (Bangkok, 1985), edited and translated by Benedict R. O'G. Anderson and Ruchira Mendiones. Anderson's introduction is excellent on the political and social background to the literature.

Another standard work of great interest is *Thai Peasant Personality* (Berkeley, 1965), by Herbert P. Phillips.

THE PHILIPPINES

The best book about the Philippines, to my mind, is Reynaldo Clemena Ileto's study of popular protest movements, *Pasyon and Revolution* (Manila, 1979). His essay on the protest movement that followed Benigno Aquino's death, published in *The Philippines After Marcos* (Sydney, 1985), edited by R. J. May and Francisco Nemenzo, is also superb.

On the Marcos years I am indebted to Reuben Canoy's *The Counterfeit Revolution: Martial Law in the Philippines* (Manila, 1980); to Carmen Navarro Pedrosa's *Imelda Marcos* (reprinted in New York, 1987); and to Ferdinand Marcos' (or his ghost's) *Today's Revolution: Democracy* (Manila, 1971).

On Philippine history I found especially interesting Renato Constantino's *The Making of a Filipino* (Manila, 1969) and also *History of the Filipino People* (Manila, 1977) by Teodoro A. Agoncillo and

Milagros C. Guerrero. The historical novels by F. Sionil Jose, especially *Po-on* (Manila, 1984), are of a high literary standard and taught me more about Philippine history than most academic books.

The uneven, flamboyant, and stimulating works by Nick Joaquin offer a great many insights into the Filipino mind. His *Aquinos of Tarlac* (Manila, 1983) was especially useful.

Jose Rizal's famous novels *Noli Me Tangere* and *El Filibusterismo* are available in different paperback editions. I quoted from Leon Ma. Guerrero's translation of the latter, published in London in 1965.

The quotation from Jose Ma. Sison, the founder of the Communist Party of the Philippines, is from his book *Struggle for National Democracy*, first published in Manila in 1969.

MALAYSIA

On Malay history I used Richard Winstedt's *The Malays—A Cultural History*, revised and updated in 1981 by Tham Seong Chee.

The quotations from Prime Minister Mahathir are from *The Malay Dilemma* (Kuala Lumpur, 1970) and *The Challenge* (Kuala Lumpur, 1986). Neither book is much fun to read, but both offer fascinating arguments for Mahathir's politics.

S. Husin Ali's *The Malays: Their Problems and Future* is interesting in that it stresses class rather than racial conflict.

Cecil Rajendra's poem "Child of the Sun" is from an anthology of his poems by the same title (London, 1986).

The cultural debate on whether Malaysian culture should be Islamic, and to what extent it should incorporate Chinese or Indian customs, is chronicled in *National Culture and Democracy*, edited by Kua Kit Soong (Kuala Lumpur, 1985).

SINGAPORE

There are several biographies of Lee Kuan Yew, some more sympathetic than others. The least sympathetic is by T. L. S. George: *Lee Kuan Yew's Singapore*, first published in Singapore in 1973. A critical, but less polemical biography is James Minchin's *No Man Is an Island: A Study of Singapore's Lee Kuan Yew* (Sydney, 1986). The most sympathetic view is offered by A. Josey: *Lee Kuan Yew* (Singapore, 1986).

All books on Singapore history that are published there are bound to be more rather than less sympathetic. J. Drysdale's *Singapore: Struggle for Success* (Singapore, 1984) is a glowing account. For a slightly more dispassionate and certainly far better written story, I turned to D. Bloodworth's *The Tiger and the Trojan Horse* (Singapore, 1986), about Lee's struggle with the communists.

TAIWAN

Harry A. Franck's travel account is entitled *Glimpses of Japan and Formosa* (New York, 1924).

I found the information on Koxinga in *Koxinga and Chinese Nationalism: History, Myth and the Hero*, by Ralph C. Crozier (Harvard, 1977).

For the Japanese period I found an excellent source in George H. Kerr's *Formosa: Licensed Revolution and the Home Rule Movement* (University of Hawaii, 1974). Kerr's *Formosa Betrayed* (London, 1966), though highly polemical, is good on the postwar "invasion" of the mainland Chinese.

KOREA

Kim Dae Jung's *Prison Writings* was published in the United States (Berkeley, 1986).

On political history the best book is still Gregory Henderson's *Korea: The Politics of the Vortex* (Harvard, 1968).

The quotation of Kim Young Soo is from *The Identity of the Korean People* (Seoul, 1983), edited by Suh Kuk-Sung et al.

For a more general history I turned to Lee Ki-baik's *A New History of Korea*, translated by Edward W. Wagner and Edward J. Shultz (Seoul, 1984).

An excellent source for the history of the Japanese period is *The Japanese Colonial Empire*, edited by Ramon H. Meyers and Mark R. Peattie (Princeton, 1984).

Kim Chi Ha's ideas on the church are from *Kim Chi Ha: Minshu no Koe* (*Kim Chi Ha: The Voice of the People*) (Tokyo, 1974).

Paek Ki Wan's *Konichi Minzokuron* (*Essay on the People's Anti-Japanese Struggle*) (Tokyo, 1975), translated into Japanese by Kosugi Katsuji, was my source for Paek's anti-foreign outburst.

The book almost confiscated by the customs officer at Pusan was *Minami Chosen no Hannichiron* (*Essays on South Korea's Anti-Japanese Line*) (Tokyo, 1973), edited and translated into Japanese by Shibuya Sentaro.

Professor Yi O Ryong's definition of *han* came from his *Kankokujin no Kokoro: Han no Bunkaron* (*The Korean Heart: Essay on the Culture of Han*) (Tokyo, 1982).

G. Cameron Hurst's essay in *UFSI Reports* (1985, No. 33), entitled "Uri Nara-ism: Cultural Nationalism in Contemporary Korea," is a rare and excellent discussion of that important topic.

JAPAN

I am indebted for much of my information on the twists and turns of Japanese intellectuals to Wagatsuma Hiroshi's chapter in *Ethnic Identity: Cultural Continuities and Change* (Chicago, 1975), edited by De Vos and Romanucci-Ross.

Donald Keene's *Dawn to the West* (New York, 1984) is a tremendous source for anything to do with modern Japanese literature.

I quoted Basil Hall Chamberlain from his book *Things Japanese* (London, 1891).

My criticism of Umehara Takeshi's theories led to a riposte from Umehara in the journal *Chuo Koron*, August 1987. My answer to his article was published in the October issue of the same magazine.

The dialogue between Umehara and the then Prime Minister, Nakasone Yasuhiro, was published in *Sekai Bunmei no Nagare to Nihon no Yakuwari* (*The Trend of World Civilization and Japan's Role*) (Tokyo, 1985).

The quotation of Takashina Shuji is from *The Japan Foundation Newsletter*, December 1986.

Kishida Shu's analysis of Japanese emperor worship was published in the journal *Voice*, May 1986.

Henry Scott Stokes's biography of Mishima Yukio is entitled *The Life and Death of Yukio Mishima* (reprinted in New York, 1982).

For the quotation of Uchimura Kanzo I turned to Tatsuo Arima's *The Failure of Freedom: A Portrait of Modern Japanese Intellectuals* (Harvard, 1969).